NORTH WIND

NORTH
WIND

David DiGilio
WRITER

Alex Cal
ARTIST

Francisco Gamboa
COLORIST - Chapter One

Renato Faccini
COLORIST - Chapters Two to Five

Marshall Dillon
and Terri Delgado
LETTERERS

Joyce El Hayek
ASSISTANT EDITOR

Marshall Dillon
MANAGING EDITOR

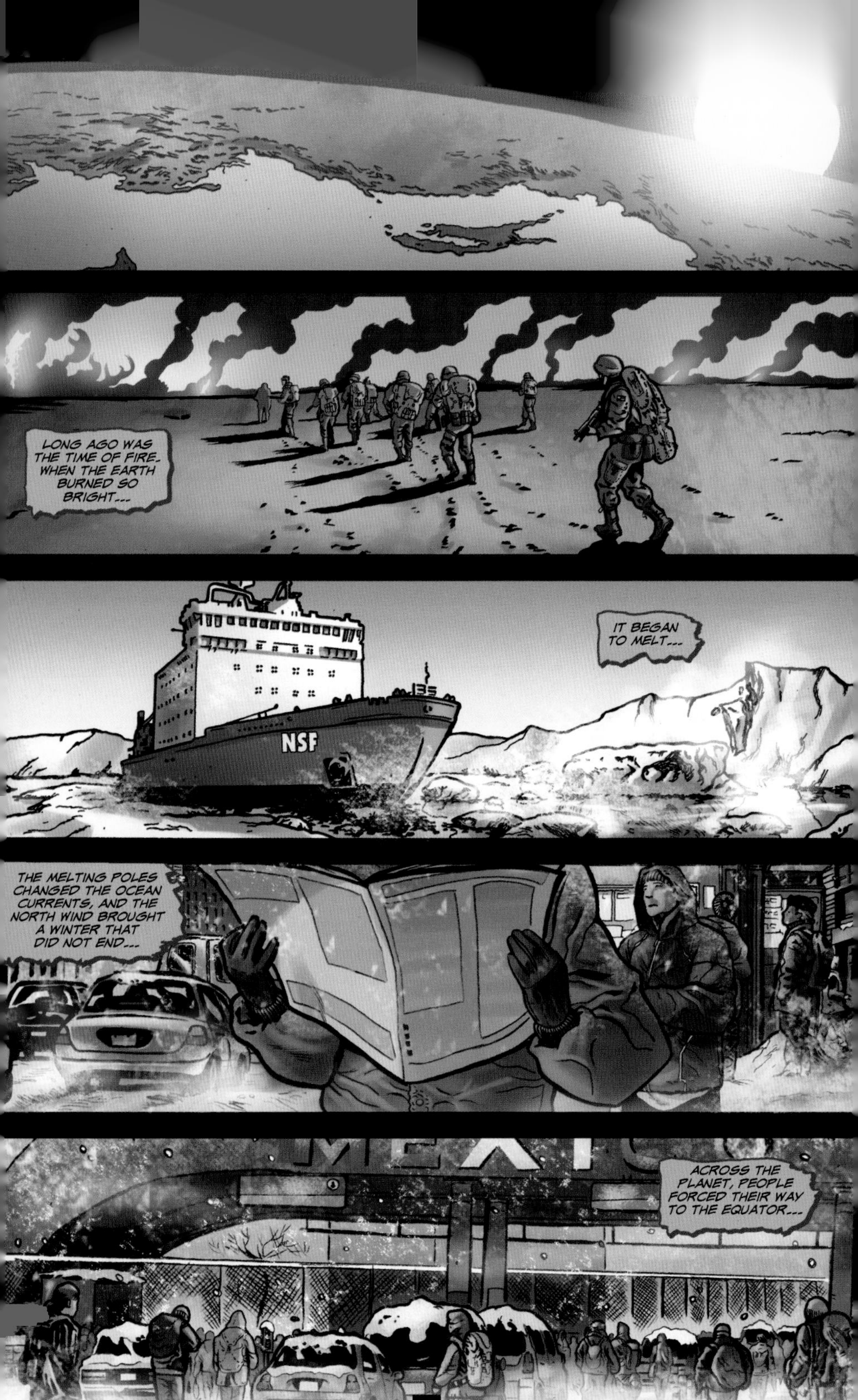
LONG AGO WAS THE TIME OF FIRE. WHEN THE EARTH BURNED SO BRIGHT...
IT BEGAN TO MELT...
NSF
THE MELTING POLES CHANGED THE OCEAN CURRENTS, AND THE NORTH WIND BROUGHT A WINTER THAT DID NOT END...
ACROSS THE PLANET, PEOPLE FORCED THEIR WAY TO THE EQUATOR...

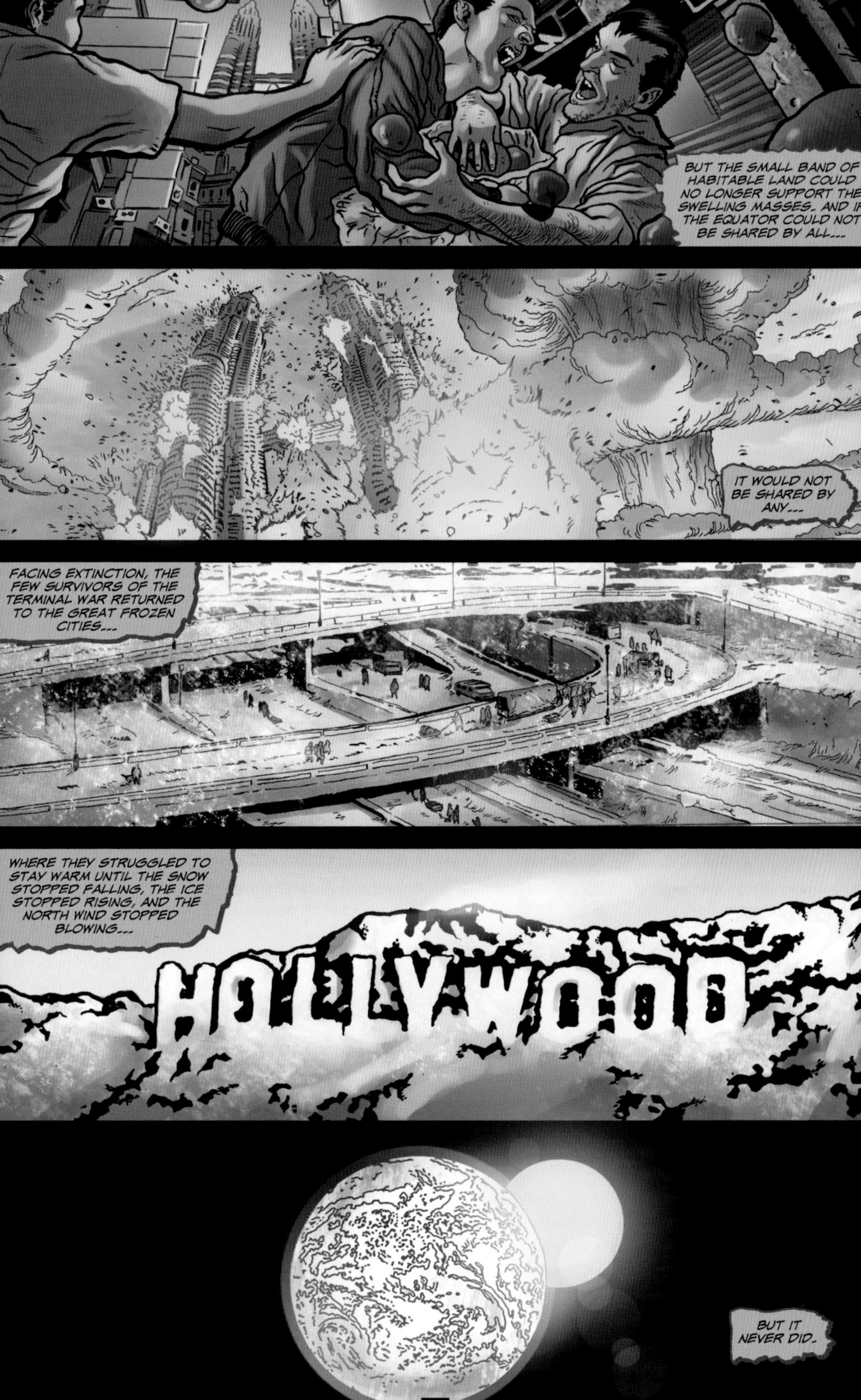
BUT THE SMALL BAND OF HABITABLE LAND COULD NO LONGER SUPPORT THE SWELLING MASSES. AND IF THE EQUATOR COULD NOT BE SHARED BY ALL...
IT WOULD NOT BE SHARED BY ANY...
FACING EXTINCTION, THE FEW SURVIVORS OF THE TERMINAL WAR RETURNED TO THE GREAT FROZEN CITIES...
WHERE THEY STRUGGLED TO STAY WARM UNTIL THE SNOW STOPPED FALLING, THE ICE STOPPED RISING, AND THE NORTH WIND STOPPED BLOWING...
HOLLYWOOD
BUT IT NEVER DID.

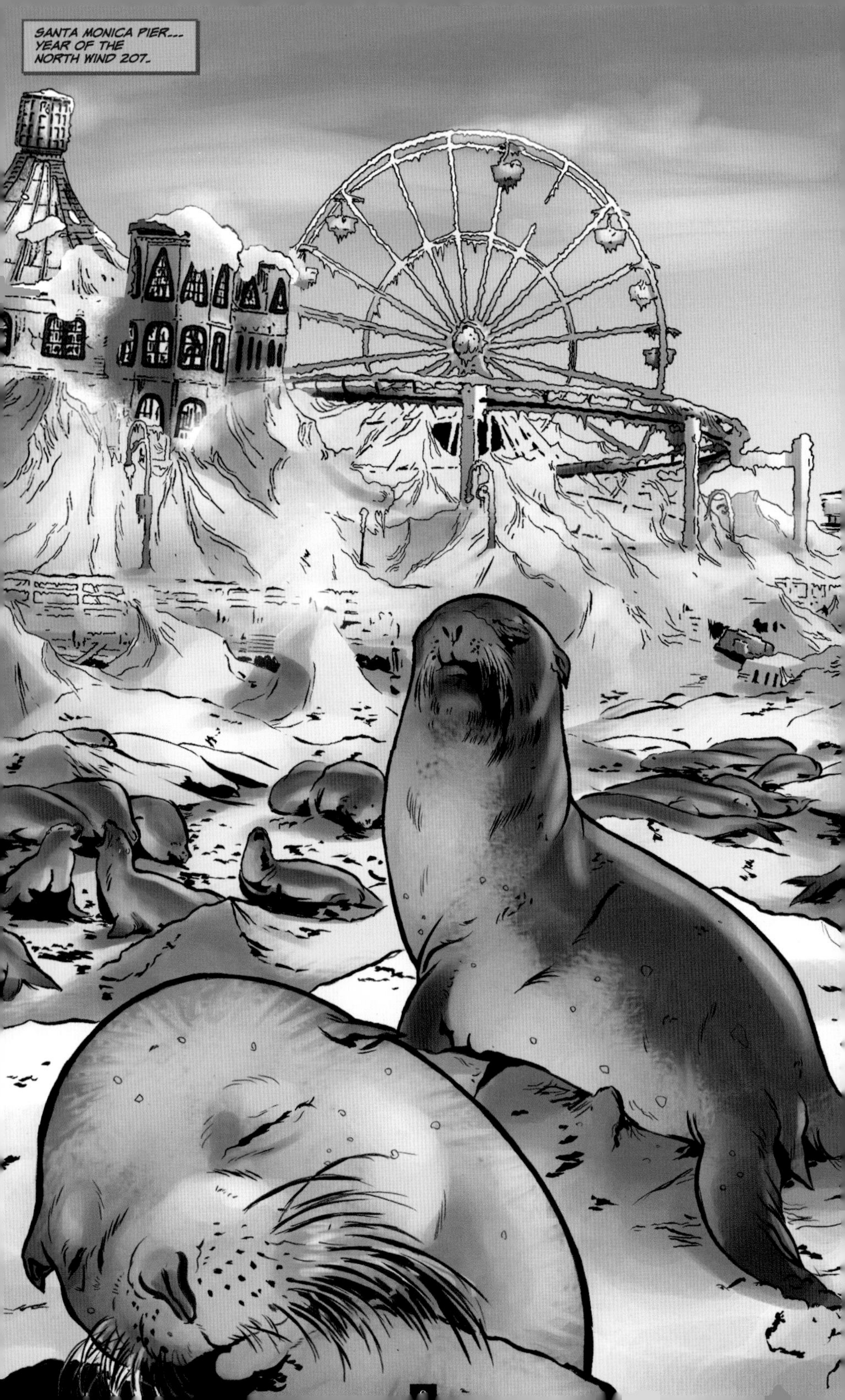
SANTA MONICA PIER... YEAR OF THE NORTH WIND 207.

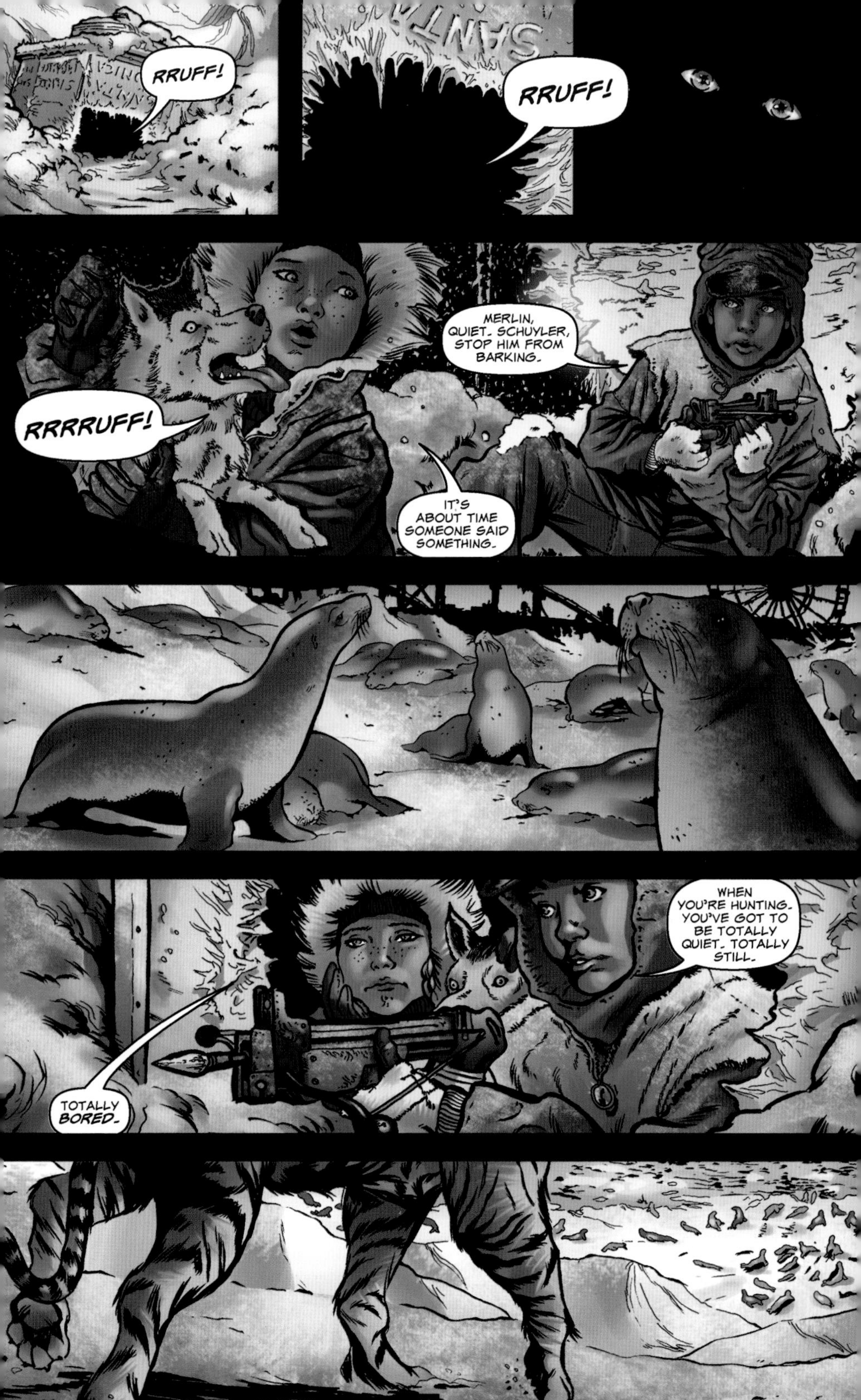
RRUFF!
RRUFF!
MERLIN, QUIET. SCHUYLER, STOP HIM FROM BARKING.
RRRRUFF!
IT'S ABOUT TIME SOMEONE SAID SOMETHING.
WHEN YOU'RE HUNTING. YOU'VE GOT TO BE TOTALLY QUIET. TOTALLY STILL.
TOTALLY BORED.

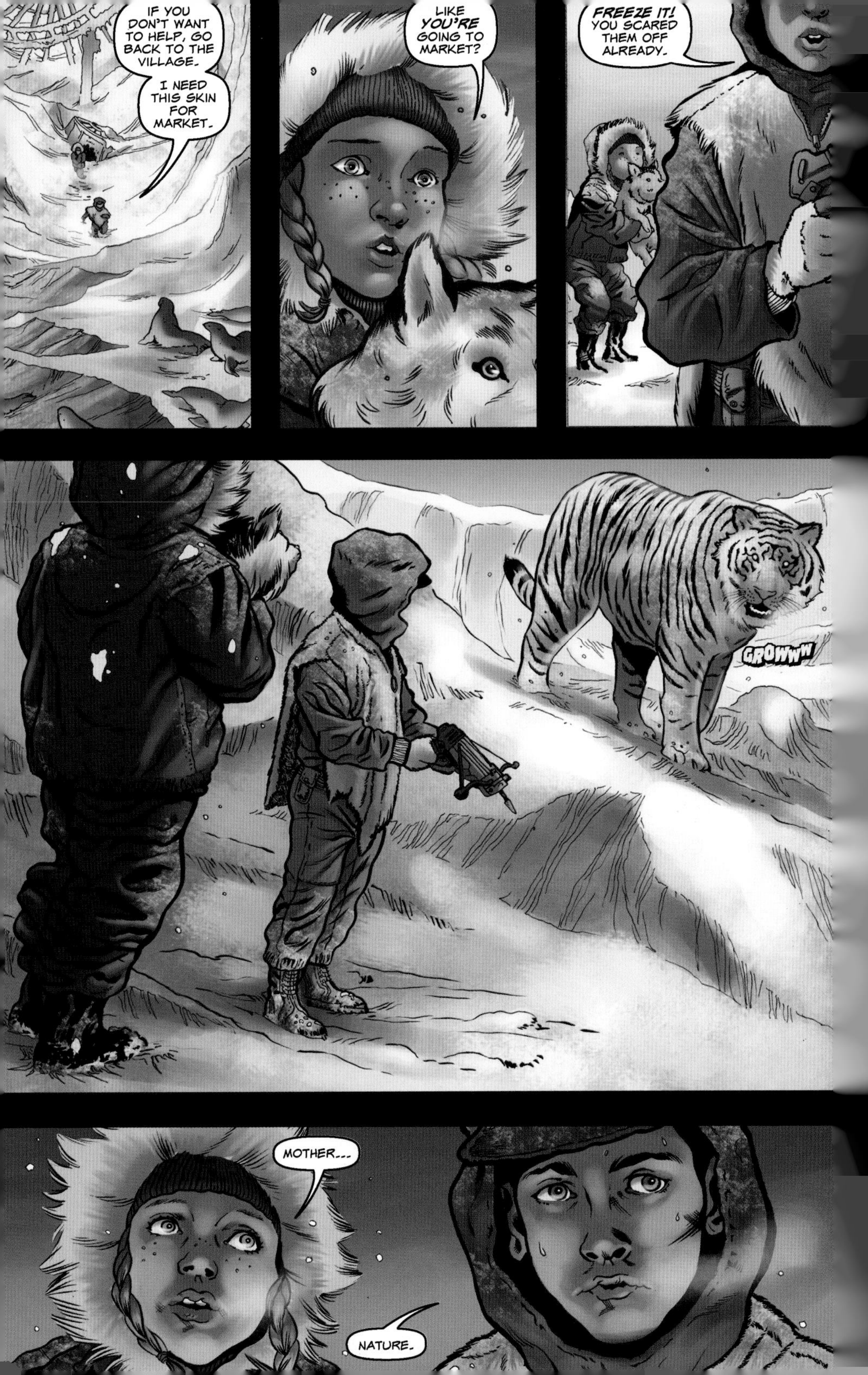
IF YOU DON'T WANT TO HELP, GO BACK TO THE VILLAGE.
I NEED THIS SKIN FOR MARKET.
LIKE *YOU'RE* GOING TO MARKET?
FREEZE IT! YOU SCARED THEM OFF ALREADY.
GROWWW
MOTHER...
NATURE.

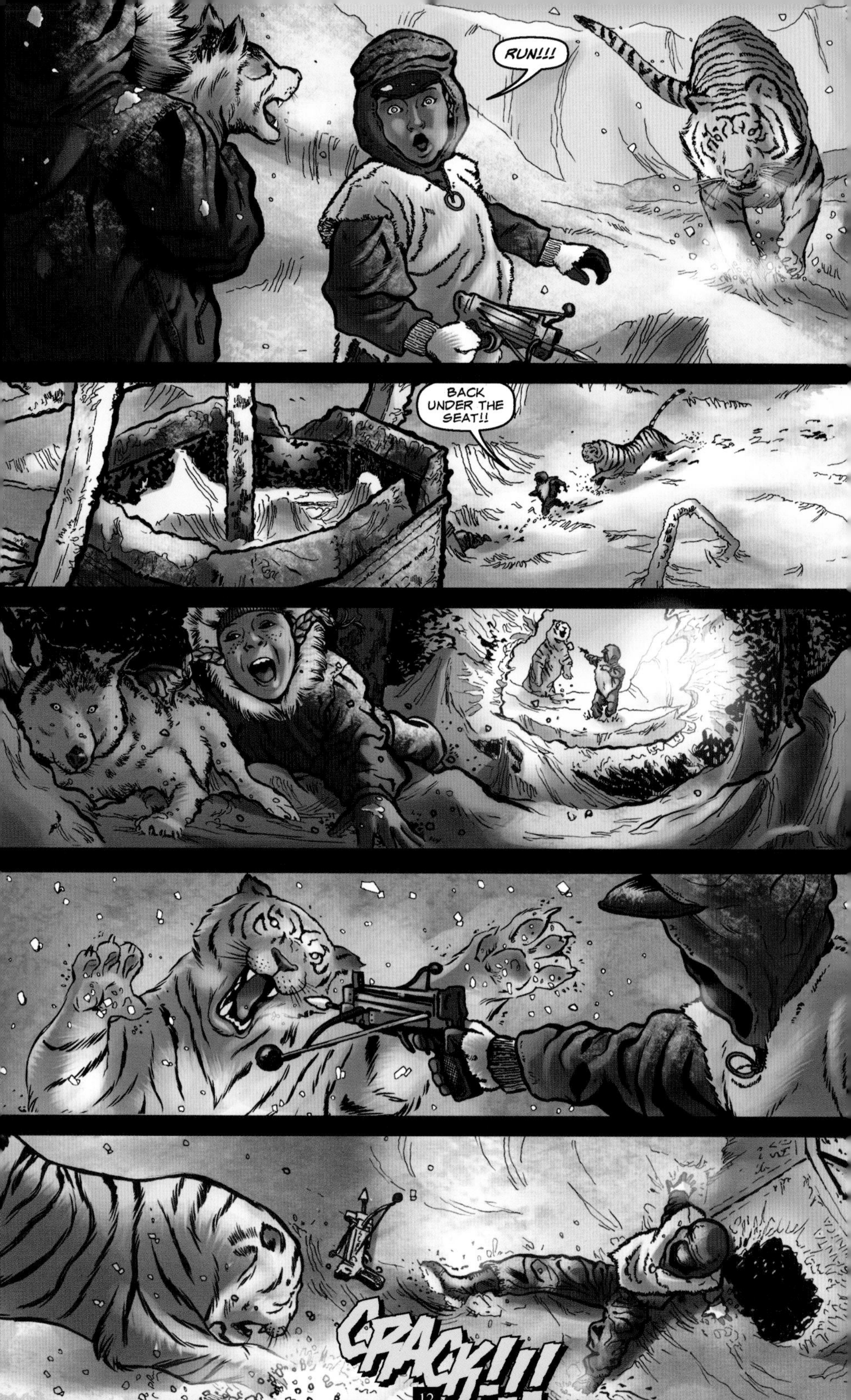
RUN!!!
BACK UNDER THE SEAT!!
CRACK!!!

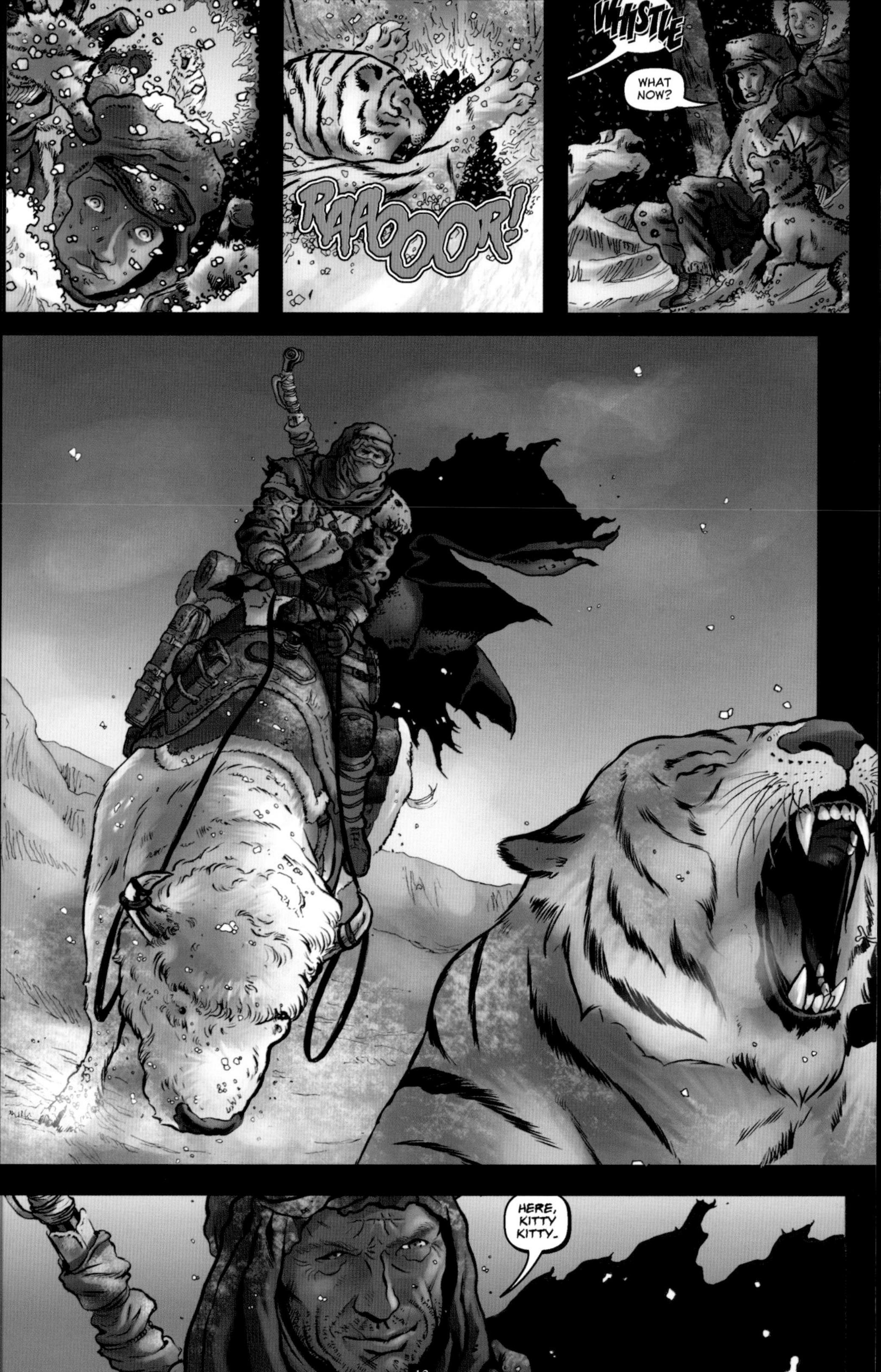

RAAOOOR!
WHISTLE
WHAT NOW?
HERE, KITTY KITTY.

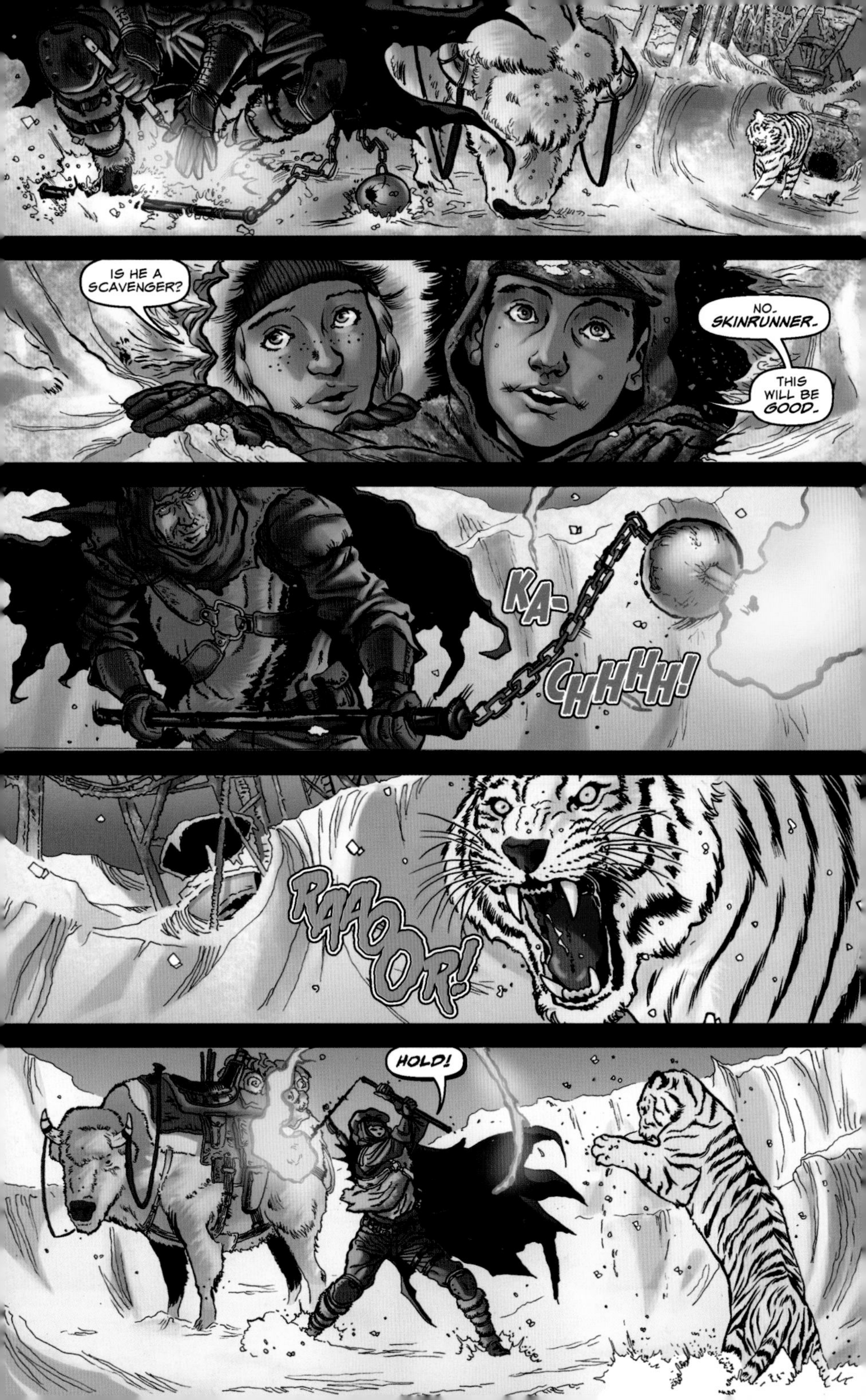
IS HE A SCAVENGER?
NO. SKINRUNNER.
THIS WILL BE GOOD.
KA-CHHHHH!
RAAOOR!
HOLD!

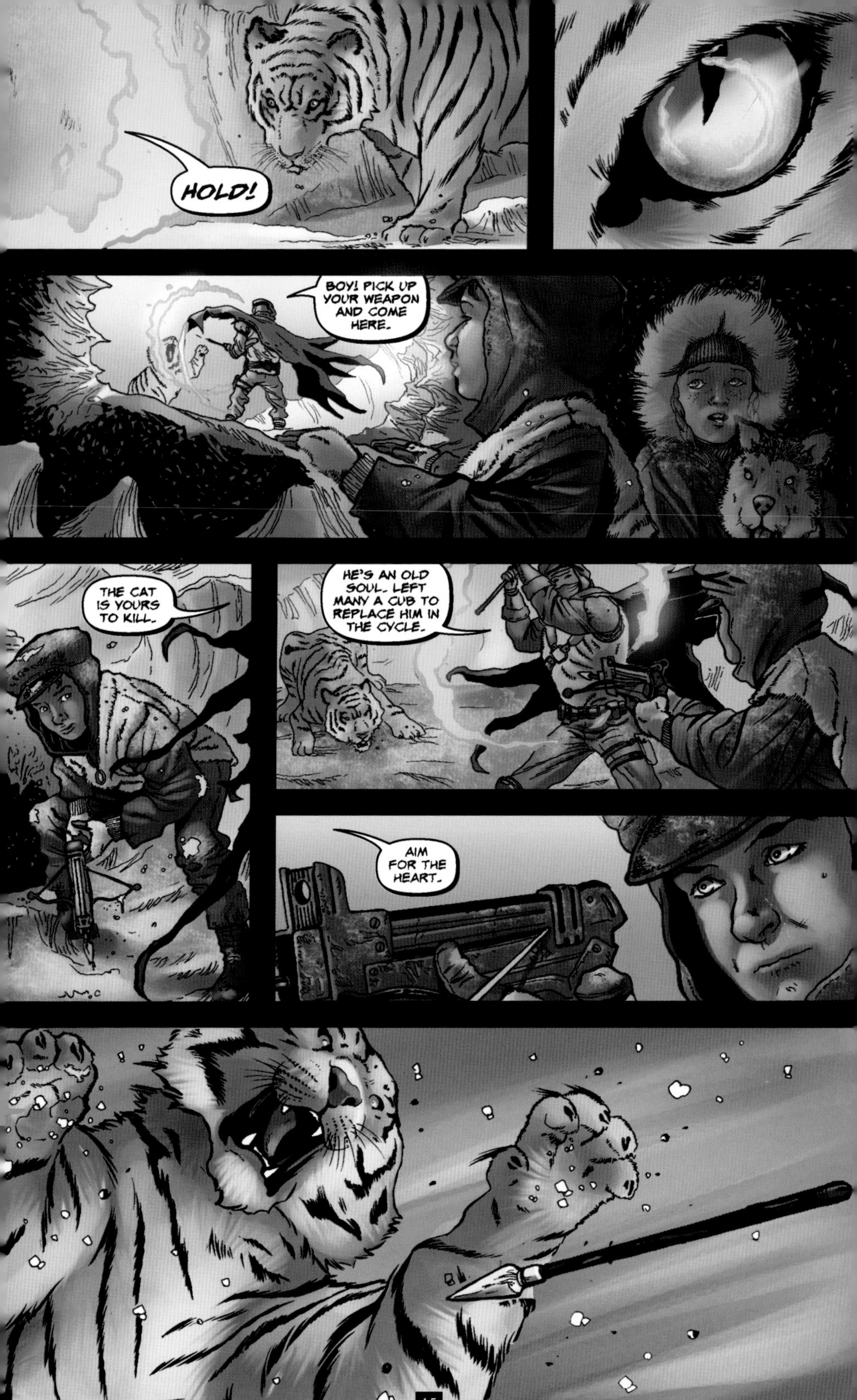
HOLD!
BOY! PICK UP YOUR WEAPON AND COME HERE.
THE CAT IS YOURS TO KILL.
HE'S AN OLD SOUL. LEFT MANY A CUB TO REPLACE HIM IN THE CYCLE.
AIM FOR THE HEART.

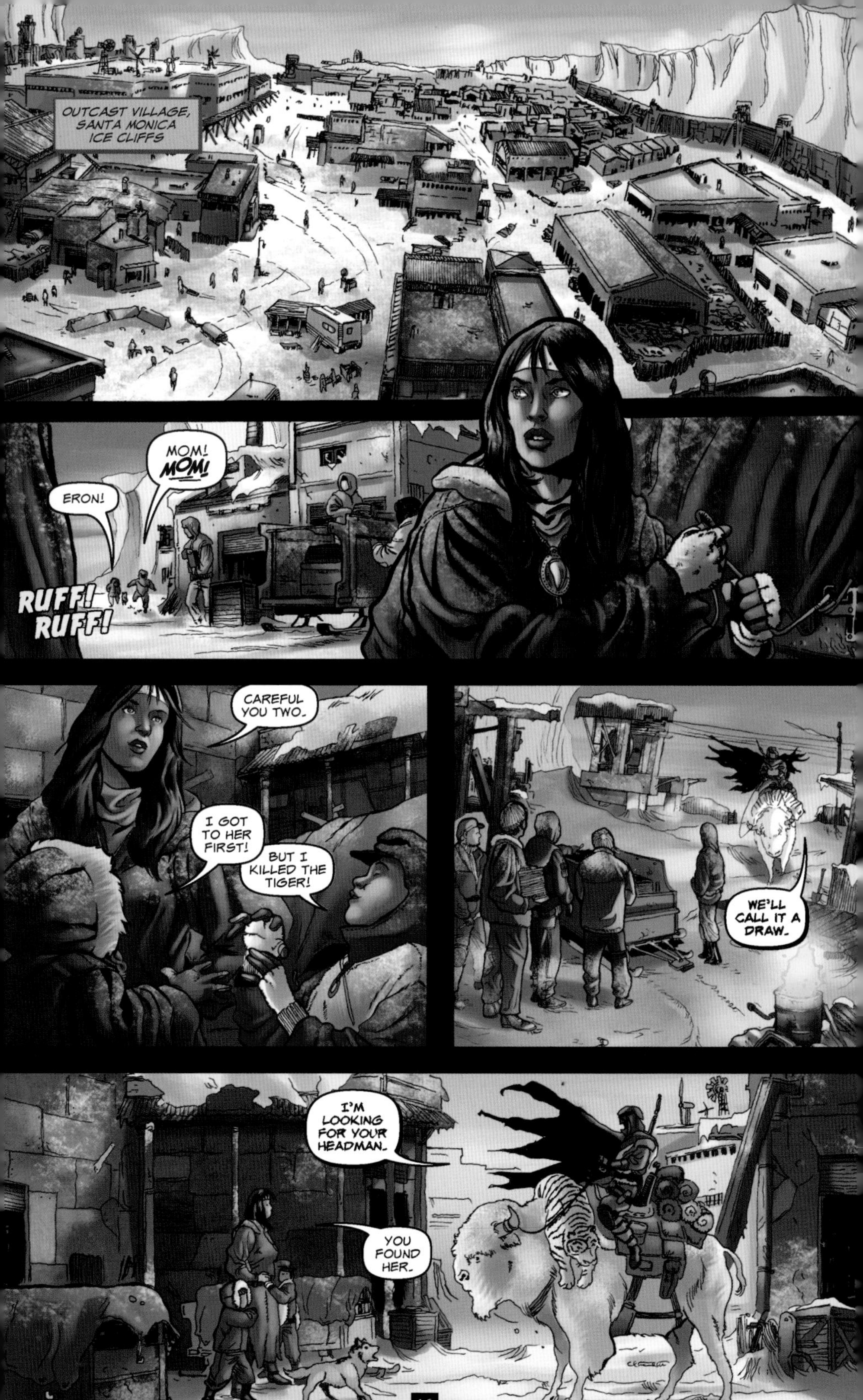
OUTCAST VILLAGE, SANTA MONICA ICE CLIFFS
MOM! MOM!
ERON!
RUFF! RUFF!
CAREFUL YOU TWO.
I GOT TO HER FIRST!
BUT I KILLED THE TIGER!
WE'LL CALL IT A DRAW.
I'M LOOKING FOR YOUR HEADMAN.
YOU FOUND HER.

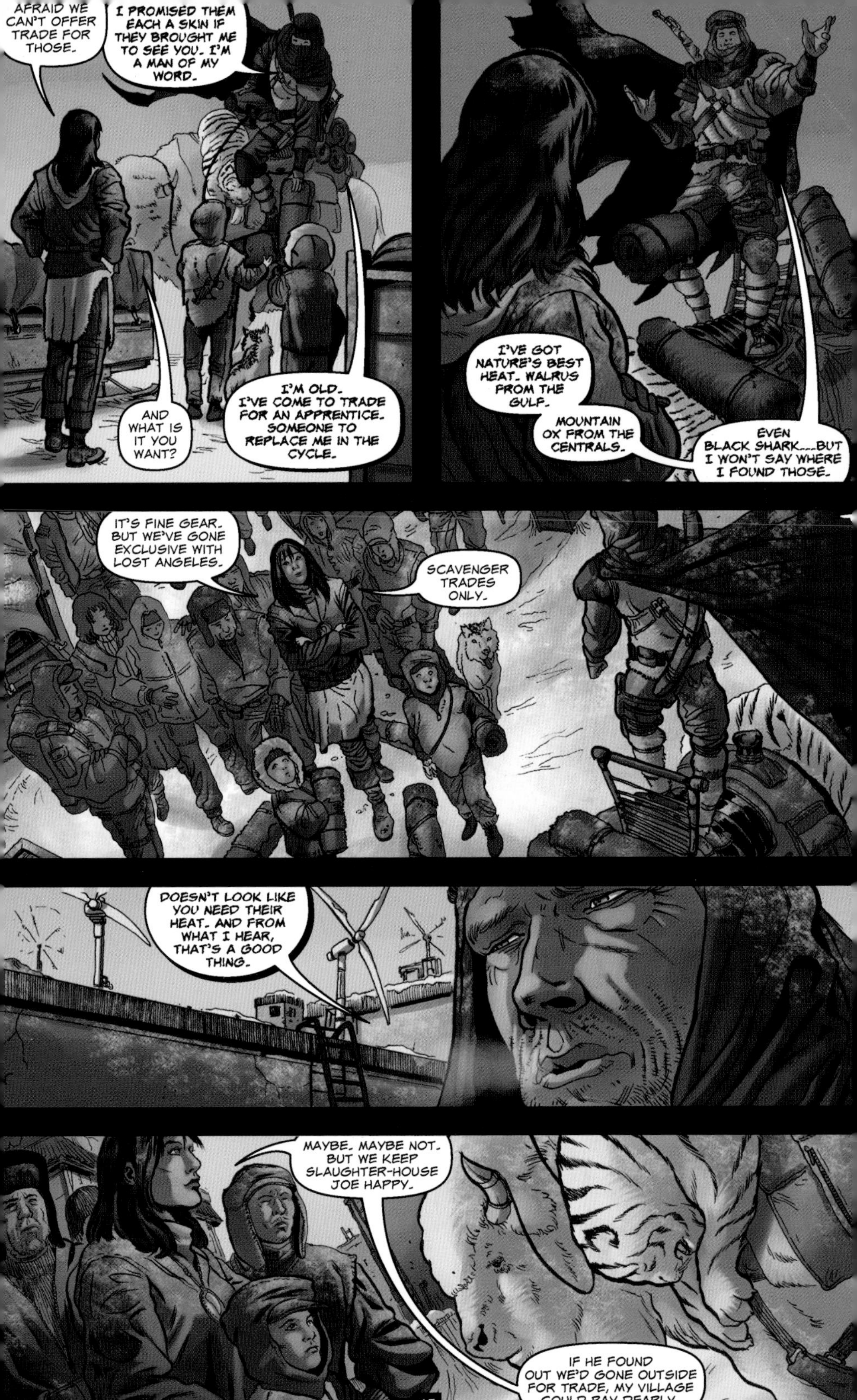
AFRAID WE CAN'T OFFER TRADE FOR THOSE.
I PROMISED THEM EACH A SKIN IF THEY BROUGHT ME TO SEE YOU. I'M A MAN OF MY WORD.
AND WHAT IS IT YOU WANT?
I'M OLD. I'VE COME TO TRADE FOR AN APPRENTICE. SOMEONE TO REPLACE ME IN THE CYCLE.
I'VE GOT NATURE'S BEST HEAT. WALRUS FROM THE GULF.
MOUNTAIN OX FROM THE CENTRALS.
EVEN BLACK SHARK... BUT I WON'T SAY WHERE I FOUND THOSE.
IT'S FINE GEAR. BUT WE'VE GONE EXCLUSIVE WITH LOST ANGELES.
SCAVENGER TRADES ONLY.
DOESN'T LOOK LIKE YOU NEED THEIR HEAT. AND FROM WHAT I HEAR, THAT'S A GOOD THING.
MAYBE. MAYBE NOT. BUT WE KEEP SLAUGHTER-HOUSE JOE HAPPY.
IF HE FOUND OUT WE'D GONE OUTSIDE FOR TRADE, MY VILLAGE COULD PAY DEARLY.

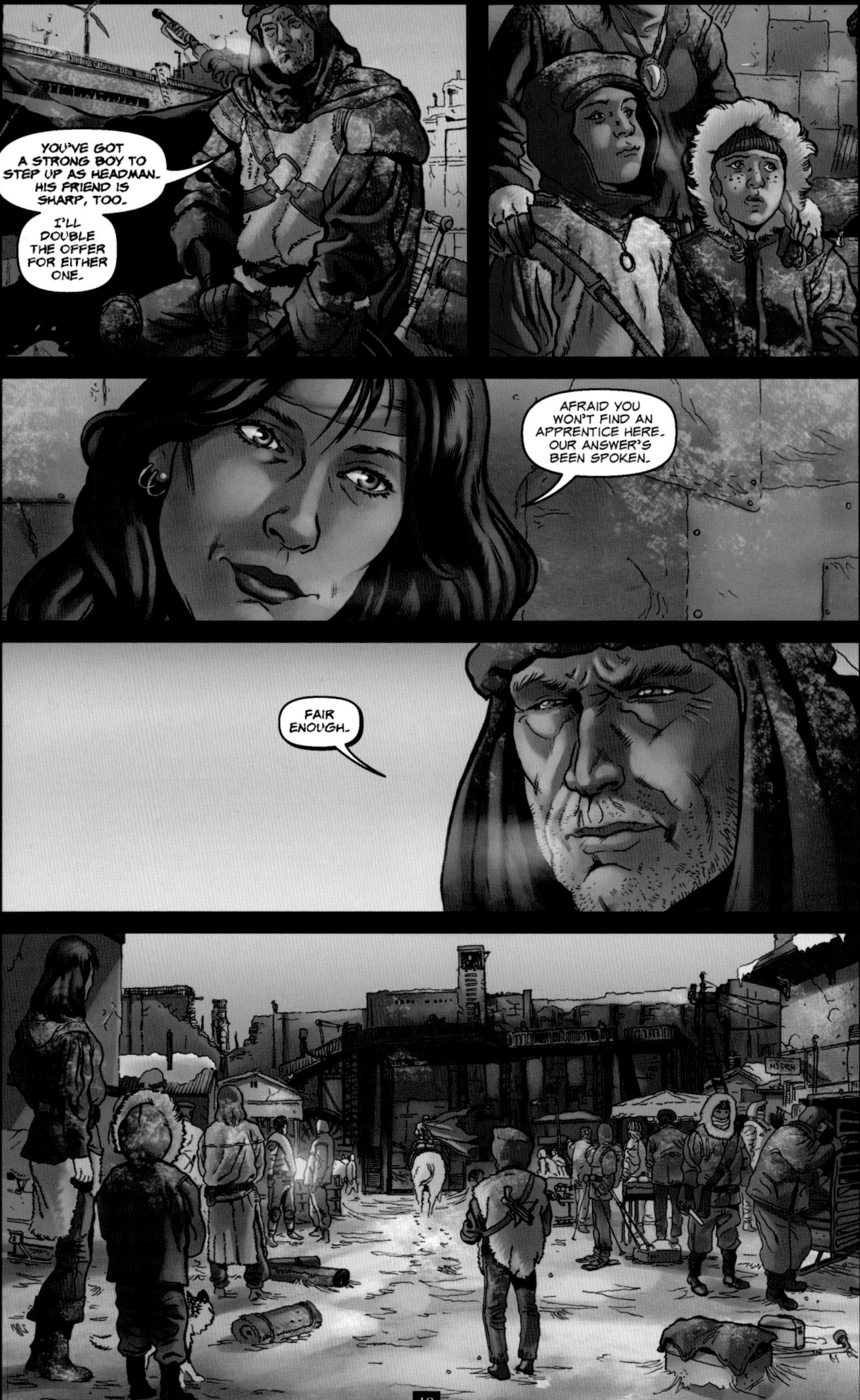
YOU'VE GOT A STRONG BOY TO STEP UP AS HEADMAN. HIS FRIEND IS SHARP, TOO.
I'LL DOUBLE THE OFFER FOR EITHER ONE.
AFRAID YOU WON'T FIND AN APPRENTICE HERE. OUR ANSWER'S BEEN SPOKEN.
FAIR ENOUGH.

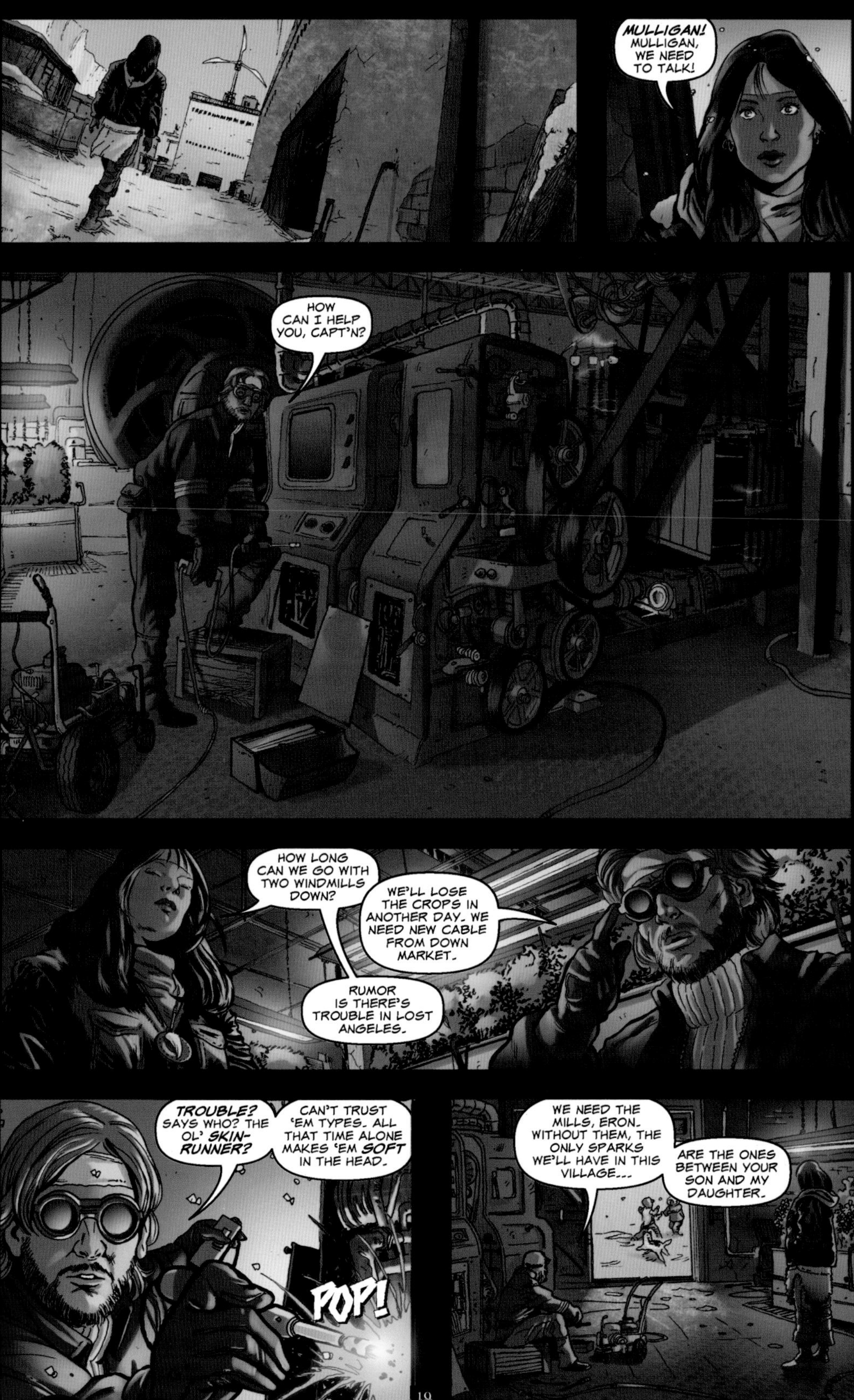
MULLIGAN! MULLIGAN, WE NEED TO TALK!
HOW CAN I HELP YOU, CAPT'N?
HOW LONG CAN WE GO WITH TWO WINDMILLS DOWN?
WE'LL LOSE THE CROPS IN ANOTHER DAY. WE NEED NEW CABLE FROM DOWN MARKET.
RUMOR IS THERE'S TROUBLE IN LOST ANGELES.
TROUBLE? SAYS WHO? THE OL' SKIN-RUNNER?
CAN'T TRUST 'EM TYPES. ALL THAT TIME ALONE MAKES 'EM SOFT IN THE HEAD.
POP!
WE NEED THE MILLS, ERON. WITHOUT THEM, THE ONLY SPARKS WE'LL HAVE IN THIS VILLAGE...
ARE THE ONES BETWEEN YOUR SON AND MY DAUGHTER.

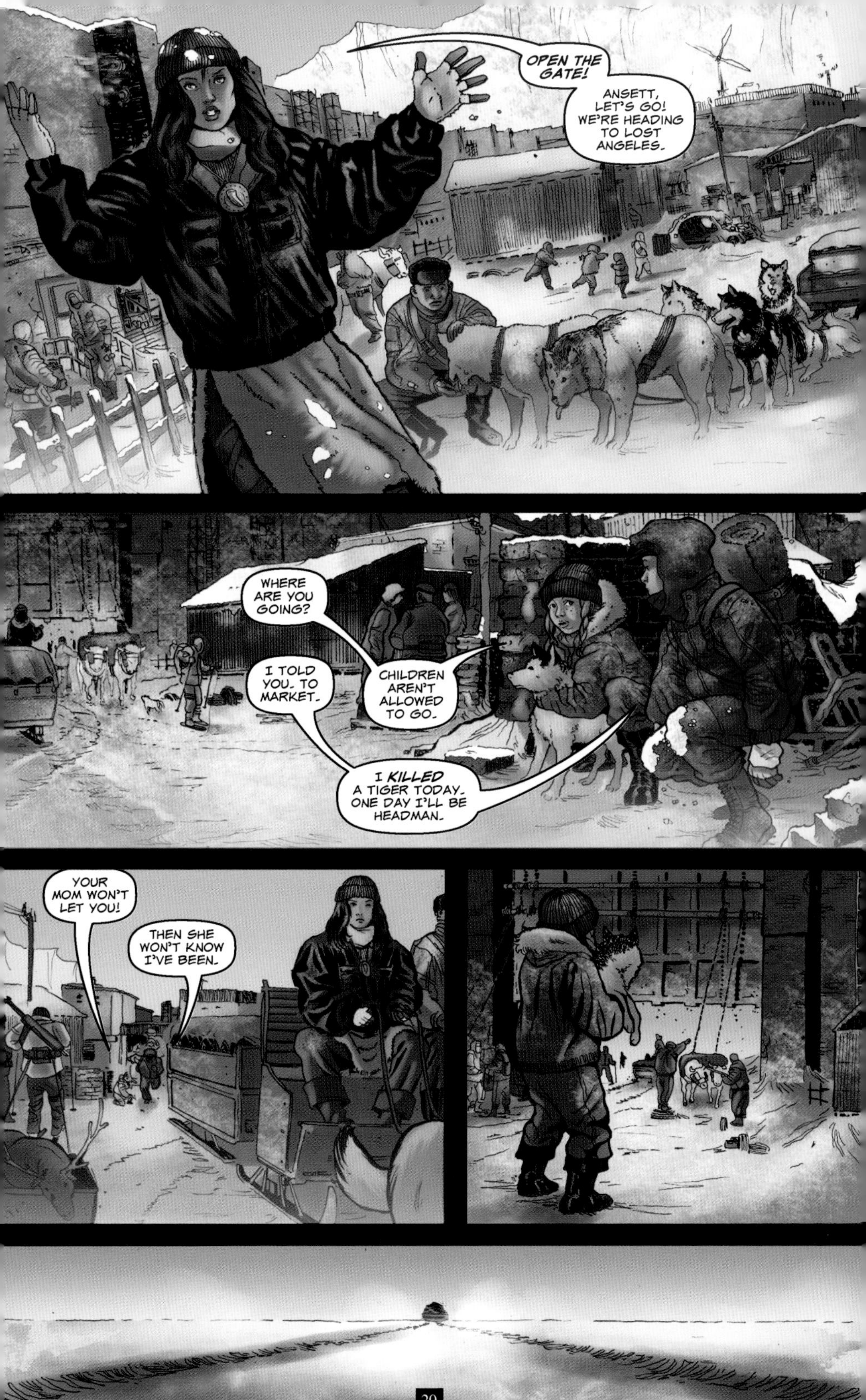
OPEN THE GATE!
ANSETT, LET'S GO! WE'RE HEADING TO LOST ANGELES.
WHERE ARE YOU GOING?
I TOLD YOU. TO MARKET.
CHILDREN AREN'T ALLOWED TO GO.
I KILLED A TIGER TODAY. ONE DAY I'LL BE HEADMAN.
YOUR MOM WON'T LET YOU!
THEN SHE WON'T KNOW I'VE BEEN.

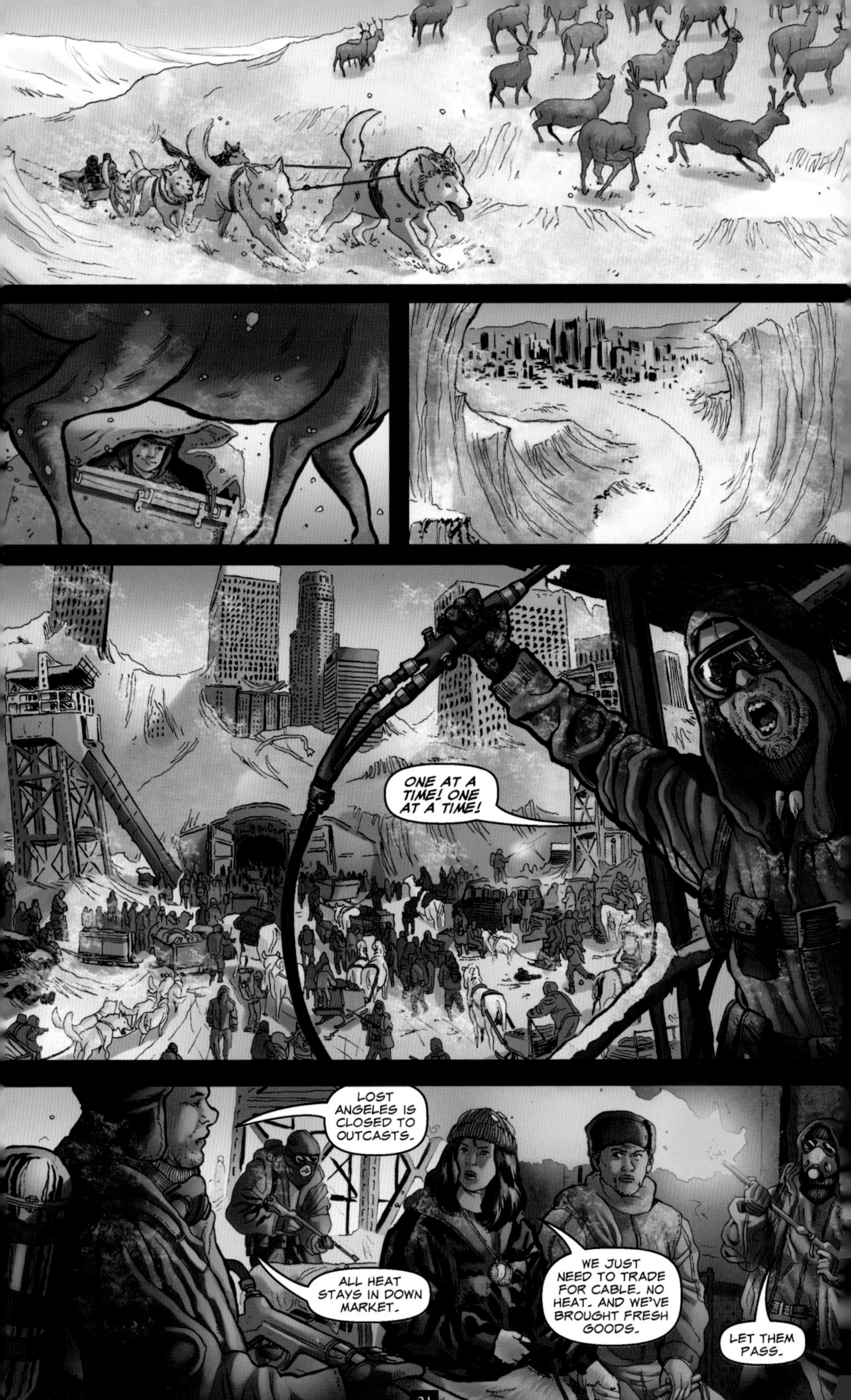
ONE AT A TIME! ONE AT A TIME!
LOST ANGELES IS CLOSED TO OUTCASTS.
ALL HEAT STAYS IN DOWN MARKET.
WE JUST NEED TO TRADE FOR CABLE. NO HEAT. AND WE'VE BROUGHT FRESH GOODS.
LET THEM PASS.

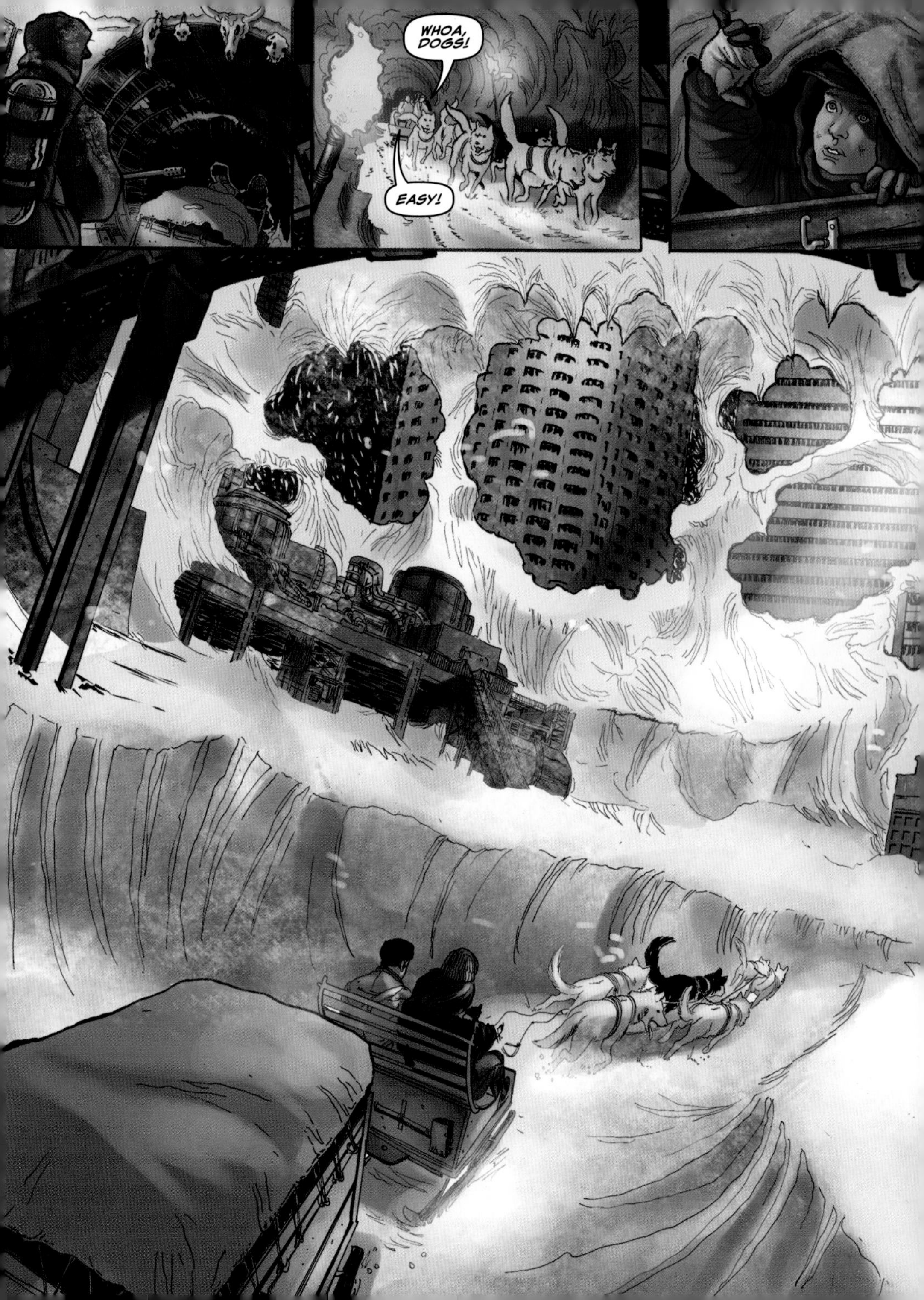
WHOA, DOGS!
EASY!

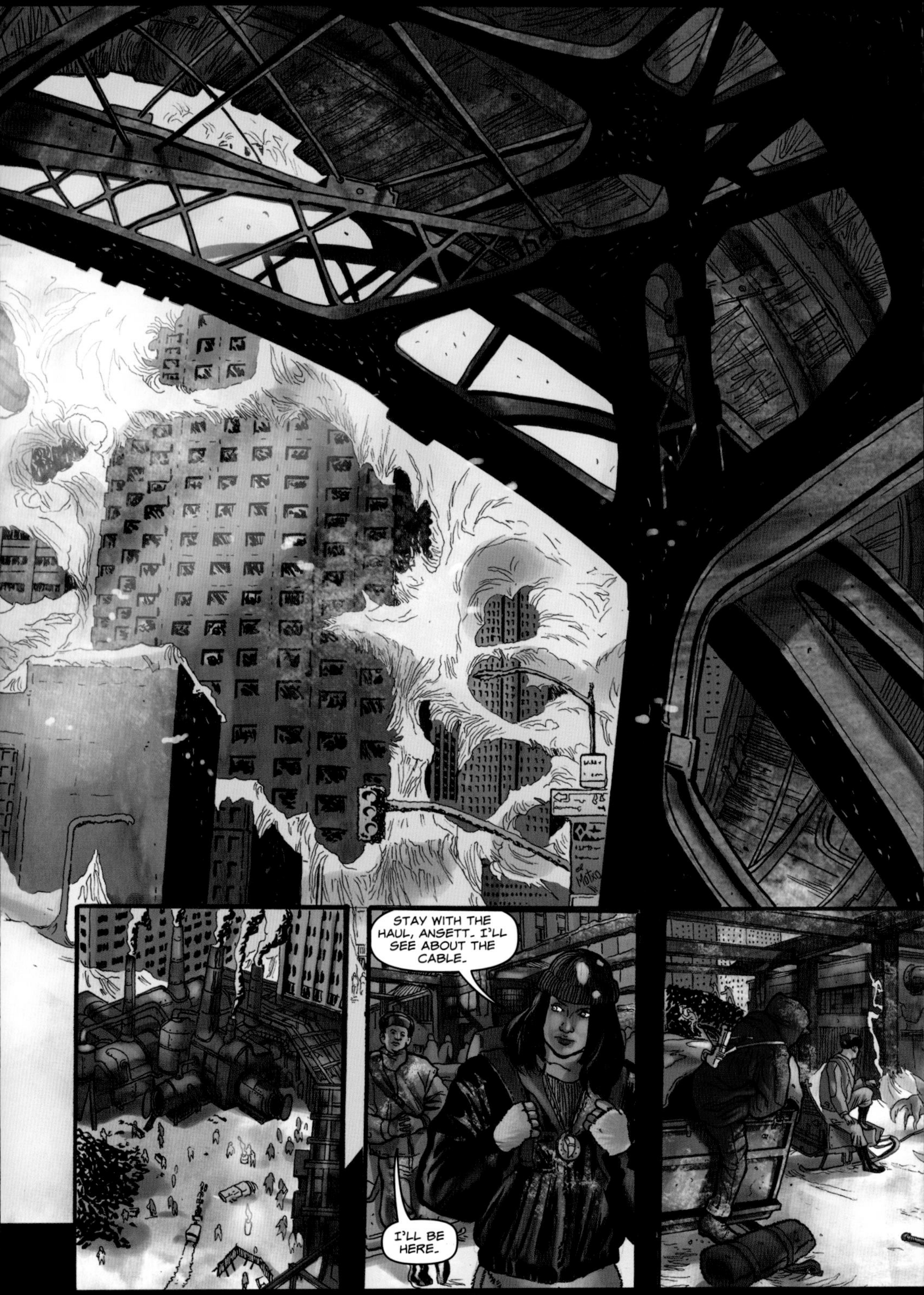
STAY WITH THE HAUL, ANSETT. I'LL SEE ABOUT THE CABLE.
I'LL BE HERE.

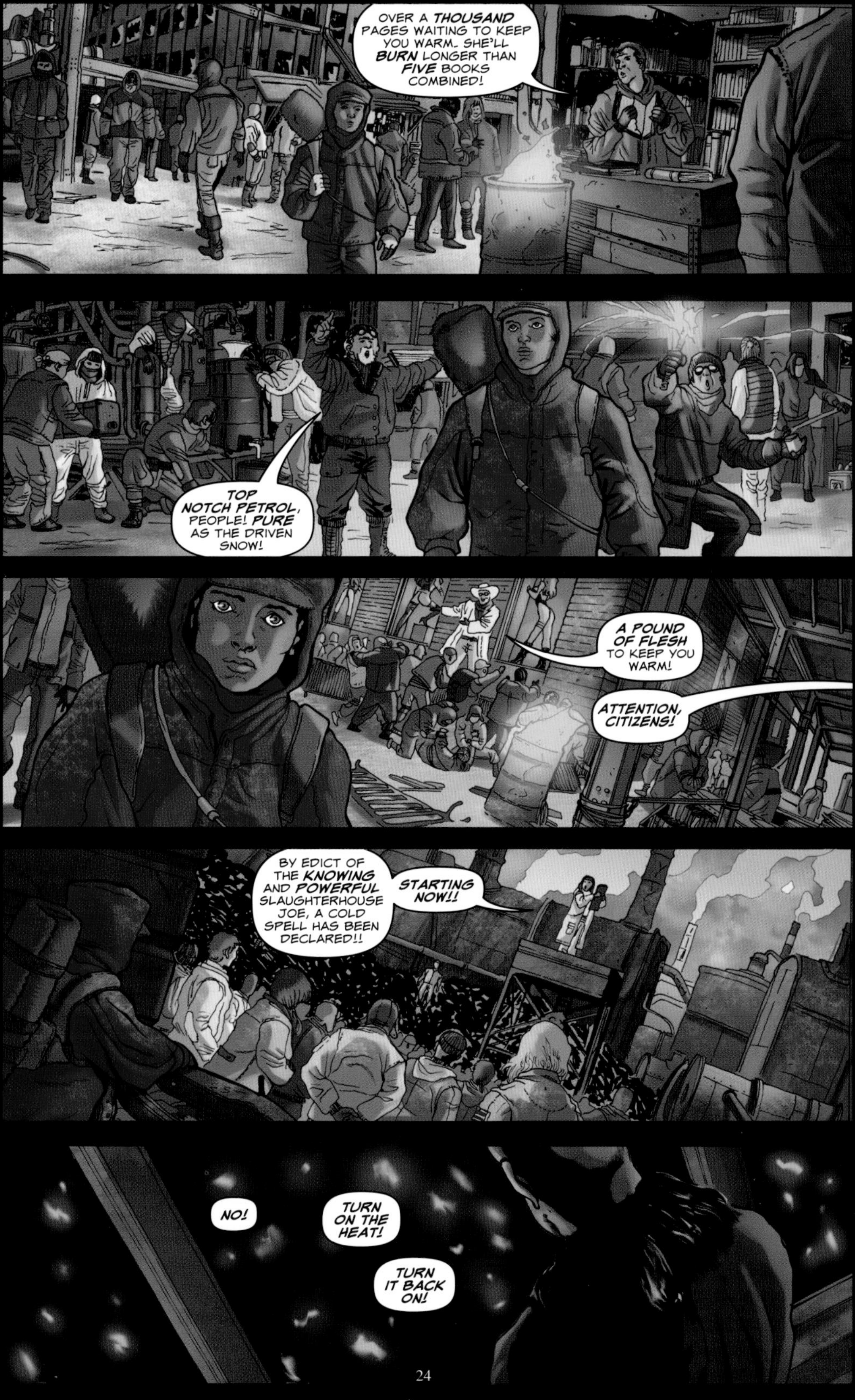
OVER A THOUSAND PAGES WAITING TO KEEP YOU WARM. SHE'LL BURN LONGER THAN FIVE BOOKS COMBINED!
TOP NOTCH PETROL, PEOPLE! PURE AS THE DRIVEN SNOW!
A POUND OF FLESH TO KEEP YOU WARM!
ATTENTION, CITIZENS!
BY EDICT OF THE KNOWING AND POWERFUL SLAUGHTERHOUSE JOE, A COLD SPELL HAS BEEN DECLARED!!
STARTING NOW!!
NO!
TURN ON THE HEAT!
TURN IT BACK ON!

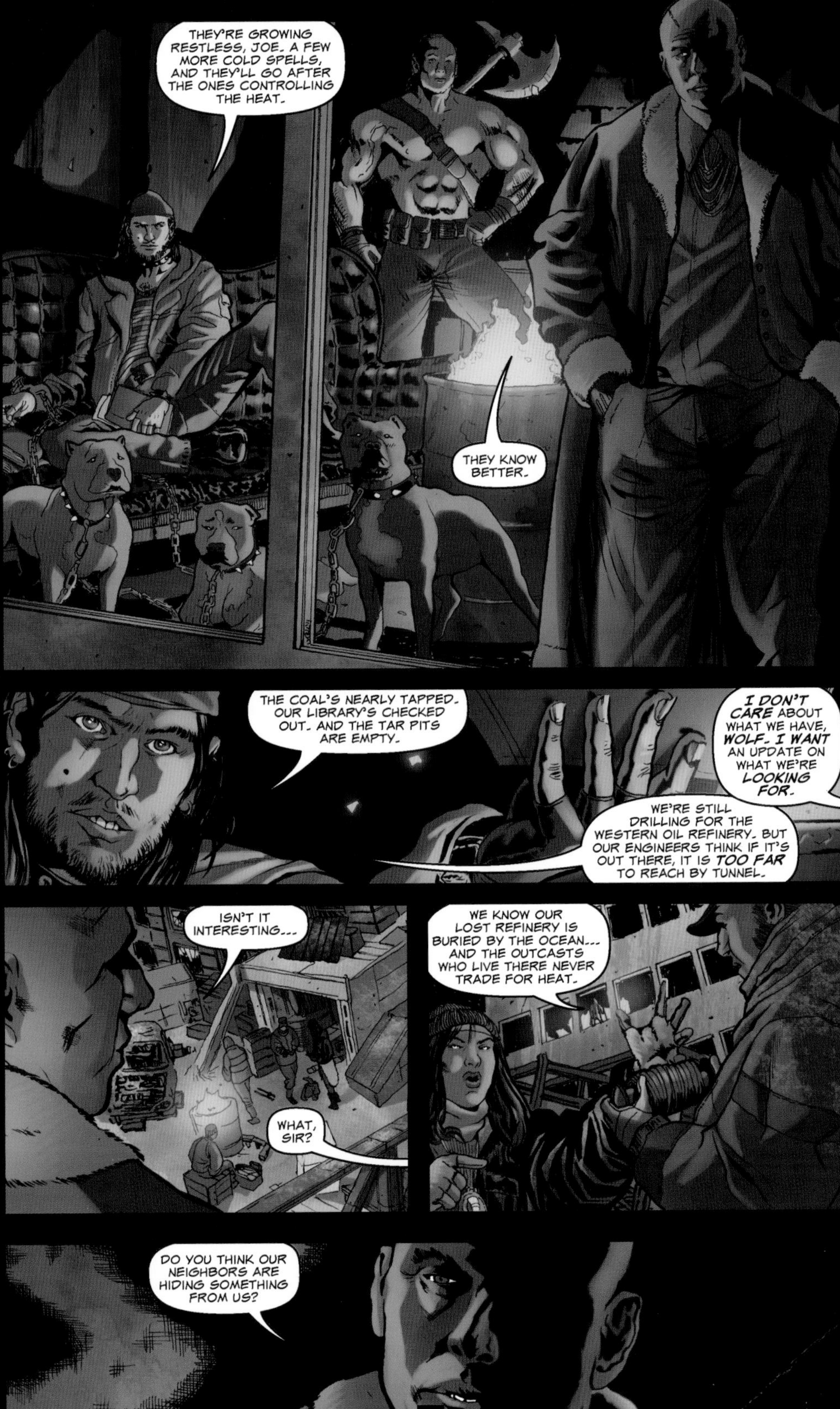
THEY'RE GROWING RESTLESS, JOE. A FEW MORE COLD SPELLS, AND THEY'LL GO AFTER THE ONES CONTROLLING THE HEAT.
THEY KNOW BETTER.
THE COAL'S NEARLY TAPPED. OUR LIBRARY'S CHECKED OUT. AND THE TAR PITS ARE EMPTY.
I DON'T CARE ABOUT WHAT WE HAVE, WOLF. I WANT AN UPDATE ON WHAT WE'RE LOOKING FOR.
WE'RE STILL DRILLING FOR THE WESTERN OIL REFINERY. BUT OUR ENGINEERS THINK IF IT'S OUT THERE, IT IS TOO FAR TO REACH BY TUNNEL.
ISN'T IT INTERESTING...
WHAT, SIR?
WE KNOW OUR LOST REFINERY IS BURIED BY THE OCEAN... AND THE OUTCASTS WHO LIVE THERE NEVER TRADE FOR HEAT.
DO YOU THINK OUR NEIGHBORS ARE HIDING SOMETHING FROM US?

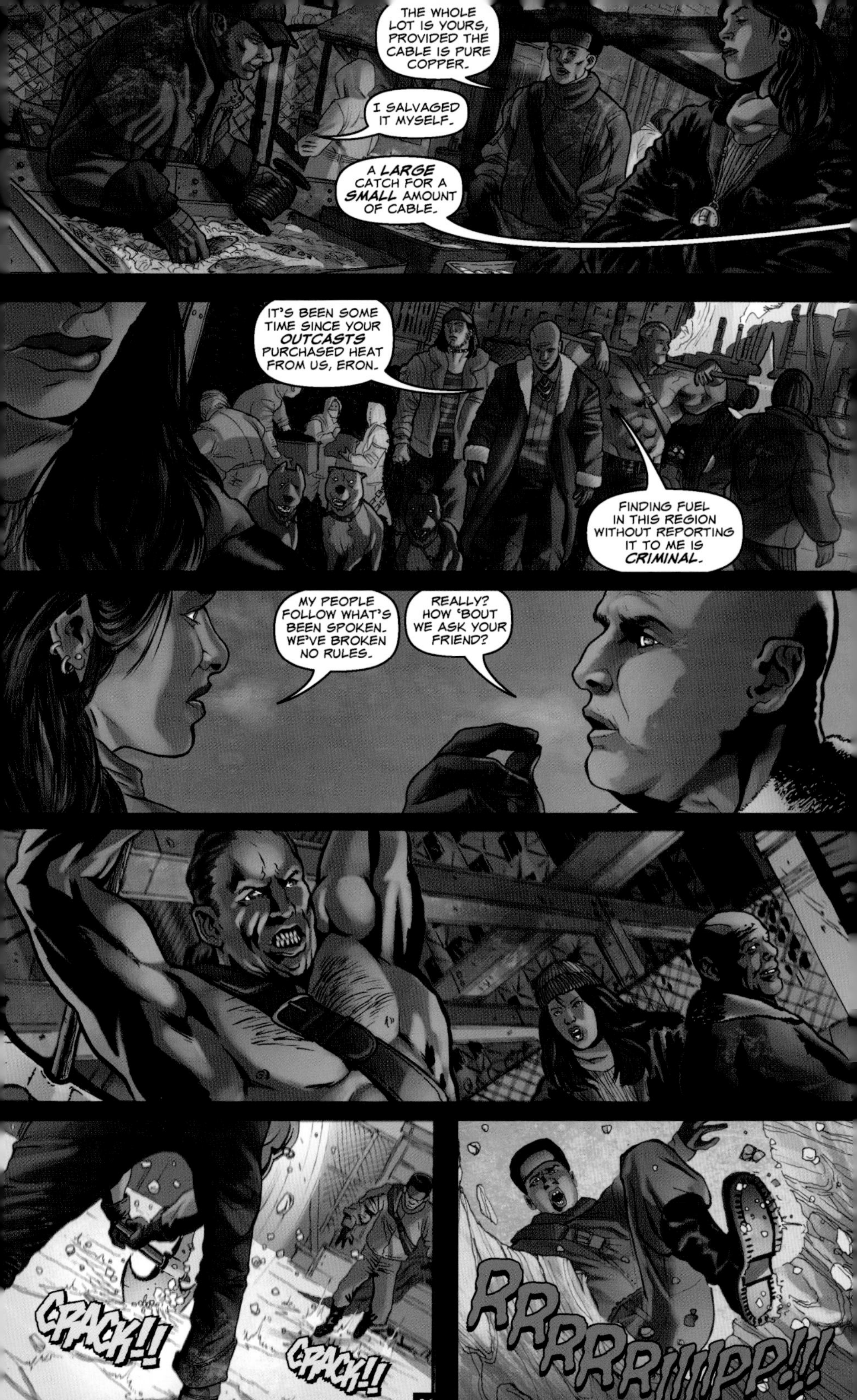
THE WHOLE LOT IS YOURS, PROVIDED THE CABLE IS PURE COPPER.
I SALVAGED IT MYSELF.
A **LARGE** CATCH FOR A **SMALL** AMOUNT OF CABLE.
IT'S BEEN SOME TIME SINCE YOUR ***OUTCASTS*** PURCHASED HEAT FROM US, ERON.
FINDING FUEL IN THIS REGION WITHOUT REPORTING IT TO ME IS ***CRIMINAL***.
MY PEOPLE FOLLOW WHAT'S BEEN SPOKEN. WE'VE BROKEN NO RULES.
REALLY? HOW 'BOUT WE ASK YOUR FRIEND?
CRACK!!!
CRACK!!!
RRRRRRIIIIPP!!!

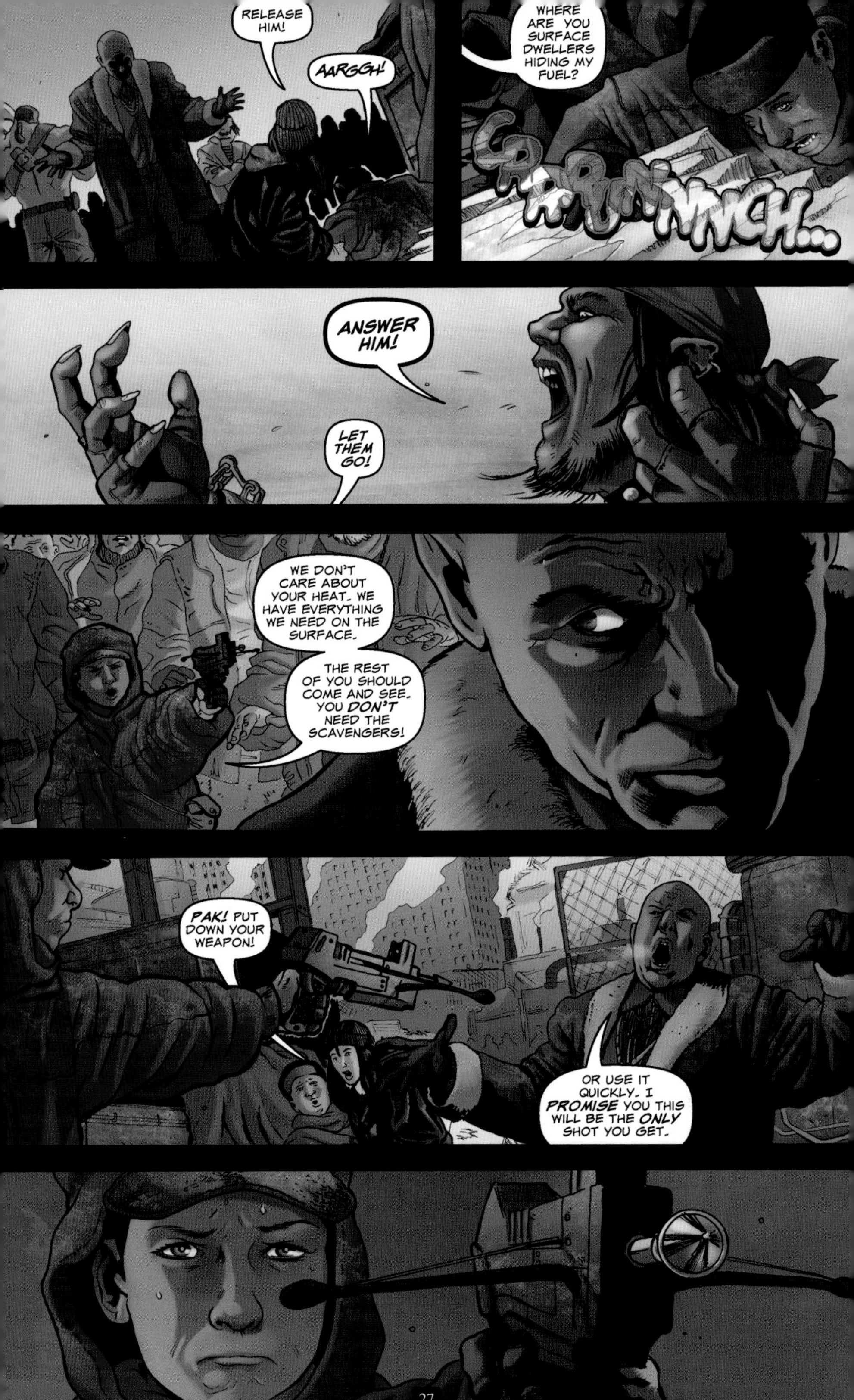
RELEASE HIM!
AARGGH!
WHERE ARE YOU SURFACE DWELLERS HIDING MY FUEL?
CRRRUNNNCH...
ANSWER HIM!
LET THEM GO!
WE DON'T CARE ABOUT YOUR HEAT. WE HAVE EVERYTHING WE NEED ON THE SURFACE.
THE REST OF YOU SHOULD COME AND SEE. YOU DON'T NEED THE SCAVENGERS!
PAK! PUT DOWN YOUR WEAPON!
OR USE IT QUICKLY. I PROMISE YOU THIS WILL BE THE ONLY SHOT YOU GET.

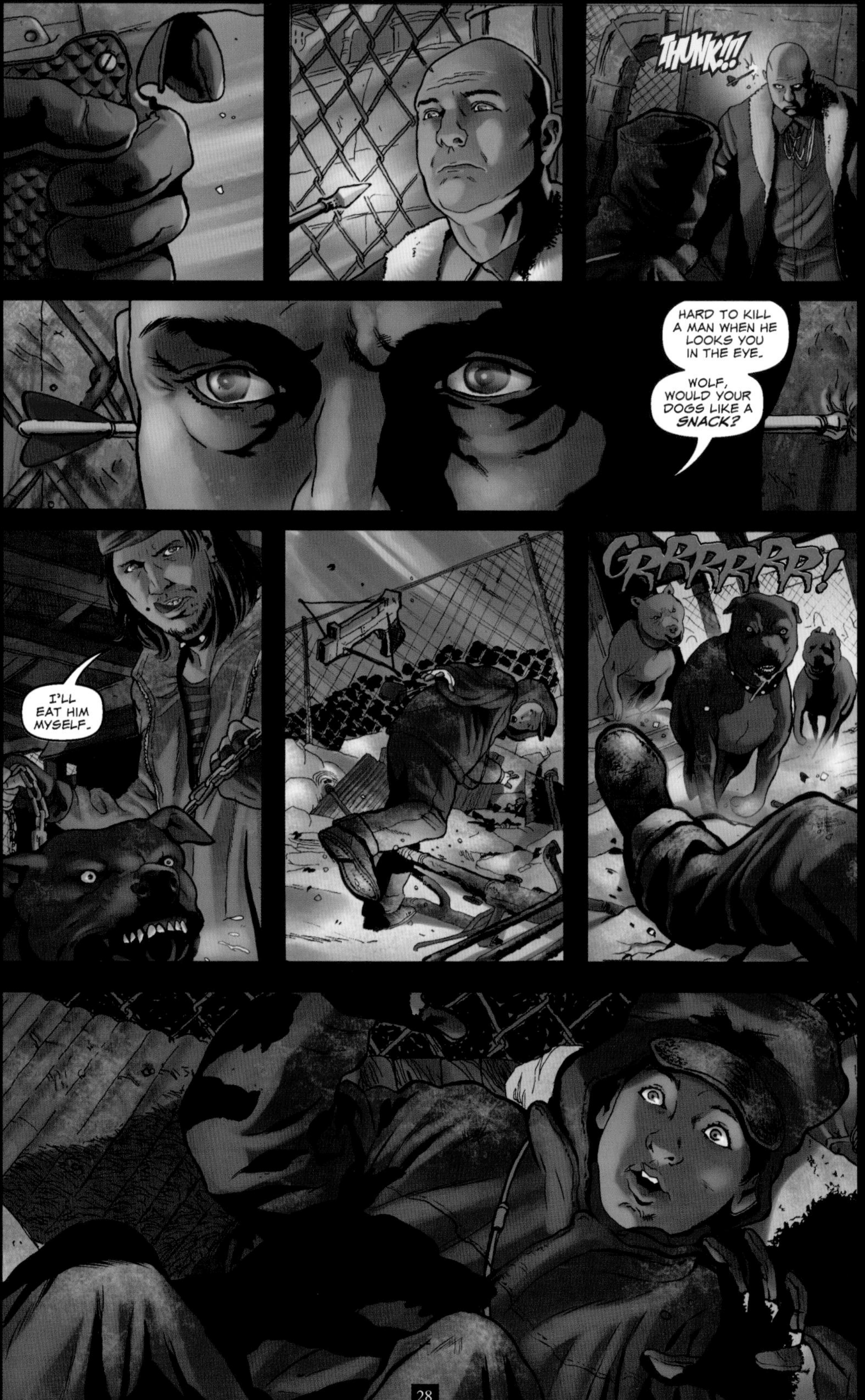
THUNK!!!
HARD TO KILL A MAN WHEN HE LOOKS YOU IN THE EYE.
WOLF, WOULD YOUR DOGS LIKE A SNACK?
I'LL EAT HIM MYSELF.
GRRRRRR!

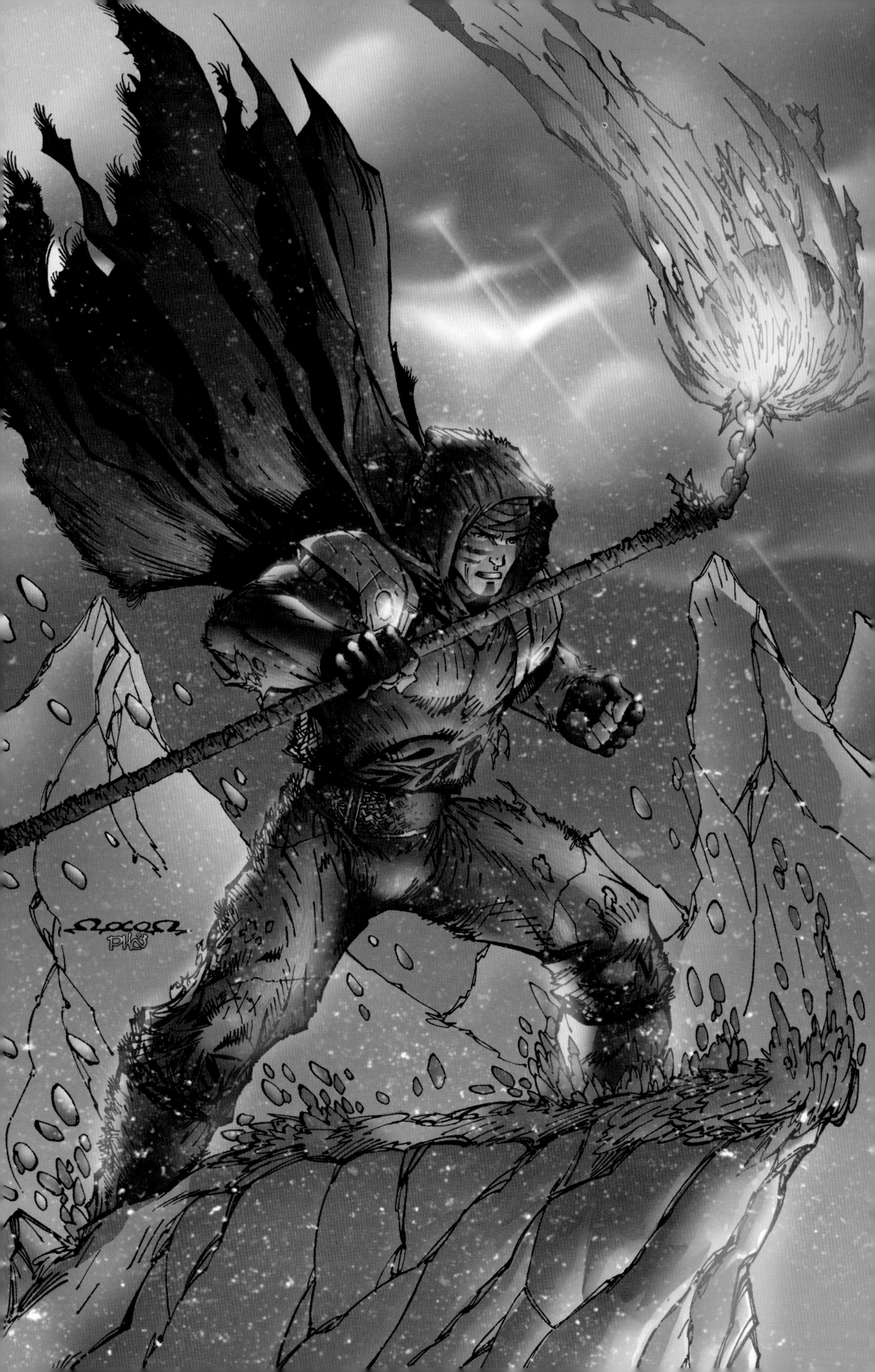

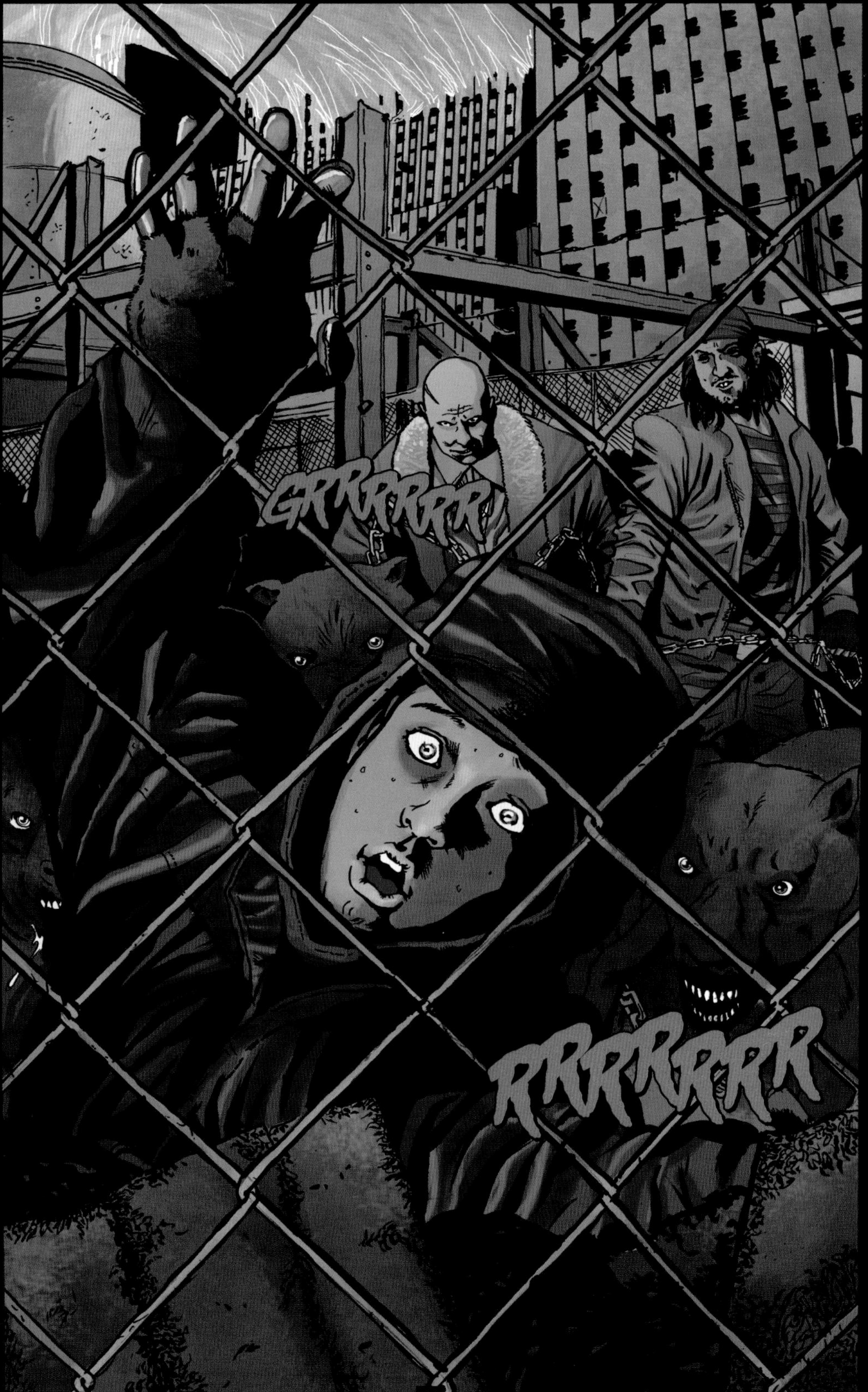
GRRRRRRR
RRRRRRRR

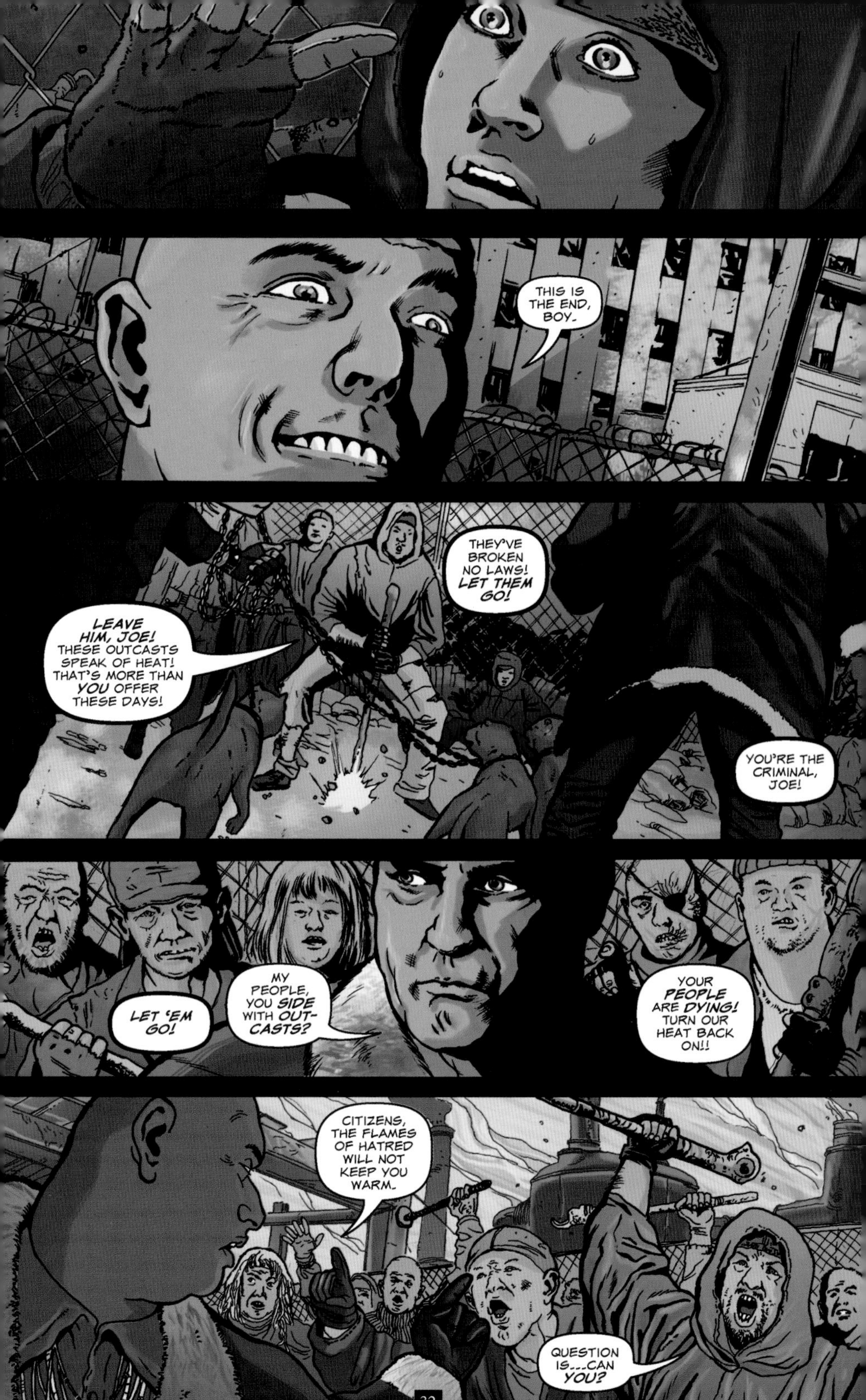

THIS IS THE END, BOY.
THEY'VE BROKEN NO LAWS! *LET THEM GO!*
LEAVE HIM, JOE! THESE OUTCASTS SPEAK OF HEAT! THAT'S MORE THAN *YOU* OFFER THESE DAYS!
YOU'RE THE CRIMINAL, JOE!
LET 'EM GO!
MY PEOPLE, YOU *SIDE* WITH *OUT-CASTS?*
YOUR *PEOPLE* ARE *DYING!* TURN OUR HEAT BACK ON!!
CITIZENS, THE FLAMES OF HATRED WILL NOT KEEP YOU WARM.
QUESTION IS...CAN *YOU?*

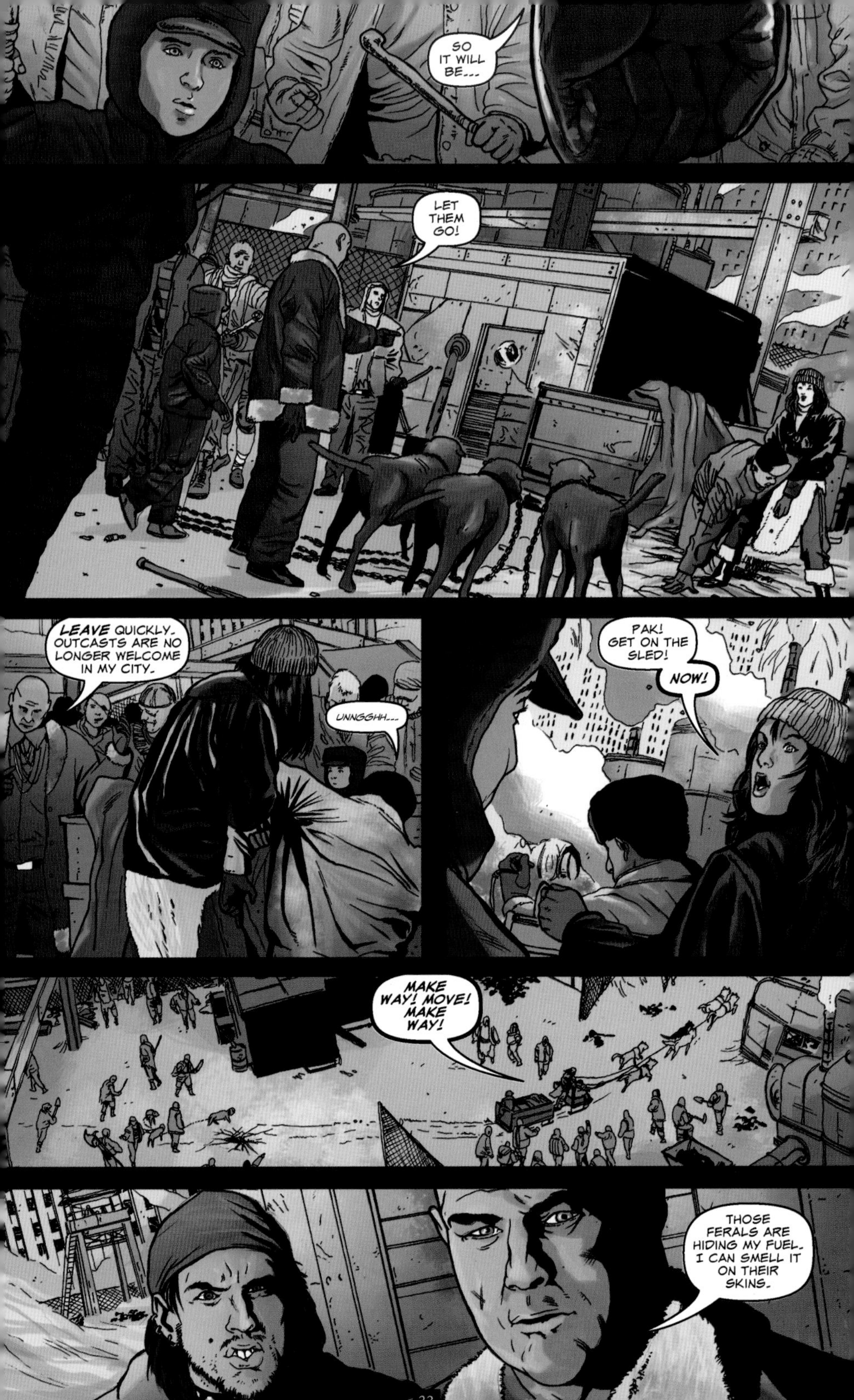
SO IT WILL BE...
LET THEM GO!
LEAVE QUICKLY. OUTCASTS ARE NO LONGER WELCOME IN MY CITY.
UNNGGHH...
PAK! GET ON THE SLED!
NOW!
MAKE WAY! MOVE! MAKE WAY!
THOSE FERALS ARE HIDING MY FUEL. I CAN SMELL IT ON THEIR SKINS.

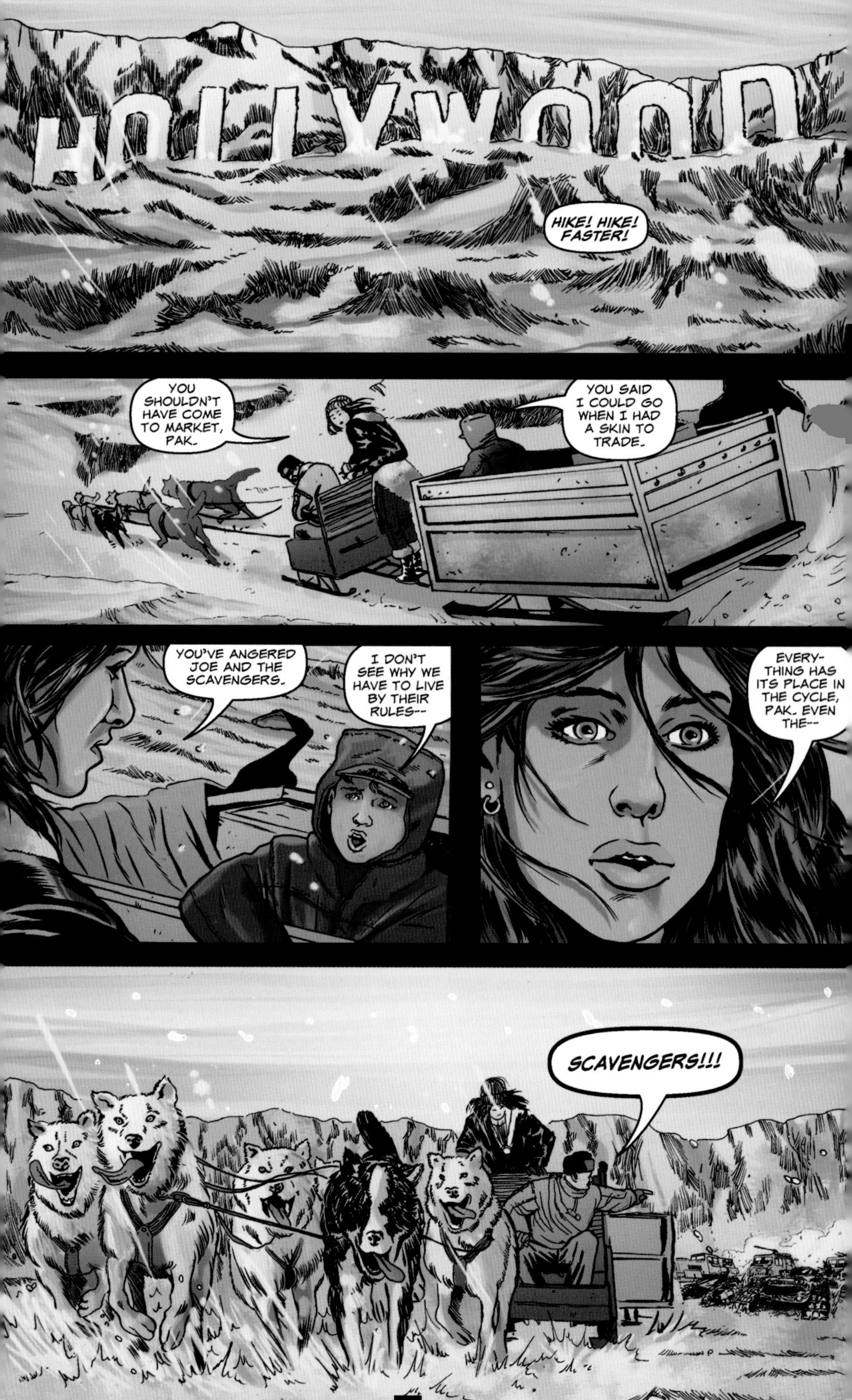
HOLLYWOOD
HIKE! HIKE! FASTER!
YOU SHOULDN'T HAVE COME TO MARKET, PAK.
YOU SAID I COULD GO WHEN I HAD A SKIN TO TRADE.
YOU'VE ANGERED JOE AND THE SCAVENGERS.
I DON'T SEE WHY WE HAVE TO LIVE BY THEIR RULES--
EVERY-THING HAS ITS PLACE IN THE CYCLE, PAK. EVEN THE--
SCAVENGERS!!!

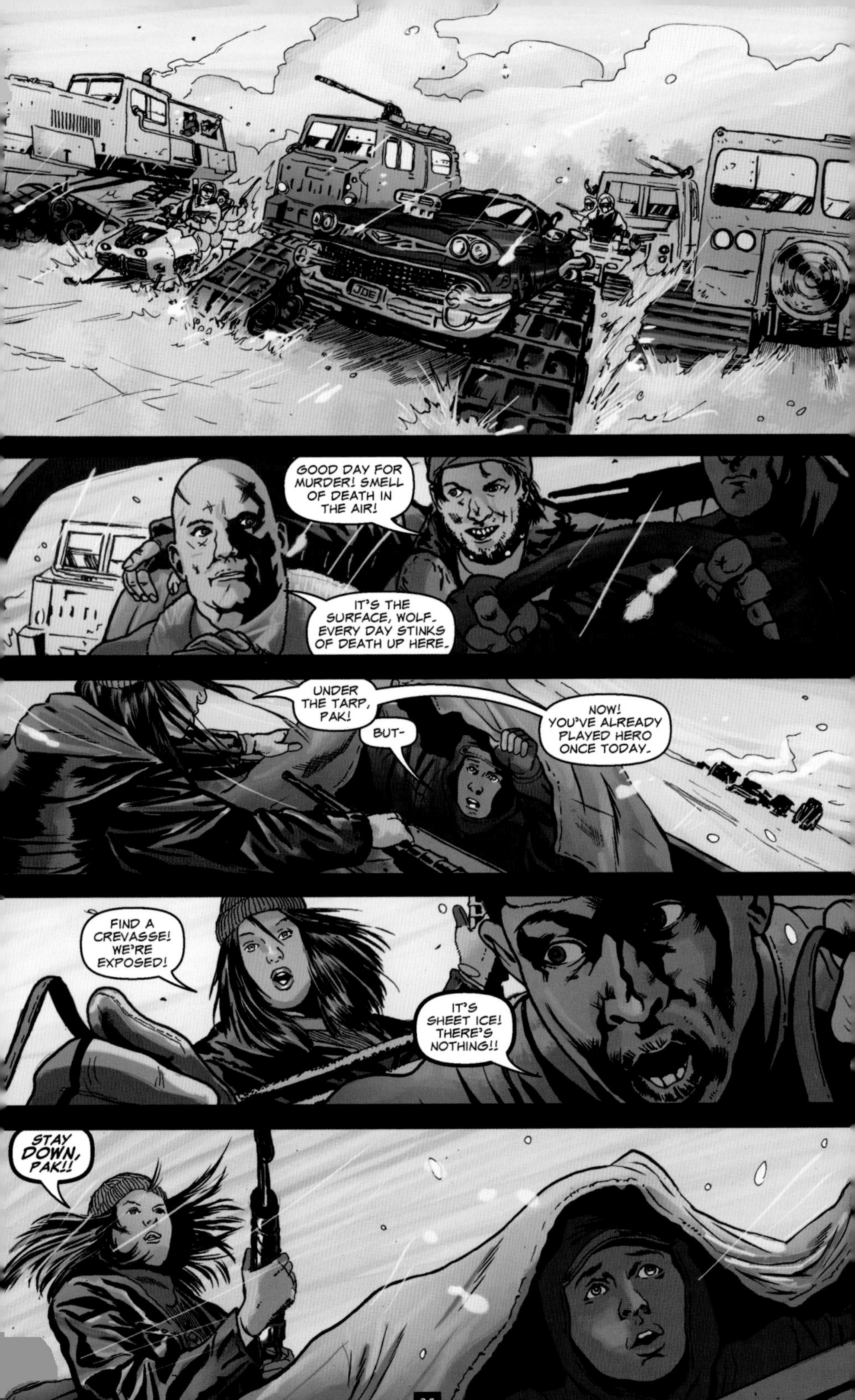
GOOD DAY FOR MURDER! SMELL OF DEATH IN THE AIR!
IT'S THE SURFACE, WOLF. EVERY DAY STINKS OF DEATH UP HERE.
UNDER THE TARP, PAK!
BUT-
NOW! YOU'VE ALREADY PLAYED HERO ONCE TODAY.
FIND A CREVASSE! WE'RE EXPOSED!
IT'S SHEET ICE! THERE'S NOTHING!!
STAY DOWN, PAK!!

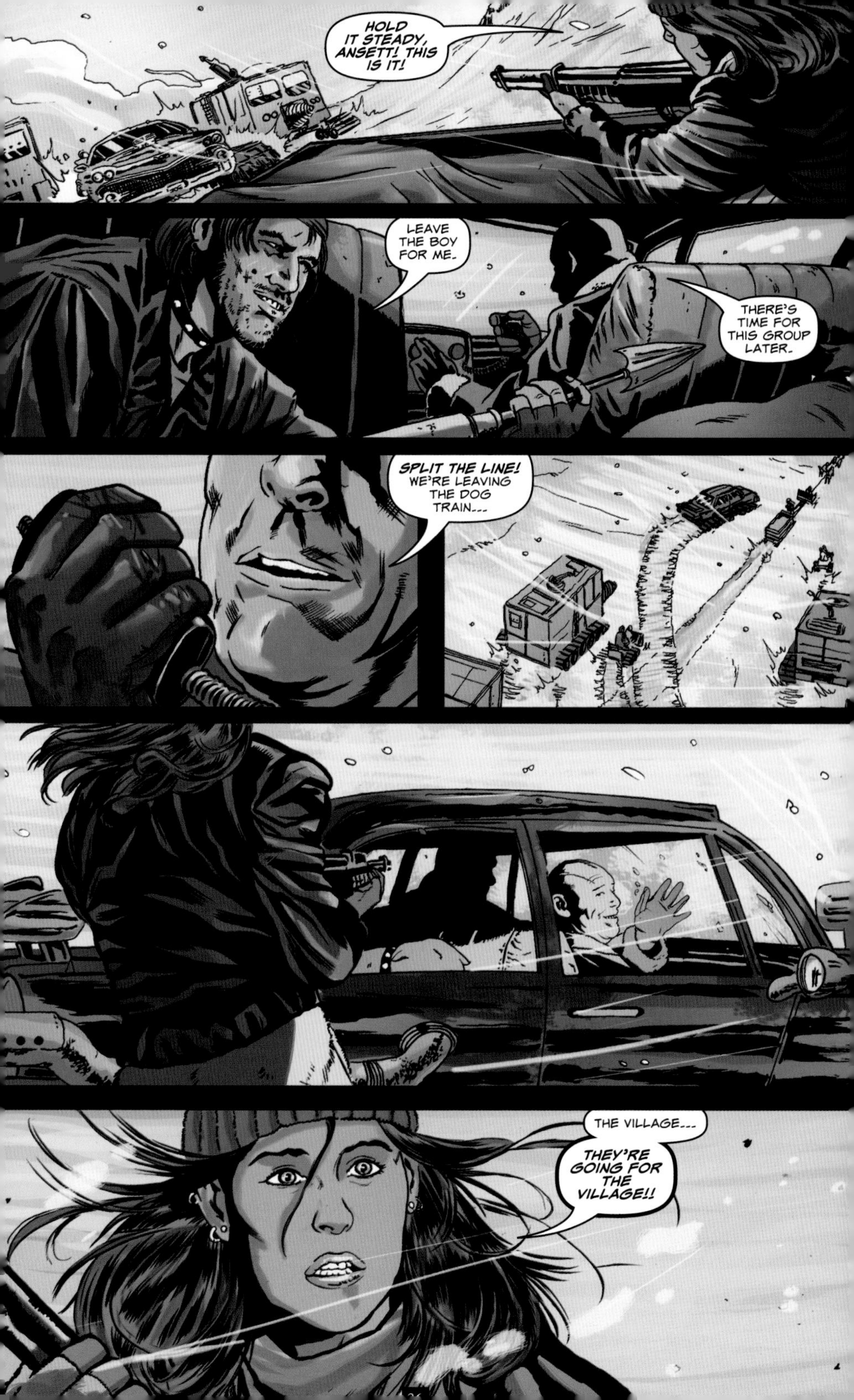
HOLD IT STEADY, ANSETT! THIS IS IT!
LEAVE THE BOY FOR ME.
THERE'S TIME FOR THIS GROUP LATER.
SPLIT THE LINE! WE'RE LEAVING THE DOG TRAIN...
THE VILLAGE...
THEY'RE GOING FOR THE VILLAGE!!

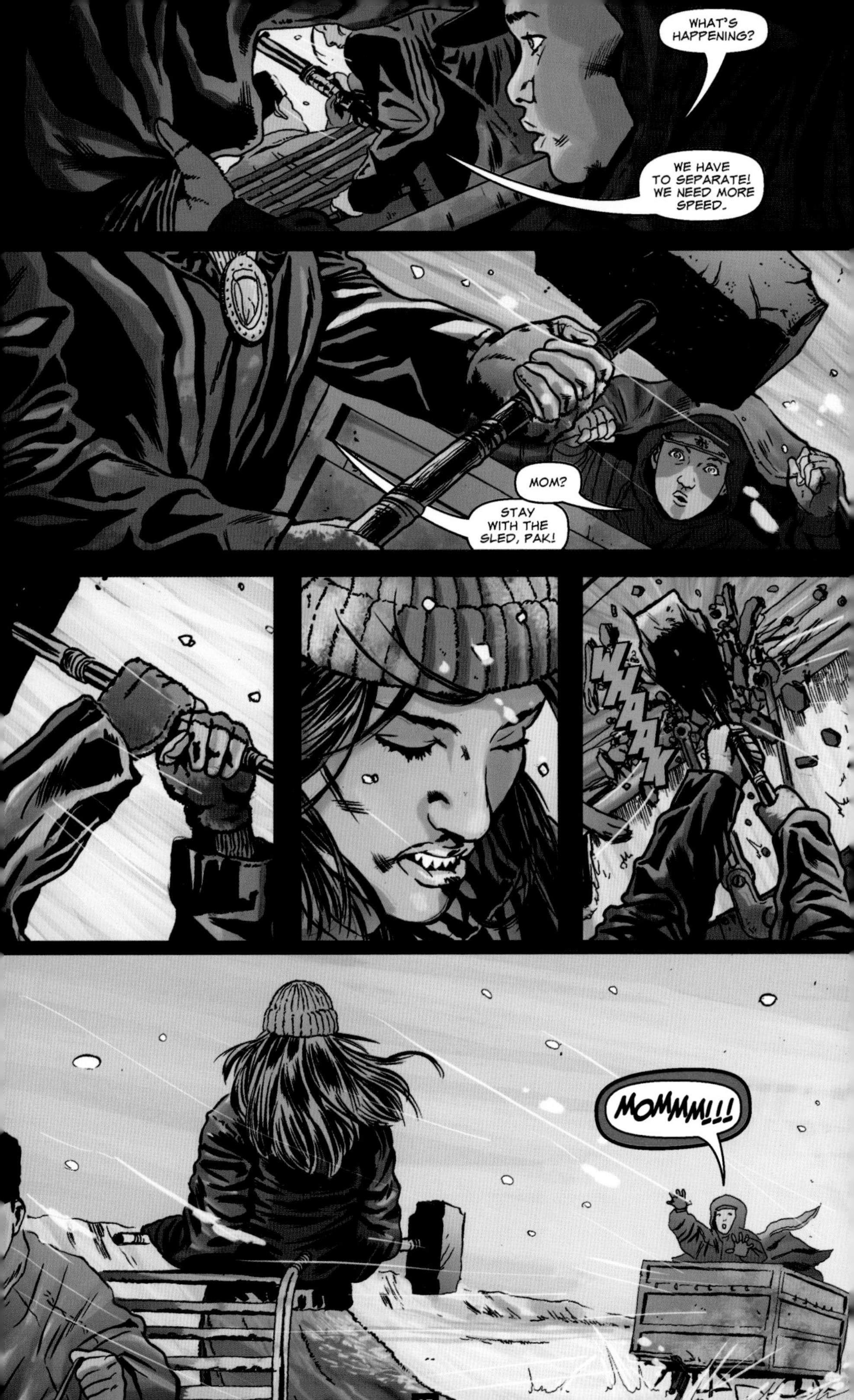
WHAT'S HAPPENING?
WE HAVE TO SEPARATE! WE NEED MORE SPEED.
MOM?
STAY WITH THE SLED, PAK!
WHAAAK
MOMMM!!!

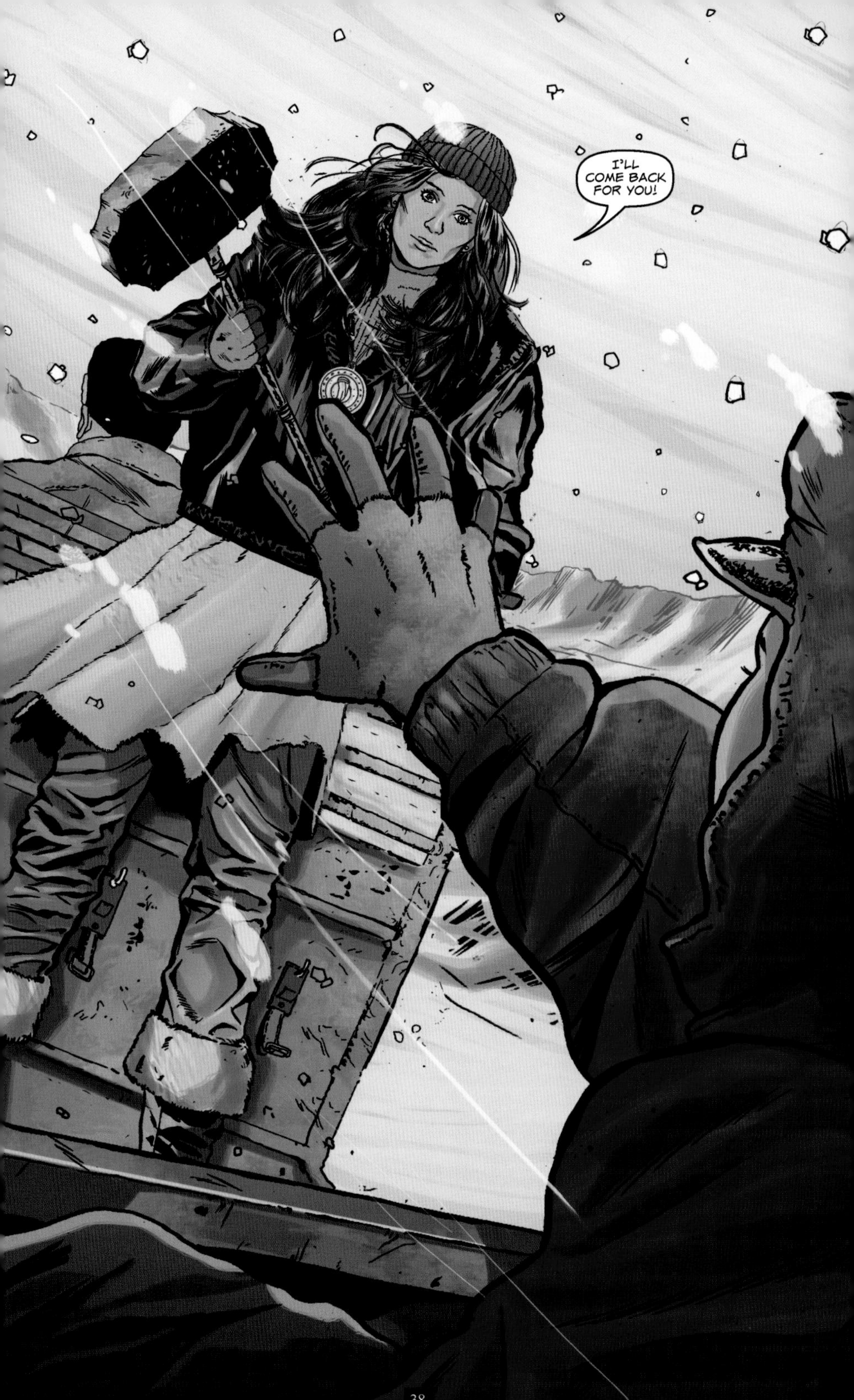
I'LL COME BACK FOR YOU!

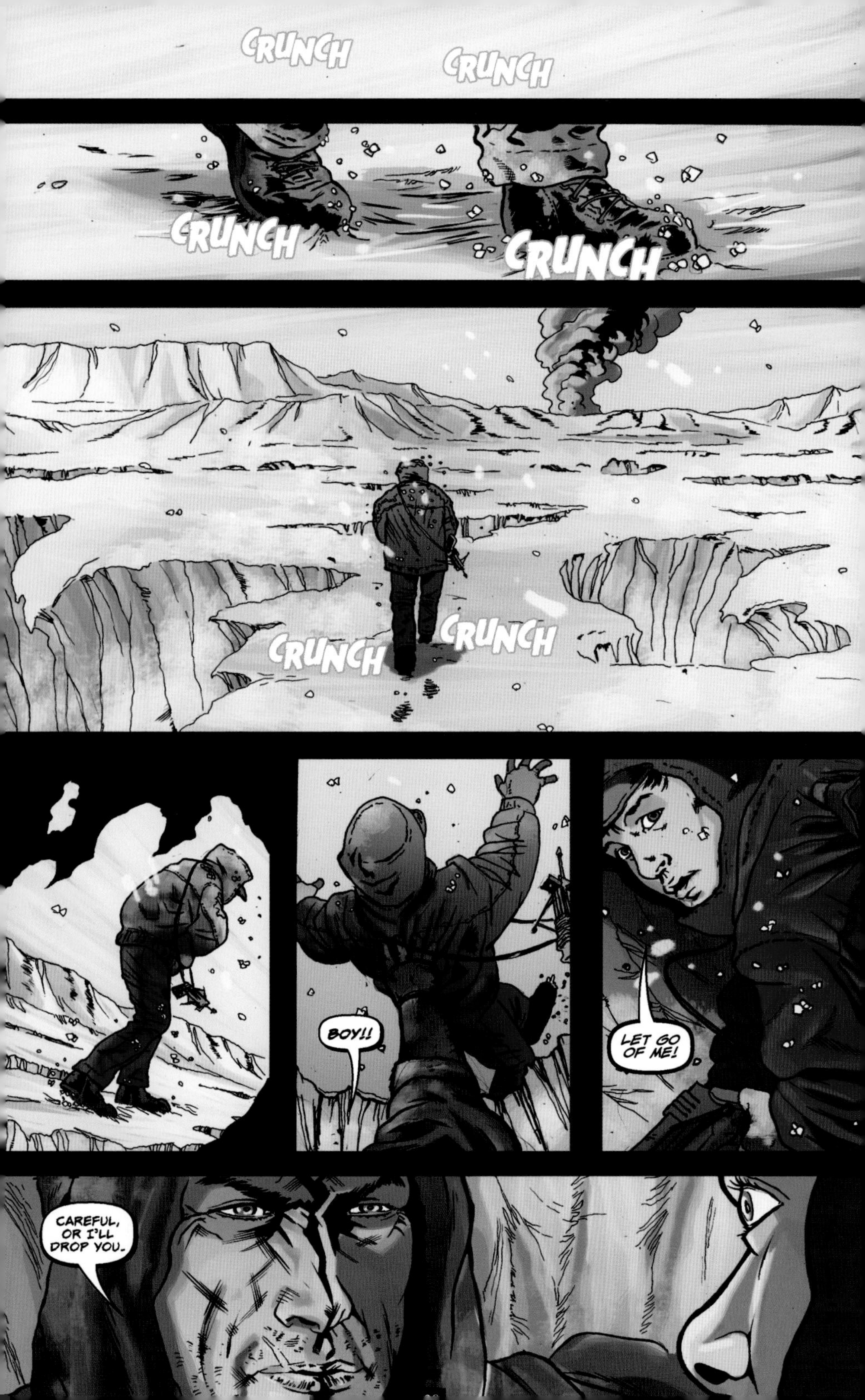
CRUNCH
CRUNCH
CRUNCH
CRUNCH
CRUNCH
CRUNCH
BOY!!
LET GO OF ME!
CAREFUL, OR I'LL DROP YOU.

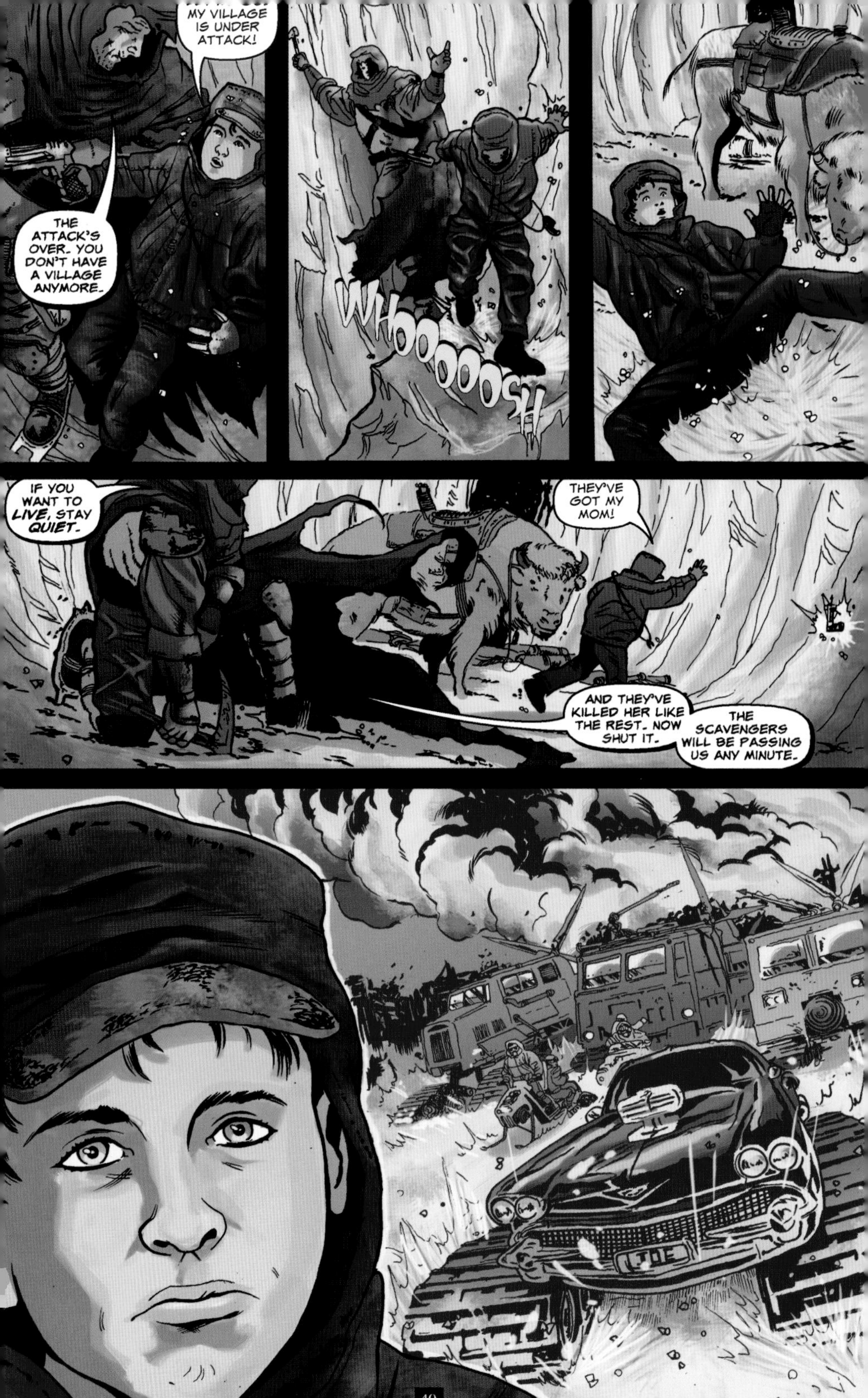
MY VILLAGE IS UNDER ATTACK!
THE ATTACK'S OVER. YOU DON'T HAVE A VILLAGE ANYMORE.
WHOOOOOOSH
IF YOU WANT TO LIVE, STAY QUIET.
THEY'VE GOT MY MOM!
AND THEY'VE KILLED HER LIKE THE REST. NOW SHUT IT.
THE SCAVENGERS WILL BE PASSING US ANY MINUTE.
JOE

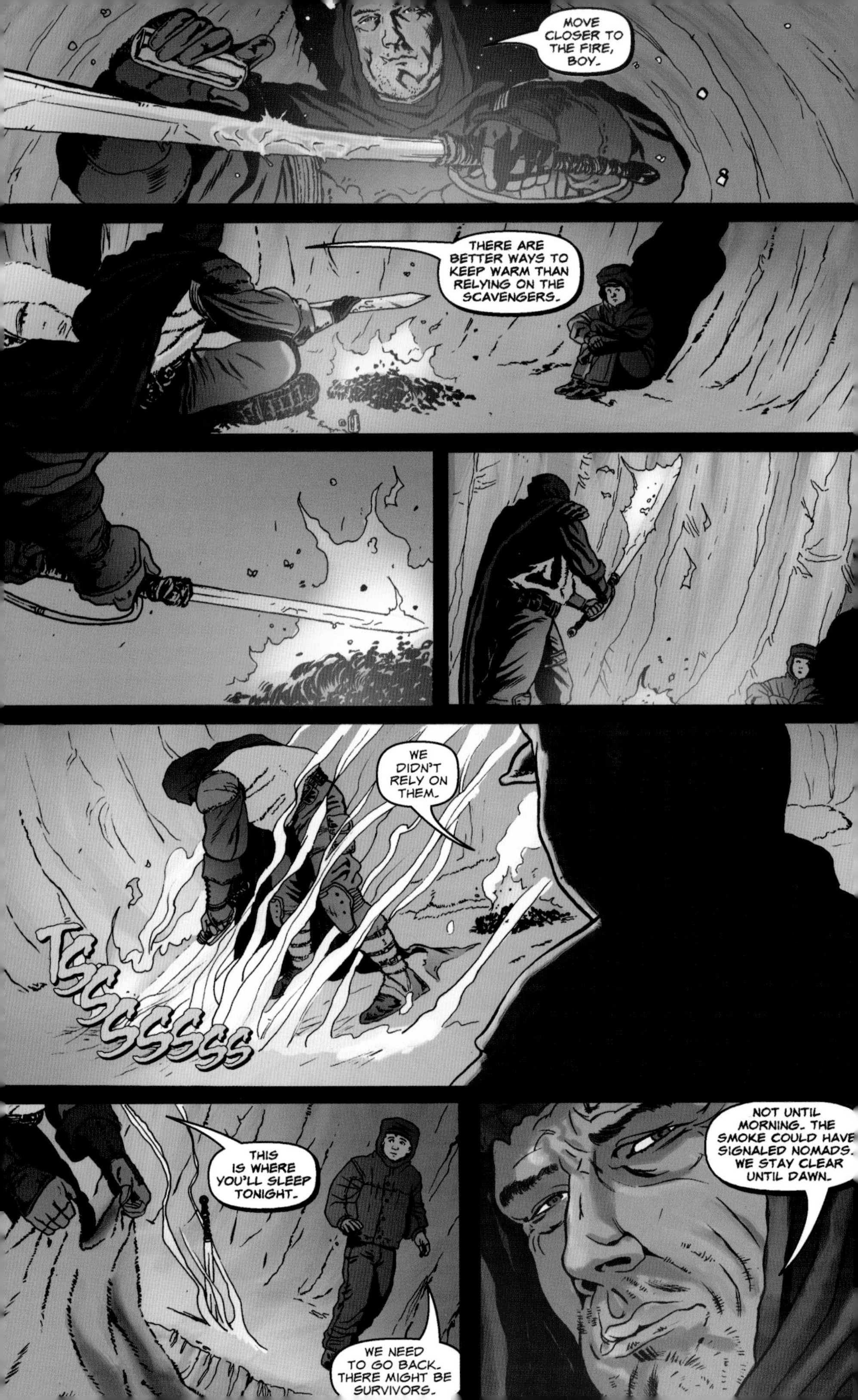
MOVE CLOSER TO THE FIRE, BOY.
THERE ARE BETTER WAYS TO KEEP WARM THAN RELYING ON THE SCAVENGERS.
WE DIDN'T RELY ON THEM.
TSSSSSSSS
THIS IS WHERE YOU'LL SLEEP TONIGHT.
WE NEED TO GO BACK. THERE MIGHT BE SURVIVORS.
NOT UNTIL MORNING. THE SMOKE COULD HAVE SIGNALED NOMADS. WE STAY CLEAR UNTIL DAWN.

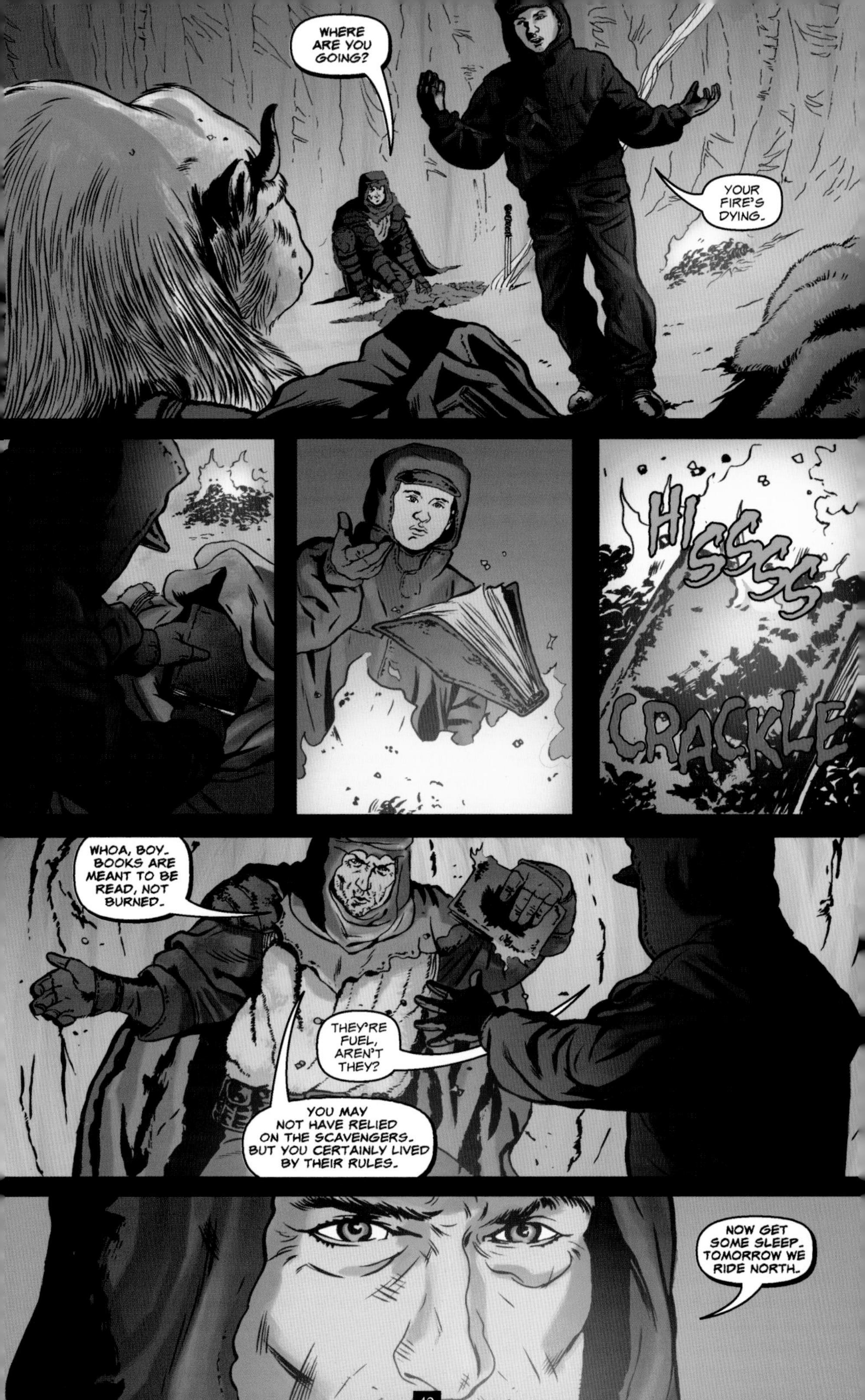
WHERE ARE YOU GOING?
YOUR FIRE'S DYING.
HISSSS
CRACKLE
WHOA, BOY. BOOKS ARE MEANT TO BE READ, NOT BURNED.
THEY'RE FUEL, AREN'T THEY?
YOU MAY NOT HAVE RELIED ON THE SCAVENGERS. BUT YOU CERTAINLY LIVED BY THEIR RULES.
NOW GET SOME SLEEP. TOMORROW WE RIDE NORTH.

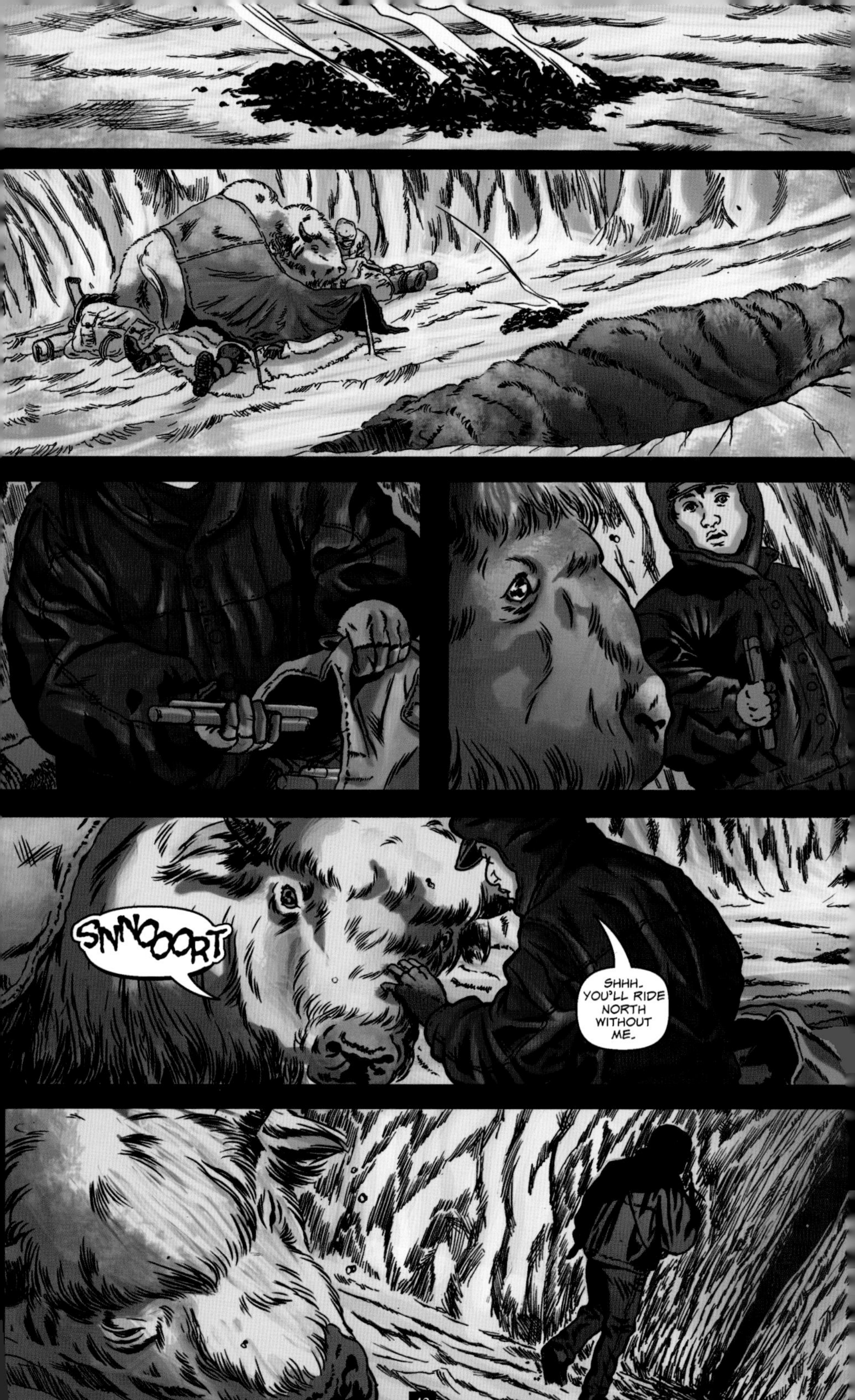
SNNOOORT
SHHH. YOU'LL RIDE NORTH WITHOUT ME.

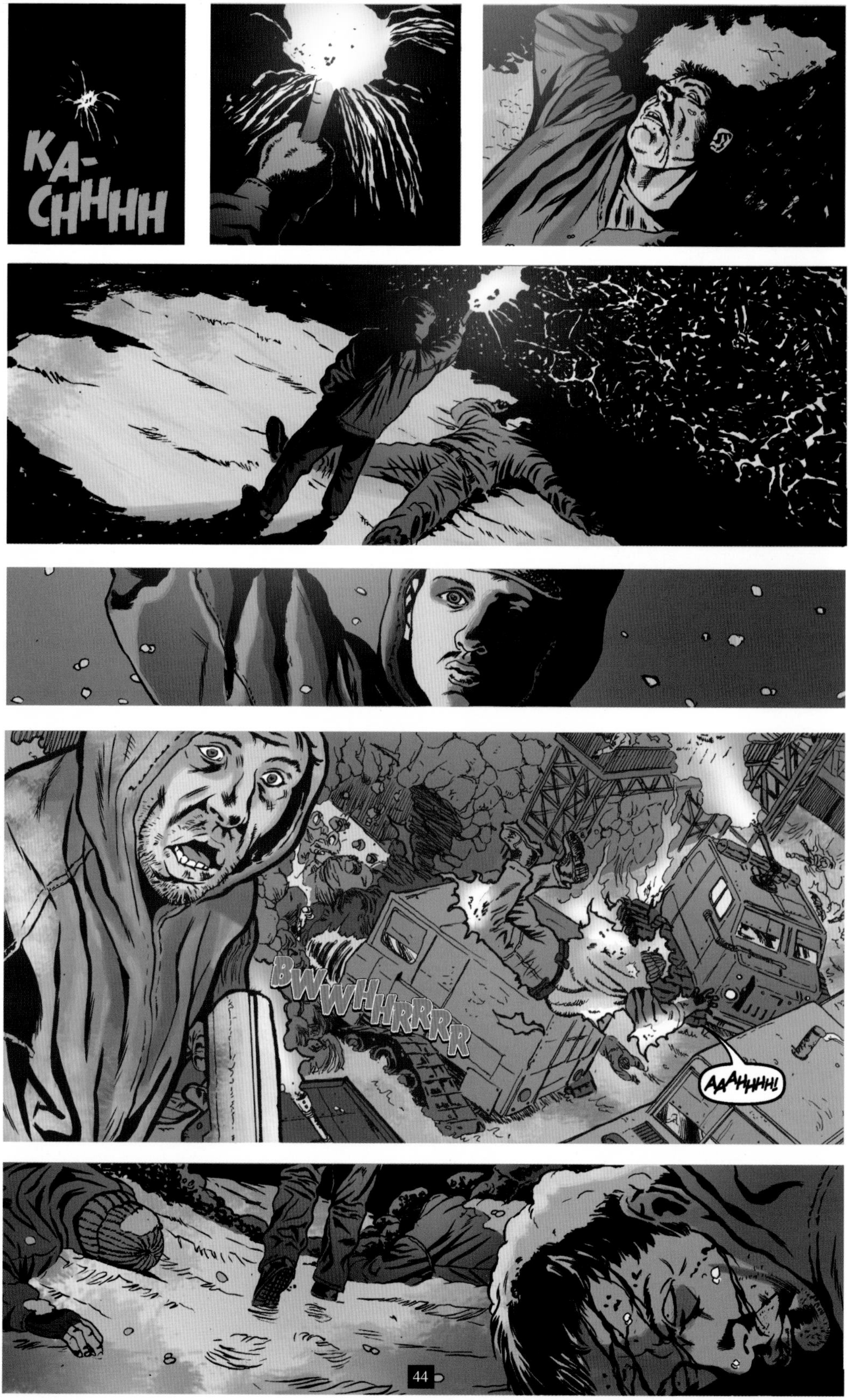
KA-
CHHHHH
BWWHHRRRRR
AAAHHHH!

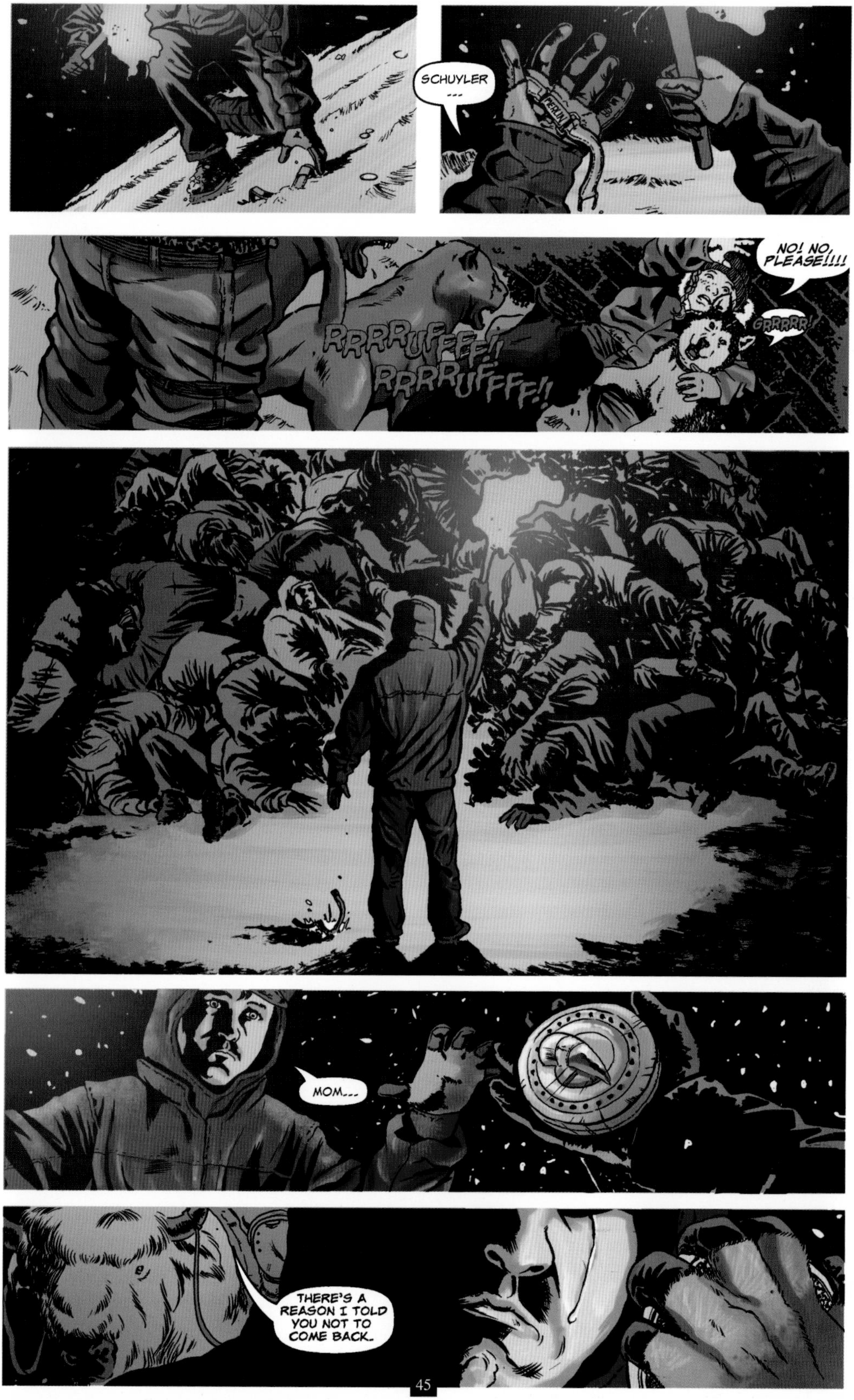
SCHUYLER ---
NO! NO, PLEASE!!!!
GRRRRR!
RRRRUFFFF!!
RRRRUFFFF!!
MOM...
THERE'S A REASON I TOLD YOU NOT TO COME BACK.

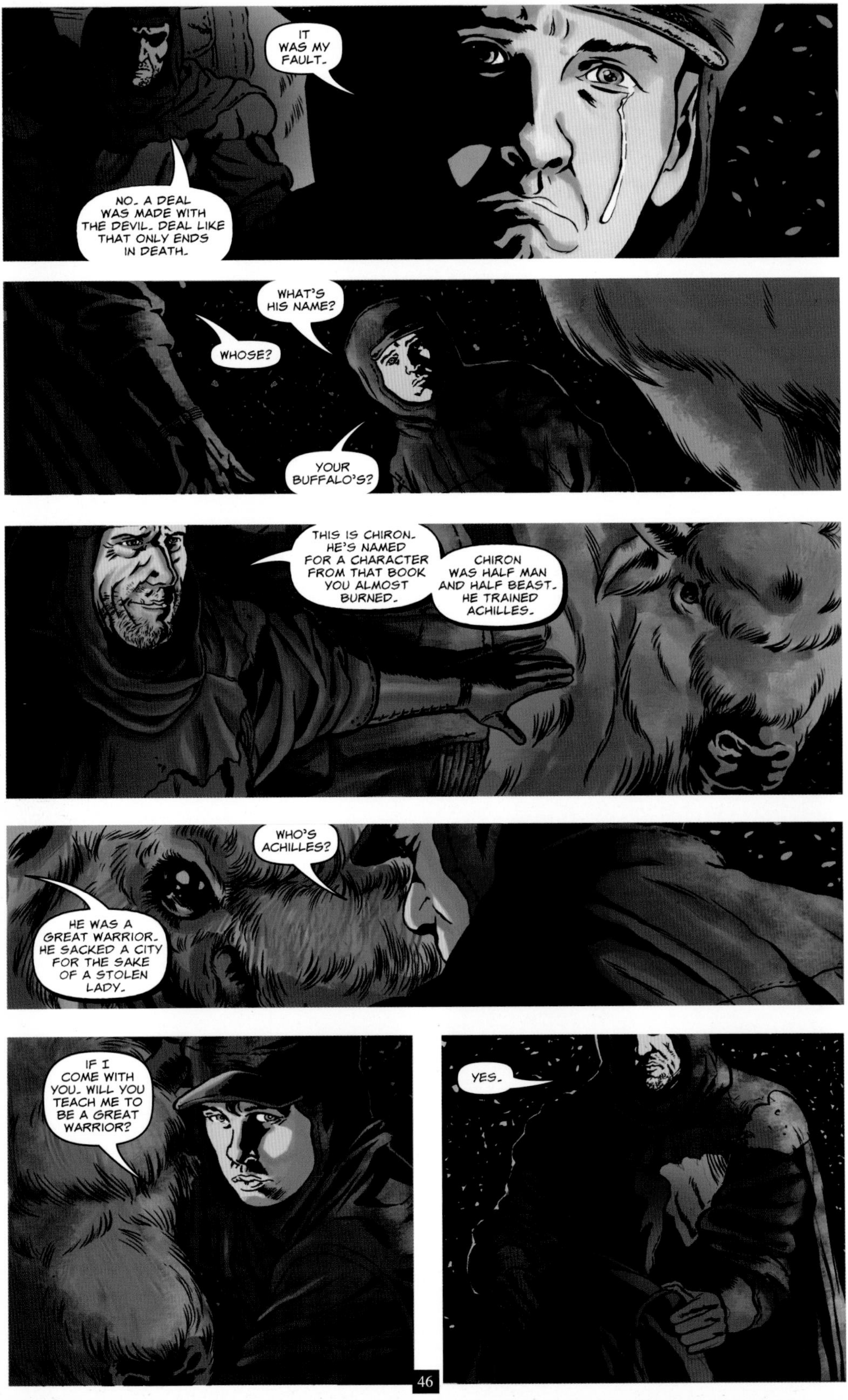
IT WAS MY FAULT.
NO. A DEAL WAS MADE WITH THE DEVIL. DEAL LIKE THAT ONLY ENDS IN DEATH.
WHAT'S HIS NAME?
WHOSE?
YOUR BUFFALO'S?
THIS IS CHIRON. HE'S NAMED FOR A CHARACTER FROM THAT BOOK YOU ALMOST BURNED.
CHIRON WAS HALF MAN AND HALF BEAST. HE TRAINED ACHILLES.
WHO'S ACHILLES?
HE WAS A GREAT WARRIOR. HE SACKED A CITY FOR THE SAKE OF A STOLEN LADY.
IF I COME WITH YOU, WILL YOU TEACH ME TO BE A GREAT WARRIOR?
YES.

SO BEGAN THE BOY'S APPRENTICESHIP WITH THE SKINRUNNER...

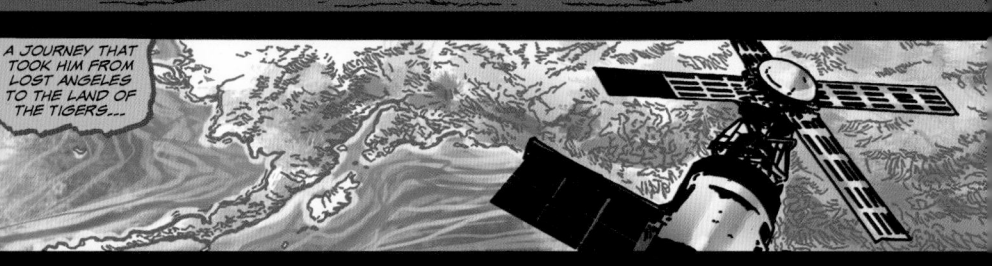

A JOURNEY THAT TOOK HIM FROM LOST ANGELES TO THE LAND OF THE TIGERS...

YOU'LL GROW INTO IT.

ALONG THE WAY, THE SKINRUNNER TAUGHT THE BOY THE USE OF HIS WEAPONS AND HIS WAYS.

WHUMPH!!

IT TOOK TIME TO CONTROL THE FLAMING STARS...

17

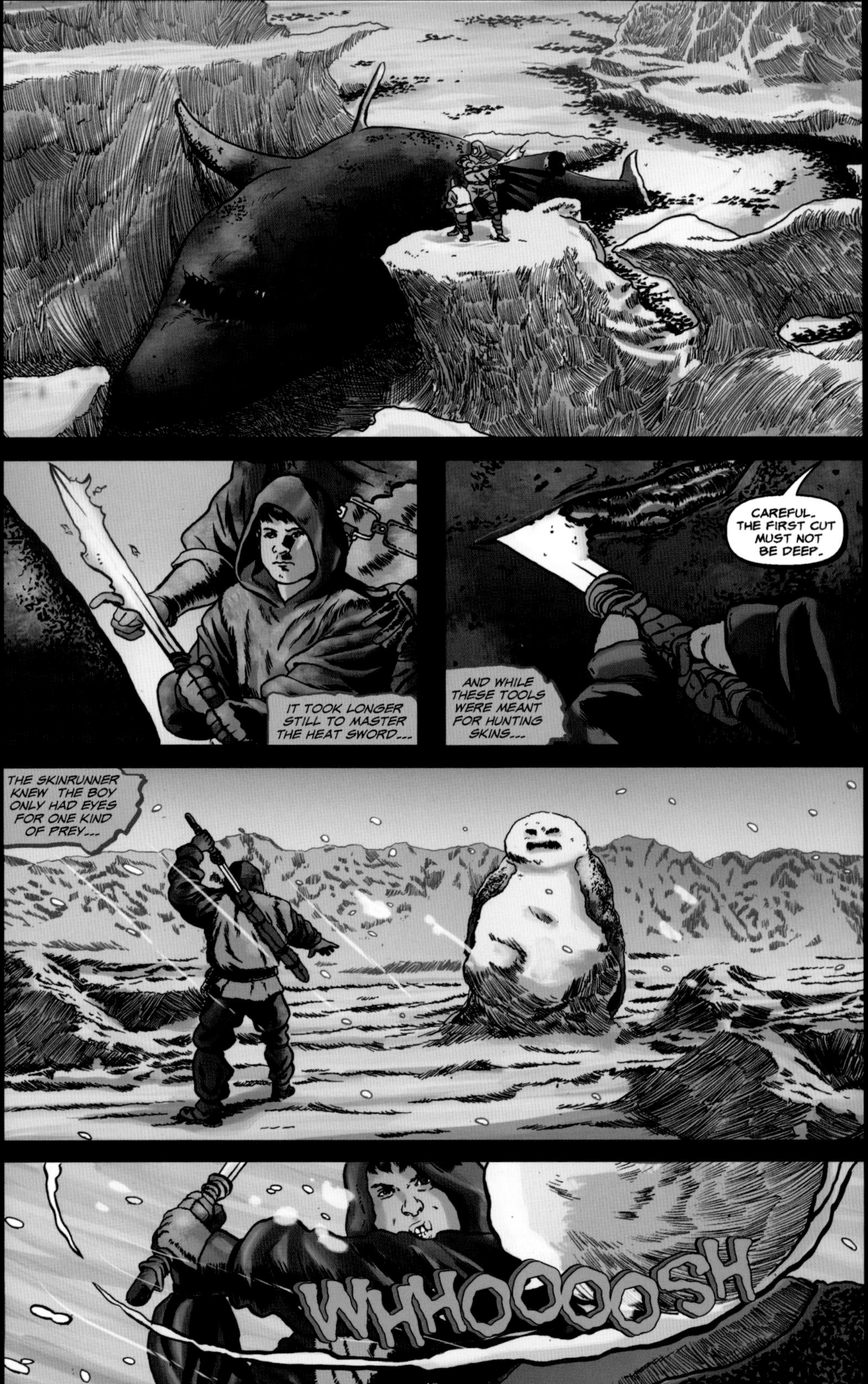
IT TOOK LONGER STILL TO MASTER THE HEAT SWORD...
AND WHILE THESE TOOLS WERE MEANT FOR HUNTING SKINS...
CAREFUL. THE FIRST CUT MUST NOT BE DEEP.
THE SKINRUNNER KNEW THE BOY ONLY HAD EYES FOR ONE KIND OF PREY...
WHHOOOOSH

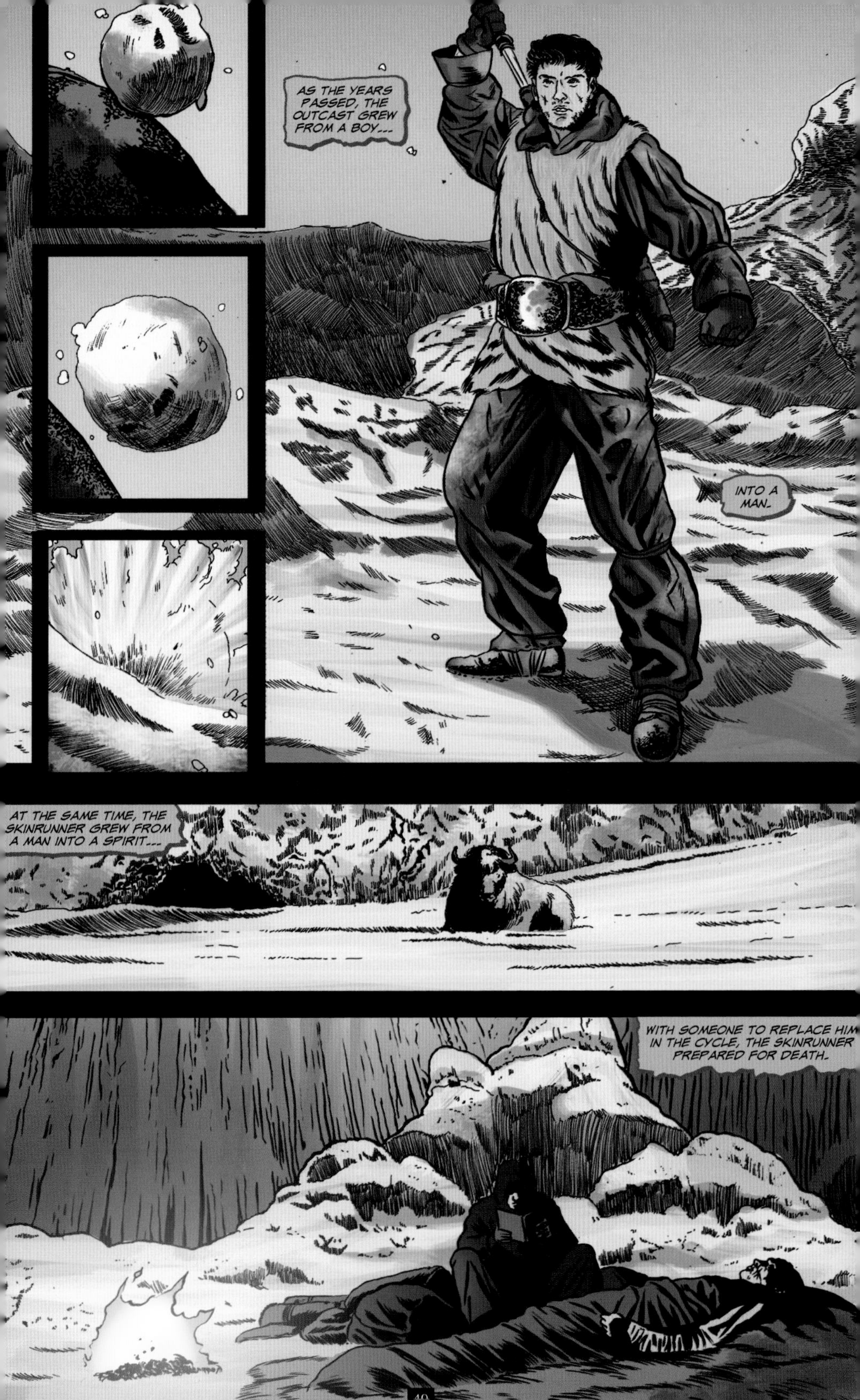
AS THE YEARS PASSED, THE OUTCAST GREW FROM A BOY...
INTO A MAN.
AT THE SAME TIME, THE SKINRUNNER GREW FROM A MAN INTO A SPIRIT...
WITH SOMEONE TO REPLACE HIM IN THE CYCLE, THE SKINRUNNER PREPARED FOR DEATH.

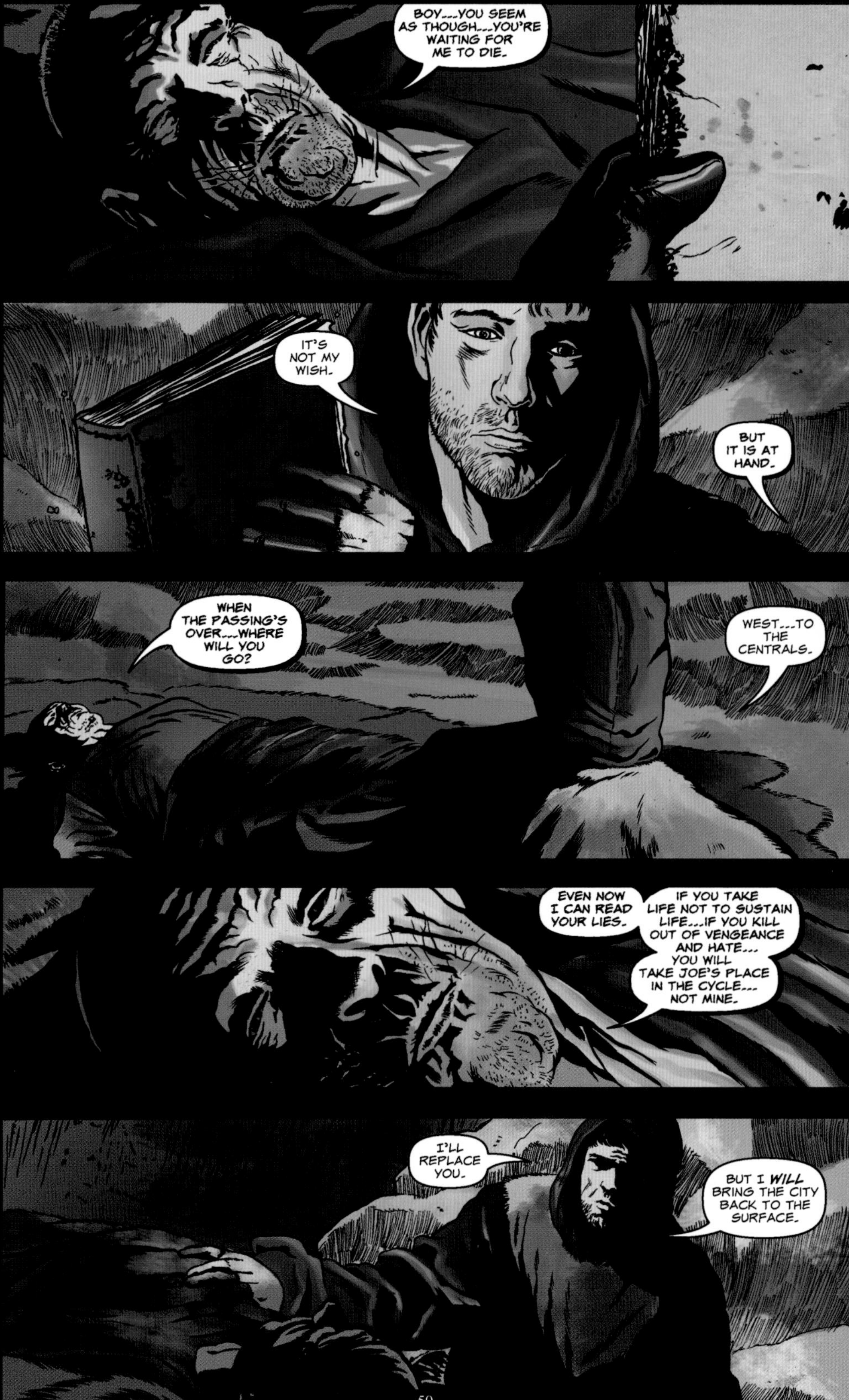

BOY...YOU SEEM AS THOUGH...YOU'RE WAITING FOR ME TO DIE.
IT'S NOT MY WISH.
BUT IT IS AT HAND.
WHEN THE PASSING'S OVER...WHERE WILL YOU GO?
WEST...TO THE CENTRALS.
EVEN NOW I CAN READ YOUR LIES.
IF YOU TAKE LIFE NOT TO SUSTAIN LIFE...IF YOU KILL OUT OF VENGEANCE AND HATE... YOU WILL TAKE JOE'S PLACE IN THE CYCLE... NOT MINE.
I'LL REPLACE YOU.
BUT I ***WILL*** BRING THE CITY BACK TO THE SURFACE.

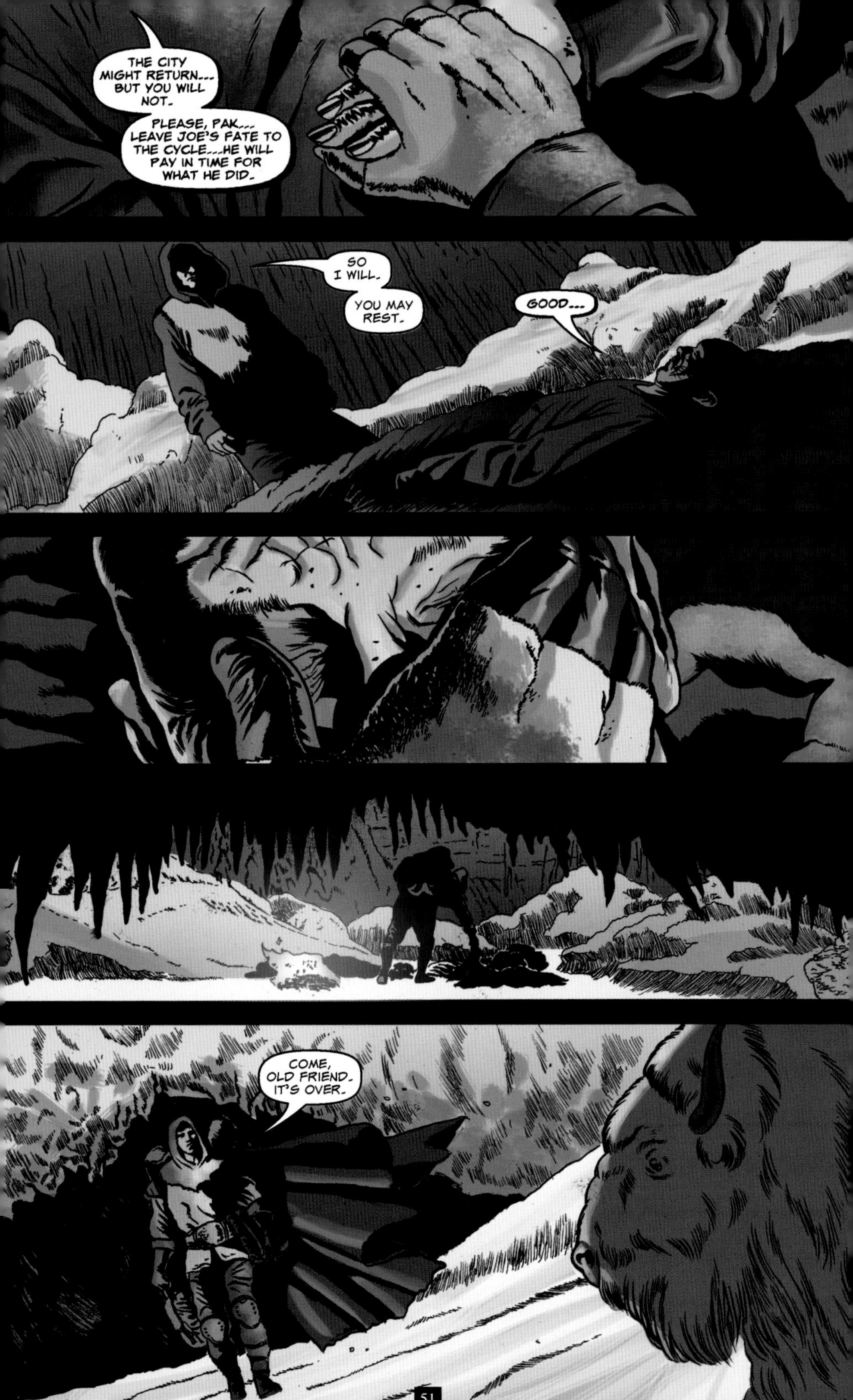
THE CITY MIGHT RETURN... BUT YOU WILL NOT.
PLEASE, PAK... LEAVE JOE'S FATE TO THE CYCLE...HE WILL PAY IN TIME FOR WHAT HE DID.
SO I WILL.
YOU MAY REST.
GOOD...
COME, OLD FRIEND. IT'S OVER.

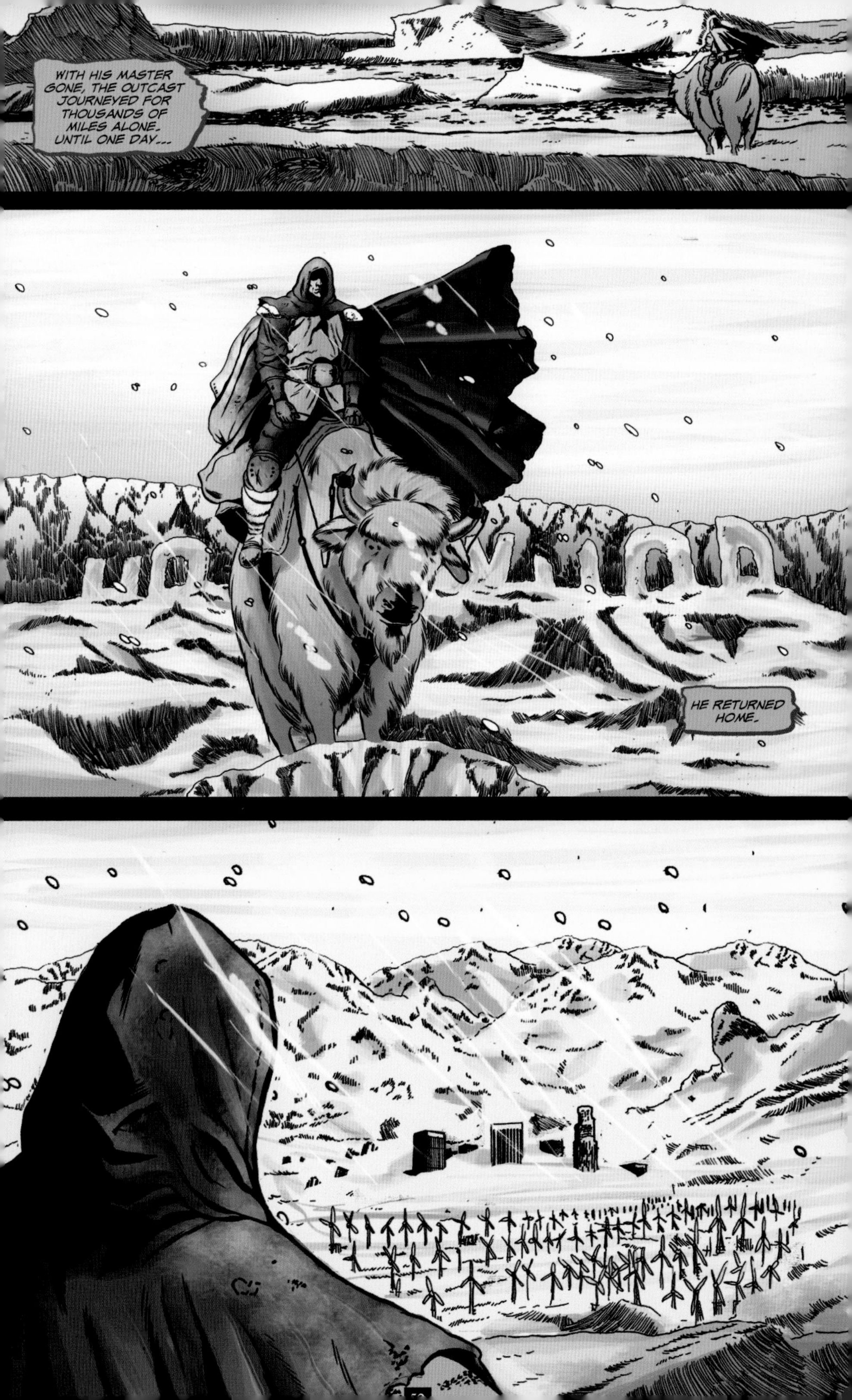
WITH HIS MASTER GONE, THE OUTCAST JOURNEYED FOR THOUSANDS OF MILES ALONE. UNTIL ONE DAY...
HE RETURNED HOME.

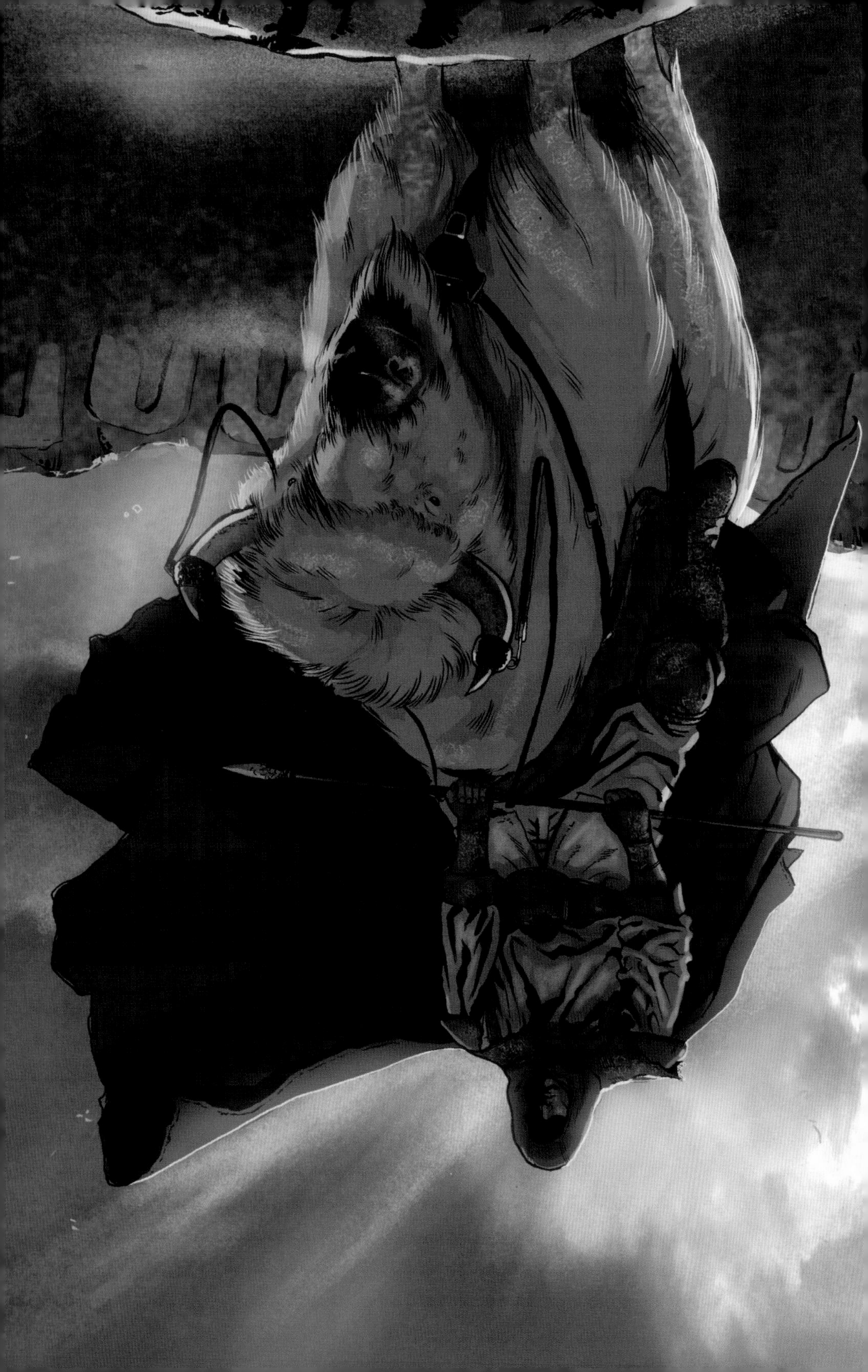

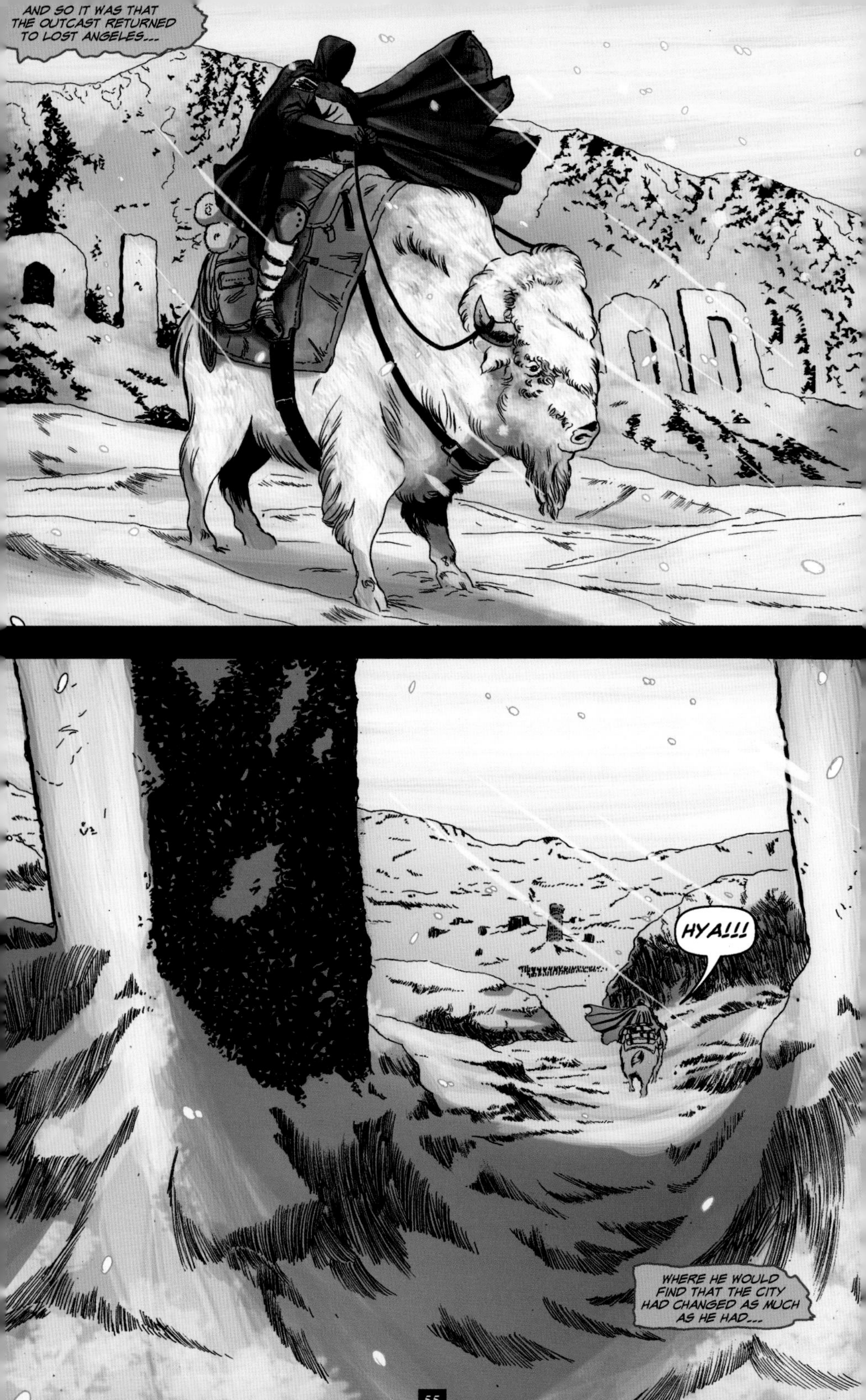
AND SO IT WAS THAT THE OUTCAST RETURNED TO LOST ANGELES...
HYA!!!
WHERE HE WOULD FIND THAT THE CITY HAD CHANGED AS MUCH AS HE HAD...

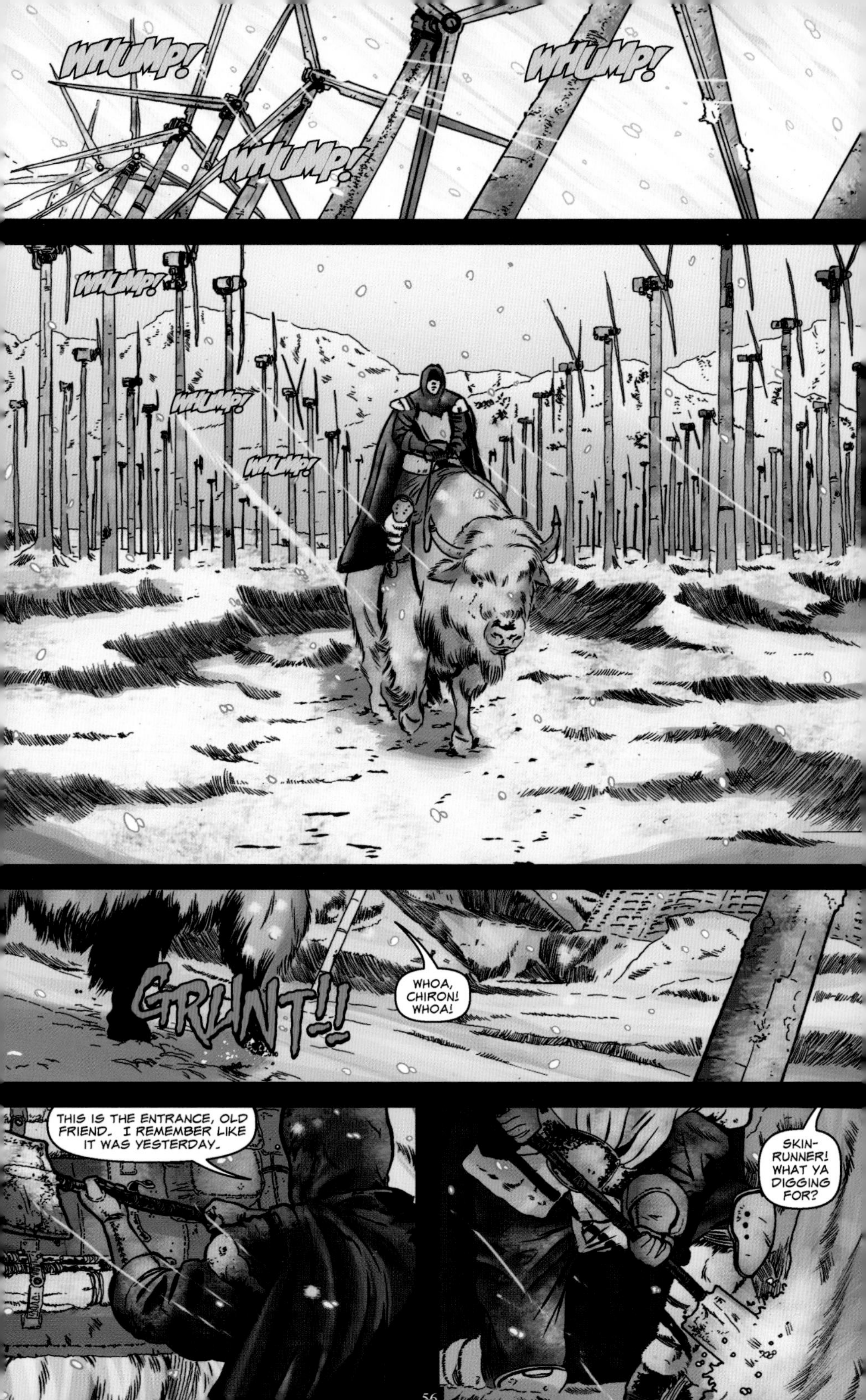
WHUMP!
WHUMP!
WHUMP!
WHUMP!
WHUMP!
WHUMP!
GRUNT!!
WHOA, CHIRON! WHOA!
THIS IS THE ENTRANCE, OLD FRIEND. I REMEMBER LIKE IT WAS YESTERDAY.
SKIN-RUNNER! WHAT YA DIGGING FOR?

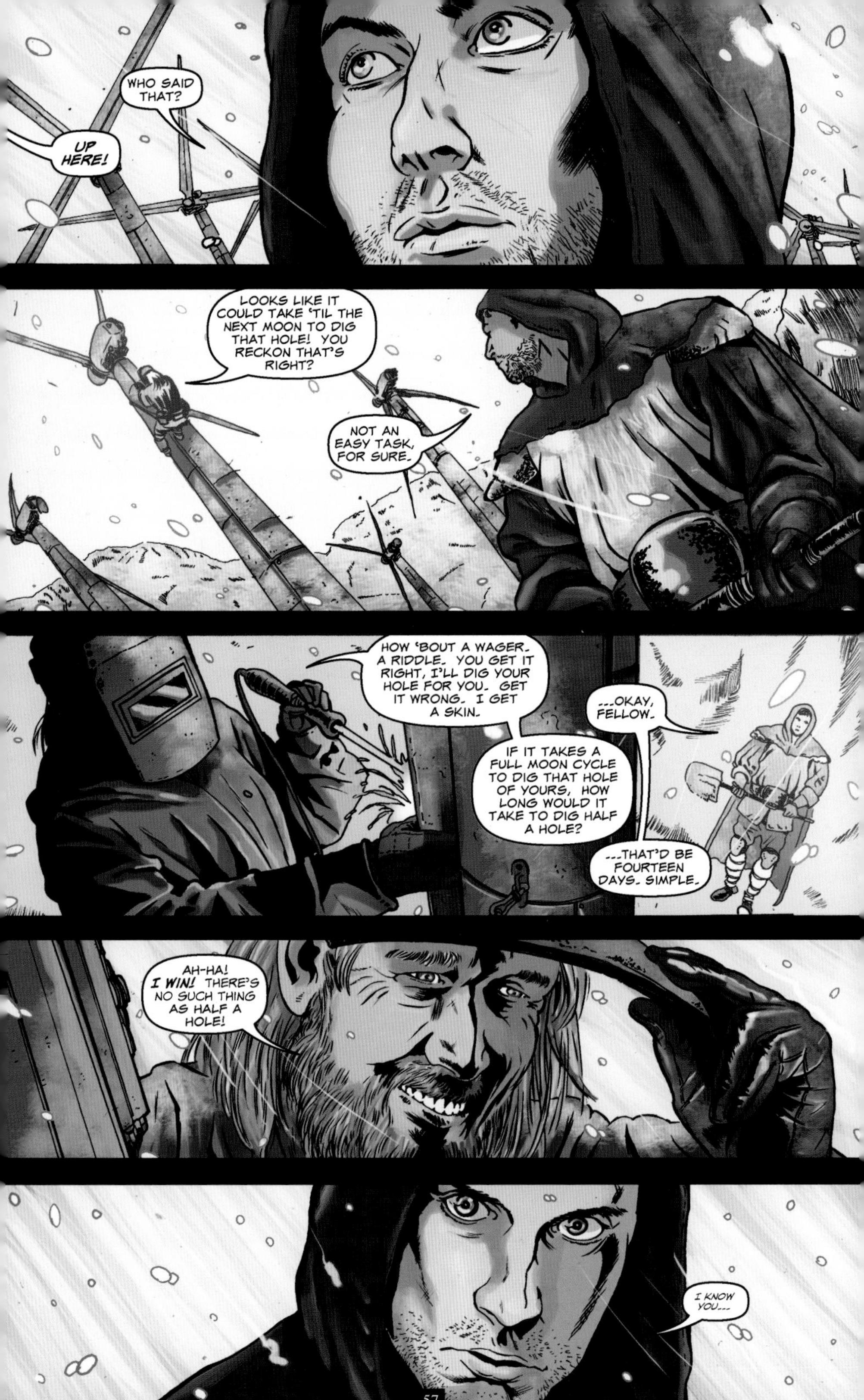
WHO SAID THAT?
UP HERE!
LOOKS LIKE IT COULD TAKE 'TIL THE NEXT MOON TO DIG THAT HOLE! YOU RECKON THAT'S RIGHT?
NOT AN EASY TASK, FOR SURE.
HOW 'BOUT A WAGER. A RIDDLE. YOU GET IT RIGHT, I'LL DIG YOUR HOLE FOR YOU. GET IT WRONG. I GET A SKIN.
IF IT TAKES A FULL MOON CYCLE TO DIG THAT HOLE OF YOURS, HOW LONG WOULD IT TAKE TO DIG HALF A HOLE?
...OKAY, FELLOW.
...THAT'D BE FOURTEEN DAYS. SIMPLE.
AH-HA! ***I WIN!*** THERE'S NO SUCH THING AS HALF A HOLE!
I KNOW YOU...

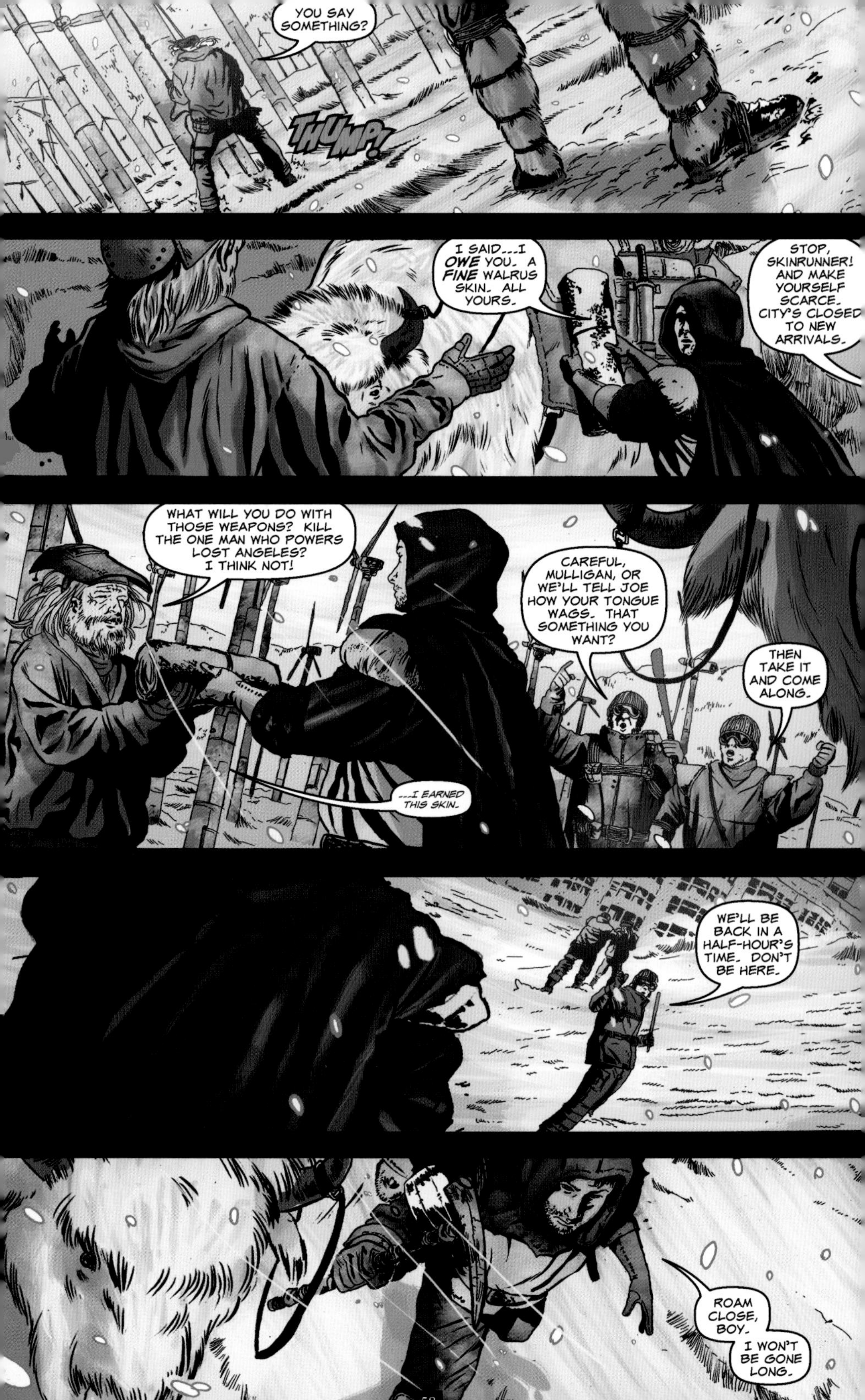
YOU SAY SOMETHING?
THUMP!
I SAID...I OWE YOU. A FINE WALRUS SKIN. ALL YOURS.
STOP, SKINRUNNER! AND MAKE YOURSELF SCARCE. CITY'S CLOSED TO NEW ARRIVALS.
WHAT WILL YOU DO WITH THOSE WEAPONS? KILL THE ONE MAN WHO POWERS LOST ANGELES? I THINK NOT!
...I EARNED THIS SKIN.
CAREFUL, MULLIGAN, OR WE'LL TELL JOE HOW YOUR TONGUE WAGS. THAT SOMETHING YOU WANT?
THEN TAKE IT AND COME ALONG.
WE'LL BE BACK IN A HALF-HOUR'S TIME. DON'T BE HERE.
ROAM CLOSE, BOY.
I WON'T BE GONE LONG.

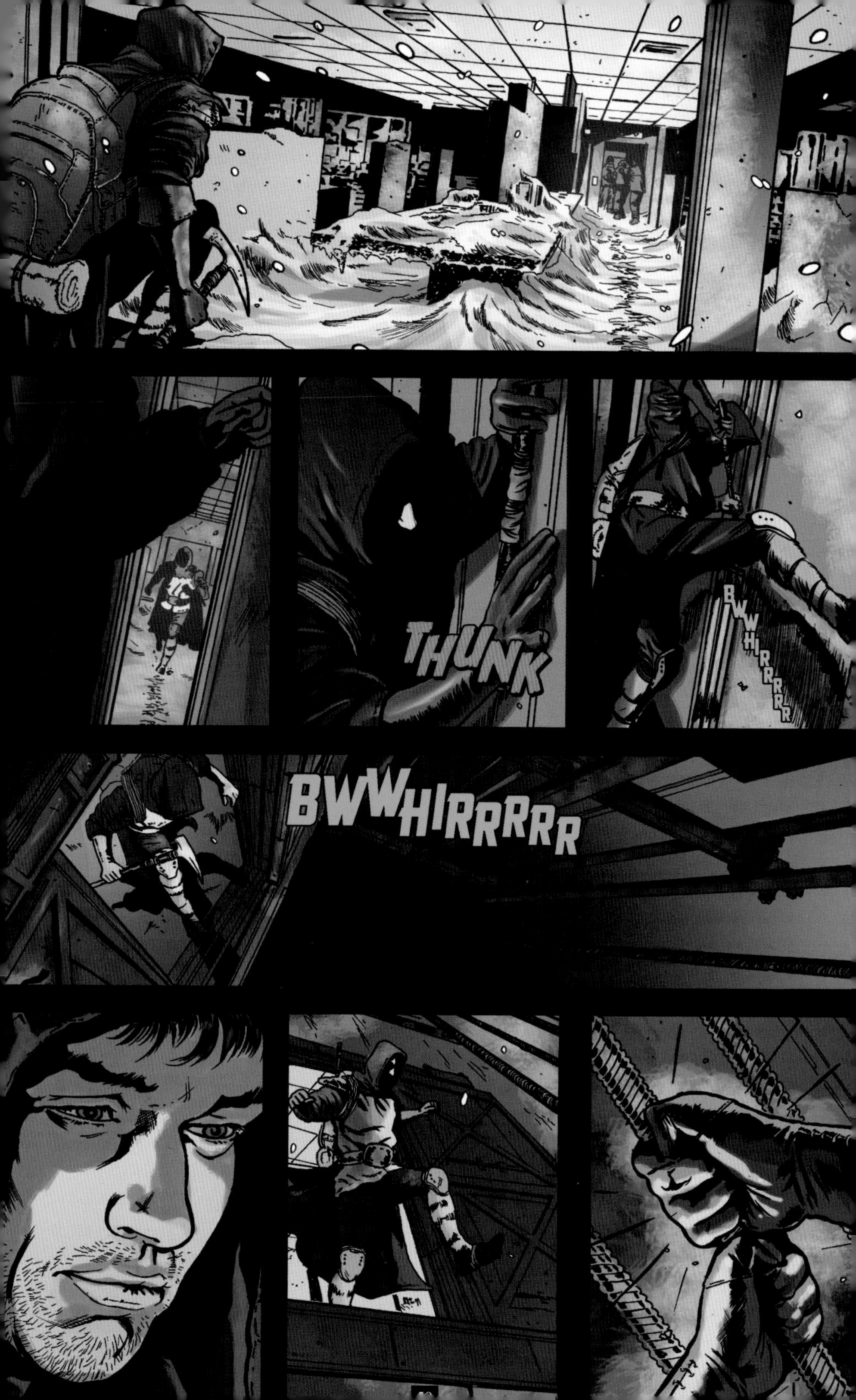
THUNK
BWWHIRRRRR
BWWHIRRRRR

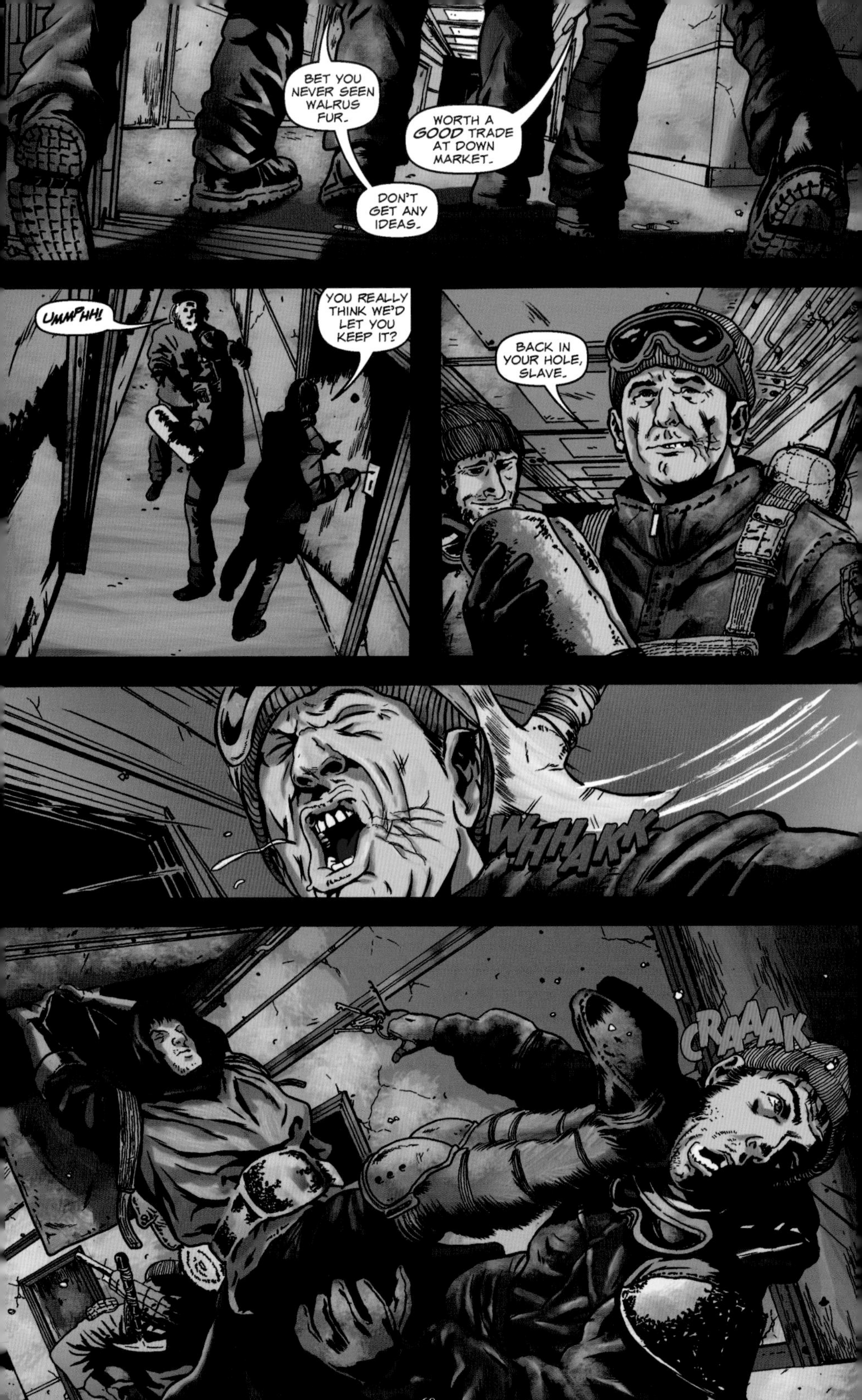
BET YOU NEVER SEEN WALRUS FUR.
WORTH A GOOD TRADE AT DOWN MARKET.
DON'T GET ANY IDEAS.
UMMPHH!
YOU REALLY THINK WE'D LET YOU KEEP IT?
BACK IN YOUR HOLE, SLAVE.
WHHAKK
CRAAAK

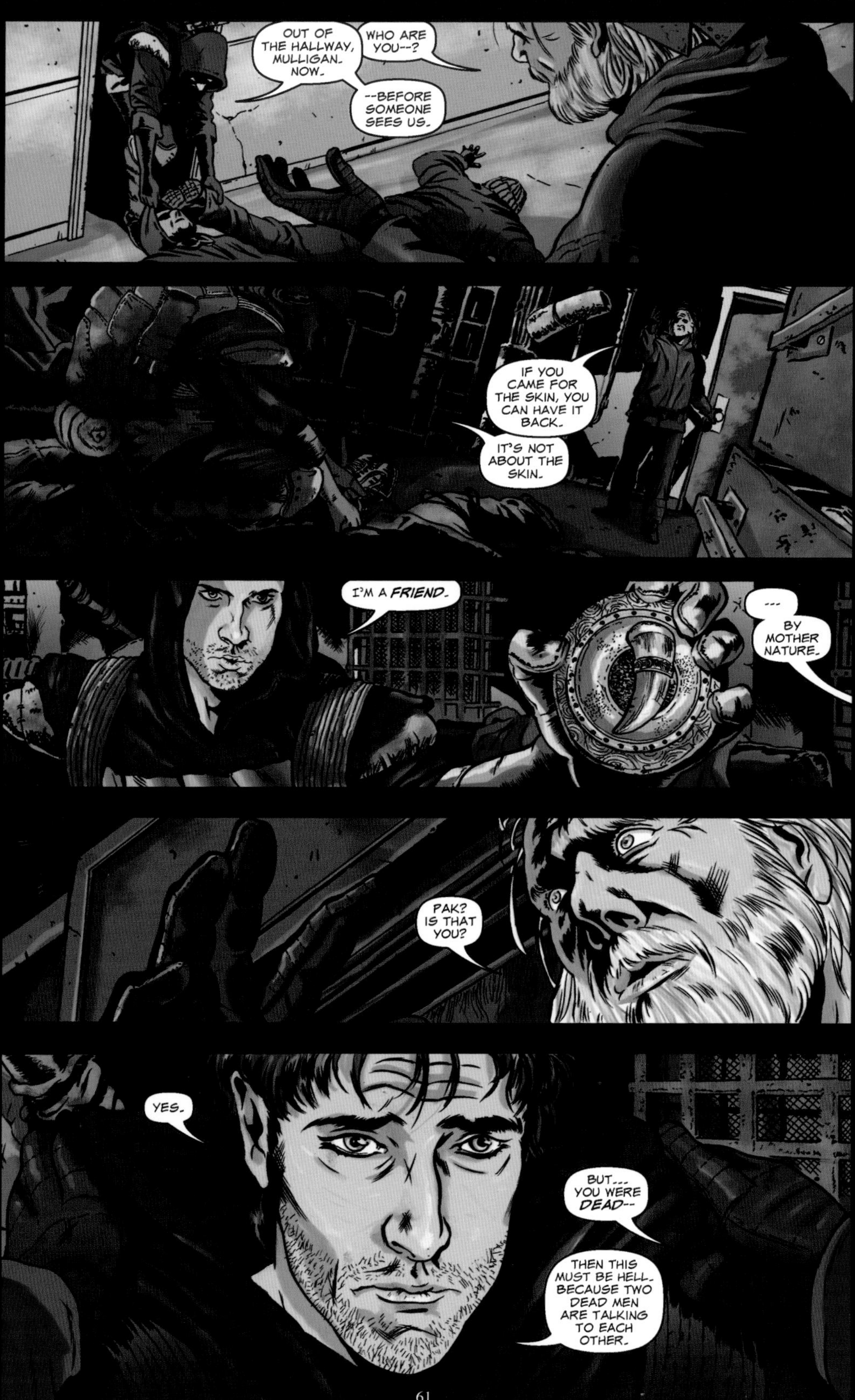
OUT OF THE HALLWAY, MULLIGAN. NOW.
WHO ARE YOU--?
--BEFORE SOMEONE SEES US.
IF YOU CAME FOR THE SKIN, YOU CAN HAVE IT BACK.
IT'S NOT ABOUT THE SKIN.
I'M A *FRIEND*.
--- BY MOTHER NATURE.
PAK? IS THAT YOU?
YES.
BUT... YOU WERE *DEAD*--
THEN THIS MUST BE HELL. BECAUSE TWO DEAD MEN ARE TALKING TO EACH OTHER.

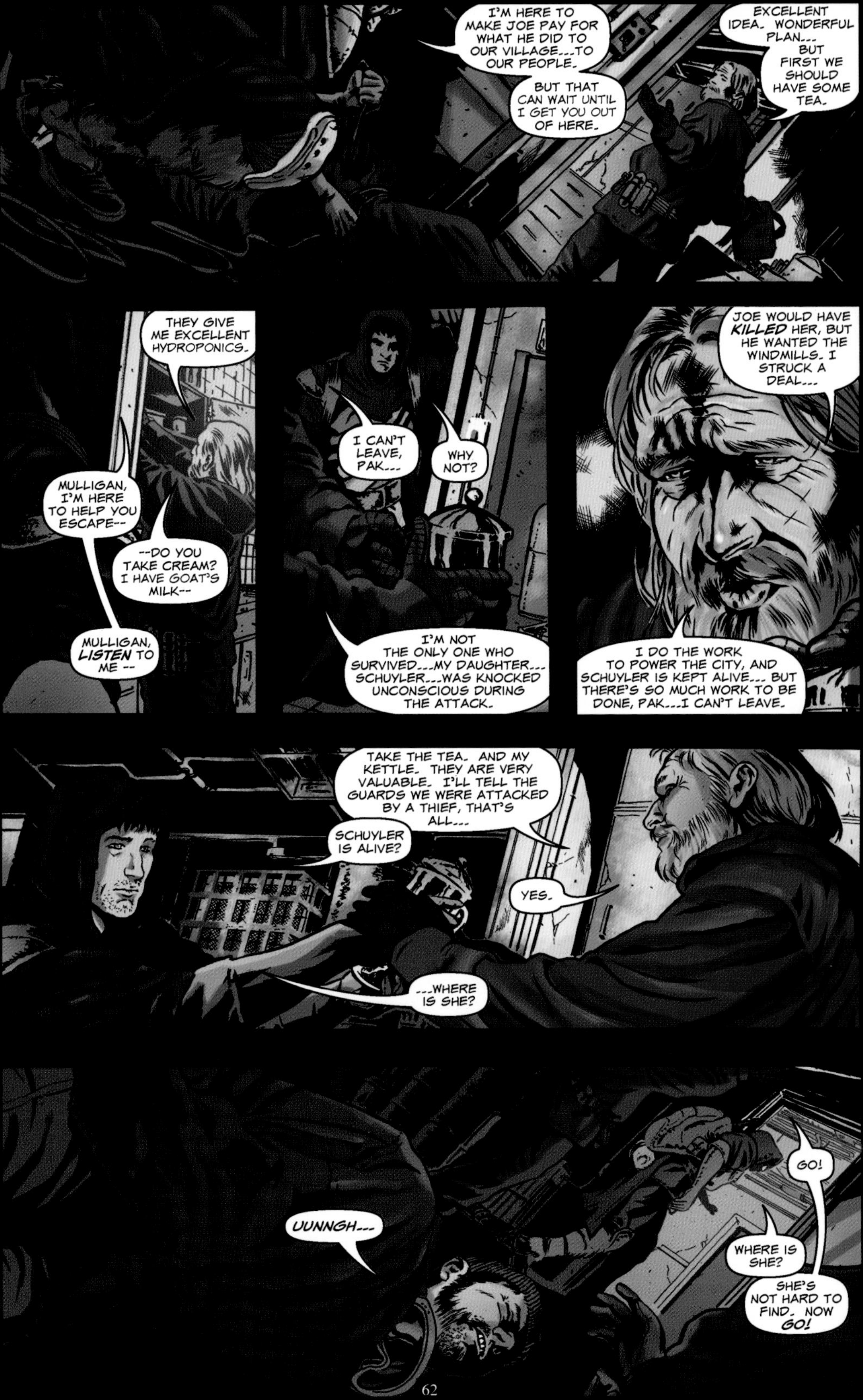
I'M HERE TO MAKE JOE PAY FOR WHAT HE DID TO OUR VILLAGE...TO OUR PEOPLE.
BUT THAT CAN WAIT UNTIL I GET YOU OUT OF HERE.
EXCELLENT IDEA. WONDERFUL PLAN... BUT FIRST WE SHOULD HAVE SOME TEA.
THEY GIVE ME EXCELLENT HYDROPONICS.
MULLIGAN, I'M HERE TO HELP YOU ESCAPE--
--DO YOU TAKE CREAM? I HAVE GOAT'S MILK--
MULLIGAN, LISTEN TO ME --
I CAN'T LEAVE, PAK...
WHY NOT?
I'M NOT THE ONLY ONE WHO SURVIVED...MY DAUGHTER... SCHUYLER...WAS KNOCKED UNCONSCIOUS DURING THE ATTACK.
JOE WOULD HAVE KILLED HER, BUT HE WANTED THE WINDMILLS. I STRUCK A DEAL...
I DO THE WORK TO POWER THE CITY, AND SCHUYLER IS KEPT ALIVE... BUT THERE'S SO MUCH WORK TO BE DONE, PAK...I CAN'T LEAVE.
TAKE THE TEA. AND MY KETTLE. THEY ARE VERY VALUABLE. I'LL TELL THE GUARDS WE WERE ATTACKED BY A THIEF, THAT'S ALL...
SCHUYLER IS ALIVE?
YES.
...WHERE IS SHE?
GO!
WHERE IS SHE?
SHE'S NOT HARD TO FIND. NOW GO!
UUNNGH...

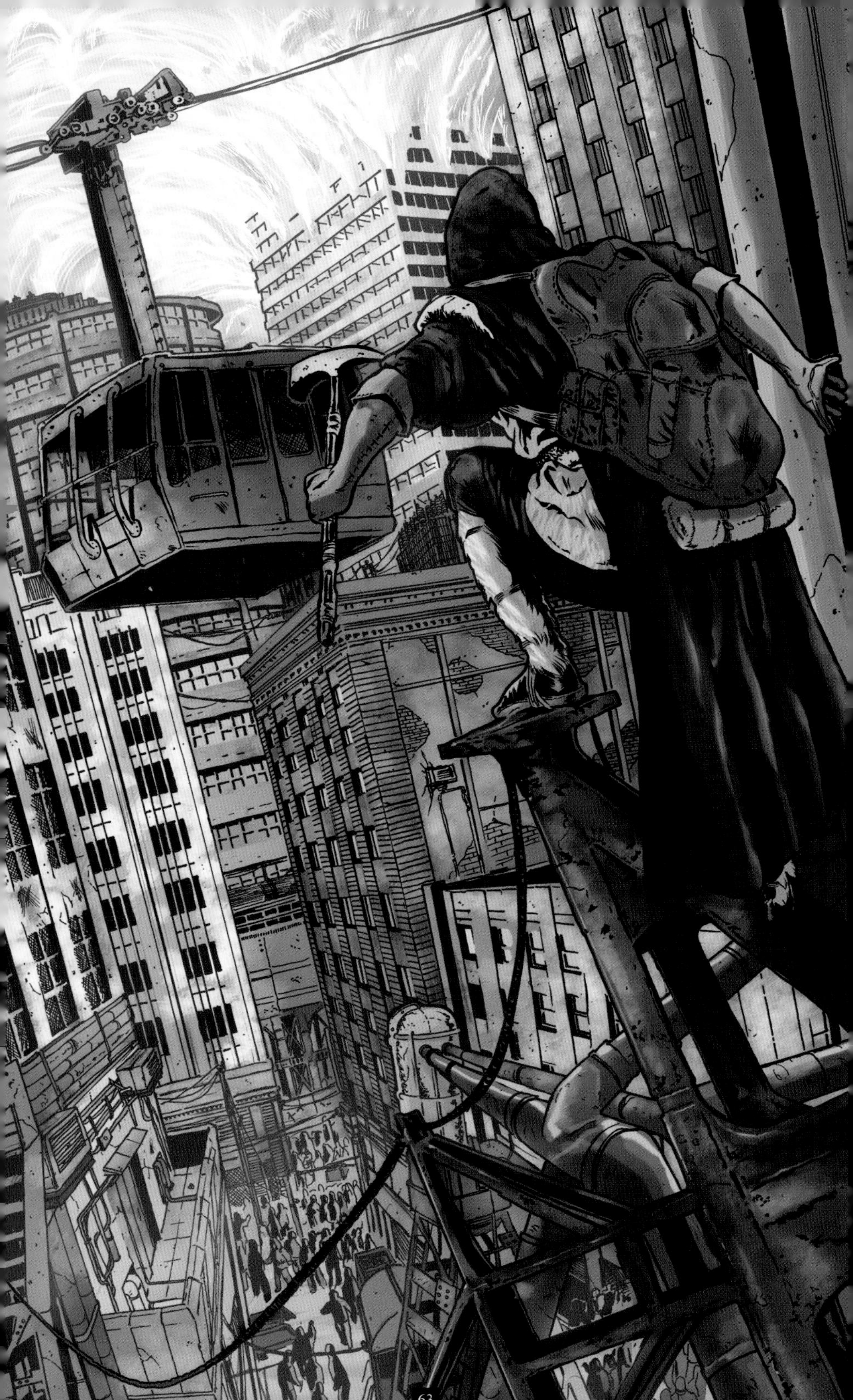

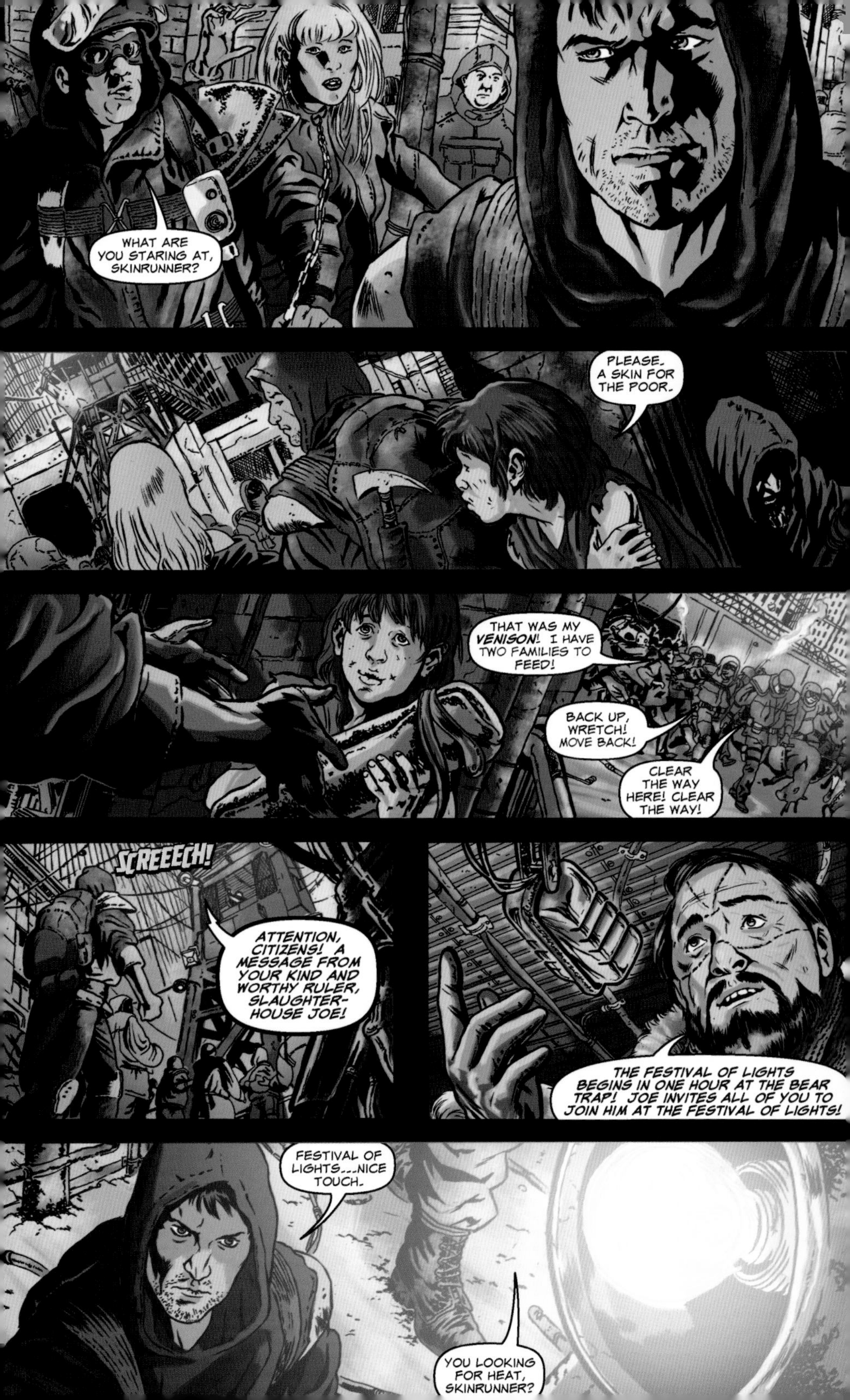
WHAT ARE YOU STARING AT, SKINRUNNER?
PLEASE. A SKIN FOR THE POOR.
THAT WAS MY *VENISON*! I HAVE TWO FAMILIES TO FEED!
BACK UP, WRETCH! MOVE BACK!
CLEAR THE WAY HERE! CLEAR THE WAY!
SCREEECH!
ATTENTION, CITIZENS! A MESSAGE FROM YOUR KIND AND WORTHY RULER, SLAUGHTER-HOUSE JOE!
THE FESTIVAL OF LIGHTS BEGINS IN ONE HOUR AT THE BEAR TRAP! JOE INVITES ALL OF YOU TO JOIN HIM AT THE FESTIVAL OF LIGHTS!
FESTIVAL OF LIGHTS...NICE TOUCH.
YOU LOOKING FOR HEAT, SKINRUNNER?

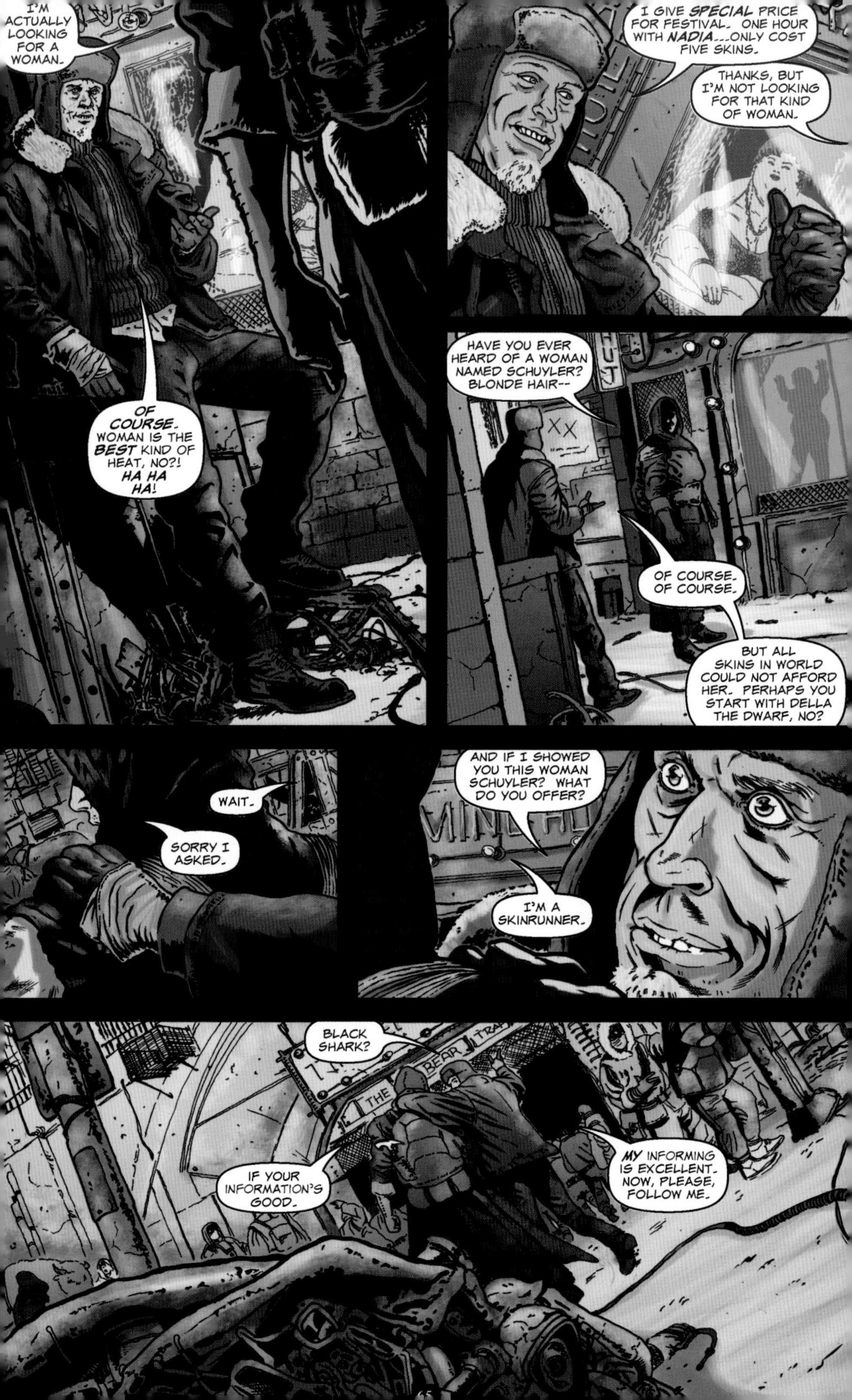
I'M ACTUALLY LOOKING FOR A WOMAN.
I GIVE ***SPECIAL*** PRICE FOR FESTIVAL. ONE HOUR WITH ***NADIA***...ONLY COST FIVE SKINS.
THANKS, BUT I'M NOT LOOKING FOR THAT KIND OF WOMAN.
OF COURSE. WOMAN IS THE ***BEST*** KIND OF HEAT, NO?! ***HA HA HA!***
HAVE YOU EVER HEARD OF A WOMAN NAMED SCHUYLER? BLONDE HAIR--
OF COURSE. OF COURSE.
BUT ALL SKINS IN WORLD COULD NOT AFFORD HER. PERHAPS YOU START WITH DELLA THE DWARF, NO?
WAIT.
SORRY I ASKED.
AND IF I SHOWED YOU THIS WOMAN SCHUYLER? WHAT DO YOU OFFER?
I'M A SKINRUNNER.
BLACK SHARK?
MY INFORMING IS EXCELLENT. NOW, PLEASE, FOLLOW ME.
IF YOUR INFORMATION'S GOOD.
THE BEAR TRA

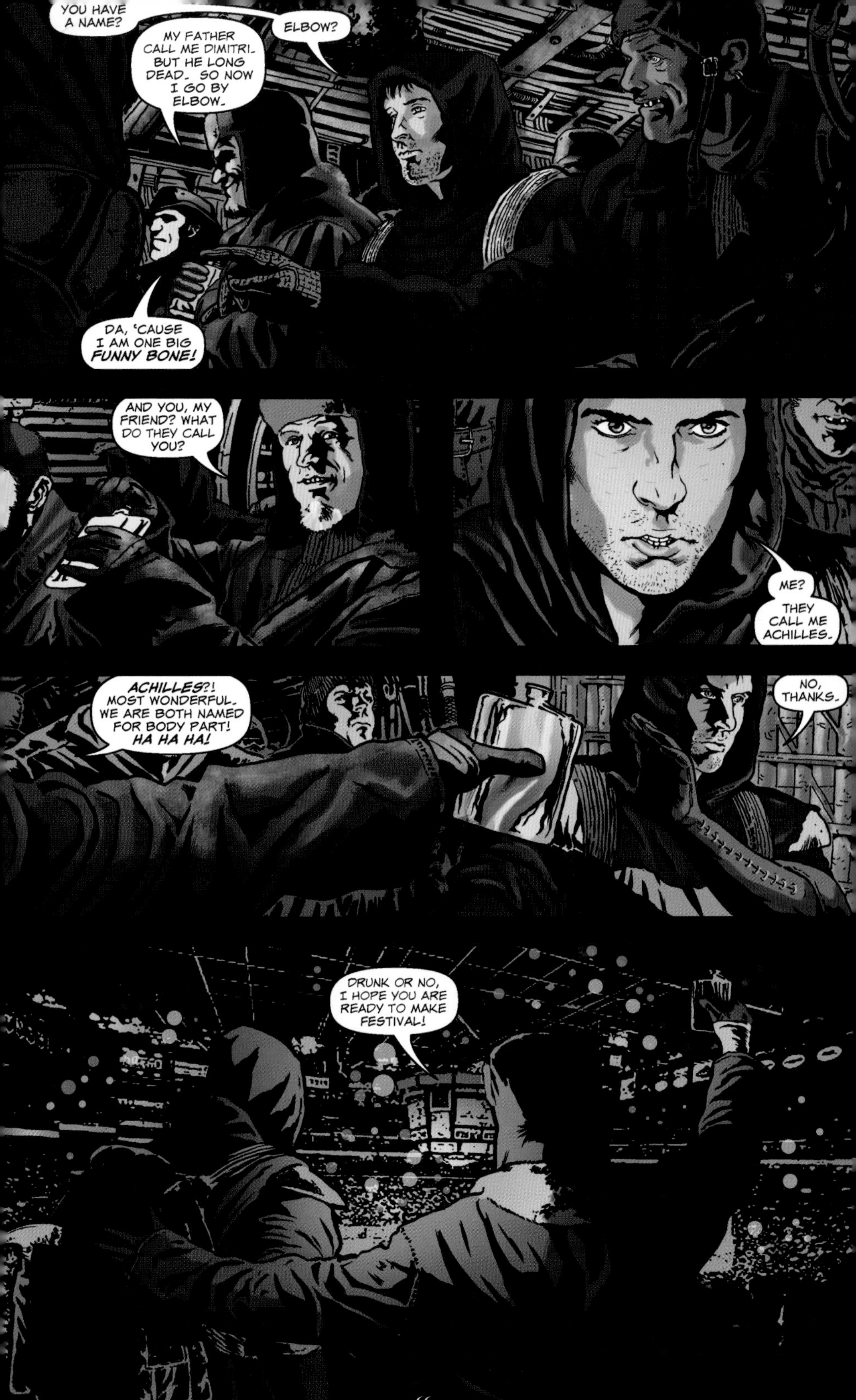
YOU HAVE A NAME?
MY FATHER CALL ME DIMITRI. BUT HE LONG DEAD. SO NOW I GO BY ELBOW.
ELBOW?
DA, 'CAUSE I AM ONE BIG FUNNY BONE!
AND YOU, MY FRIEND? WHAT DO THEY CALL YOU?
ME? THEY CALL ME ACHILLES.
ACHILLES?! MOST WONDERFUL. WE ARE BOTH NAMED FOR BODY PART! HA HA HA!
NO, THANKS.
DRUNK OR NO, I HOPE YOU ARE READY TO MAKE FESTIVAL!

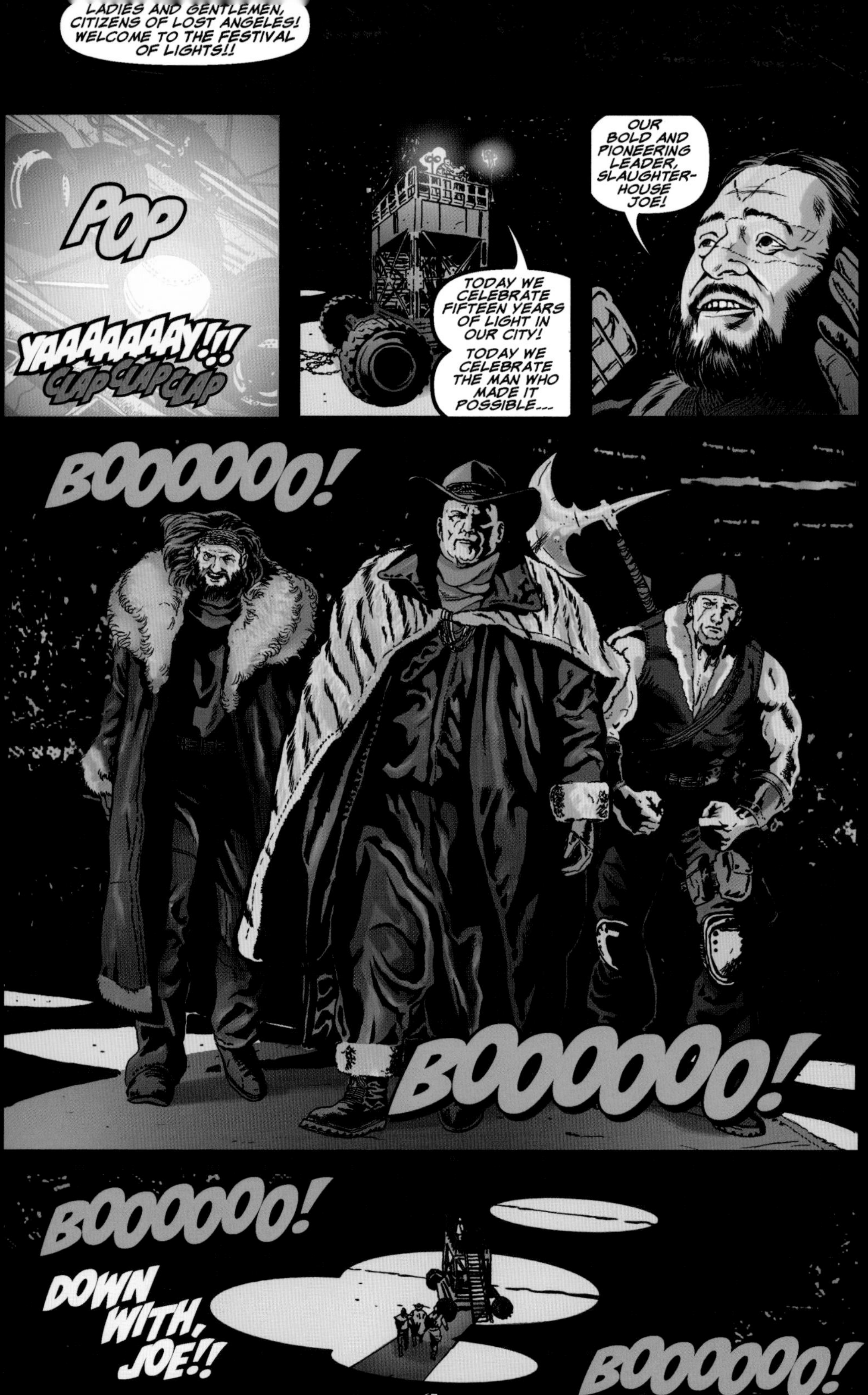
LADIES AND GENTLEMEN, CITIZENS OF LOST ANGELES! WELCOME TO THE FESTIVAL OF LIGHTS!!
POP
YAAAAAAAY!!!
CLAP CLAP CLAP
TODAY WE CELEBRATE FIFTEEN YEARS OF LIGHT IN OUR CITY!
TODAY WE CELEBRATE THE MAN WHO MADE IT POSSIBLE...
OUR BOLD AND PIONEERING LEADER, SLAUGHTER-HOUSE JOE!
BOOOOOO!
BOOOOOO!
BOOOOOO!
DOWN WITH, JOE!!
BOOOOOO!

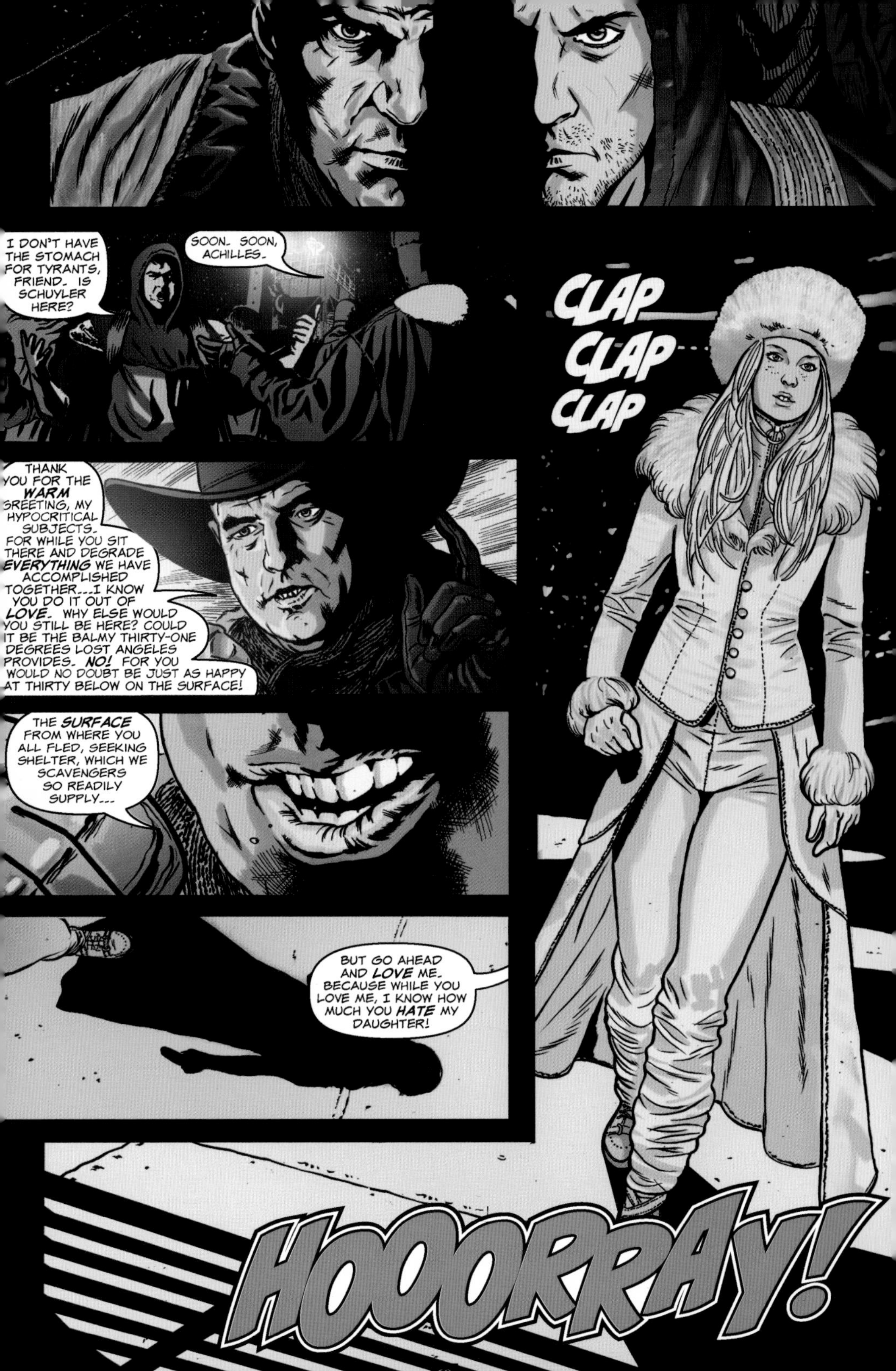
I DON'T HAVE THE STOMACH FOR TYRANTS, FRIEND. IS SCHUYLER HERE?
SOON. SOON, ACHILLES.
THANK YOU FOR THE WARM GREETING, MY HYPOCRITICAL SUBJECTS. FOR WHILE YOU SIT THERE AND DEGRADE EVERYTHING WE HAVE ACCOMPLISHED TOGETHER...I KNOW YOU DO IT OUT OF LOVE. WHY ELSE WOULD YOU STILL BE HERE? COULD IT BE THE BALMY THIRTY-ONE DEGREES LOST ANGELES PROVIDES. NO! FOR YOU WOULD NO DOUBT BE JUST AS HAPPY AT THIRTY BELOW ON THE SURFACE!
THE SURFACE FROM WHERE YOU ALL FLED, SEEKING SHELTER, WHICH WE SCAVENGERS SO READILY SUPPLY...
BUT GO AHEAD AND LOVE ME. BECAUSE WHILE YOU LOVE ME, I KNOW HOW MUCH YOU HATE MY DAUGHTER!
CLAP
CLAP
CLAP
HOOORRAY!

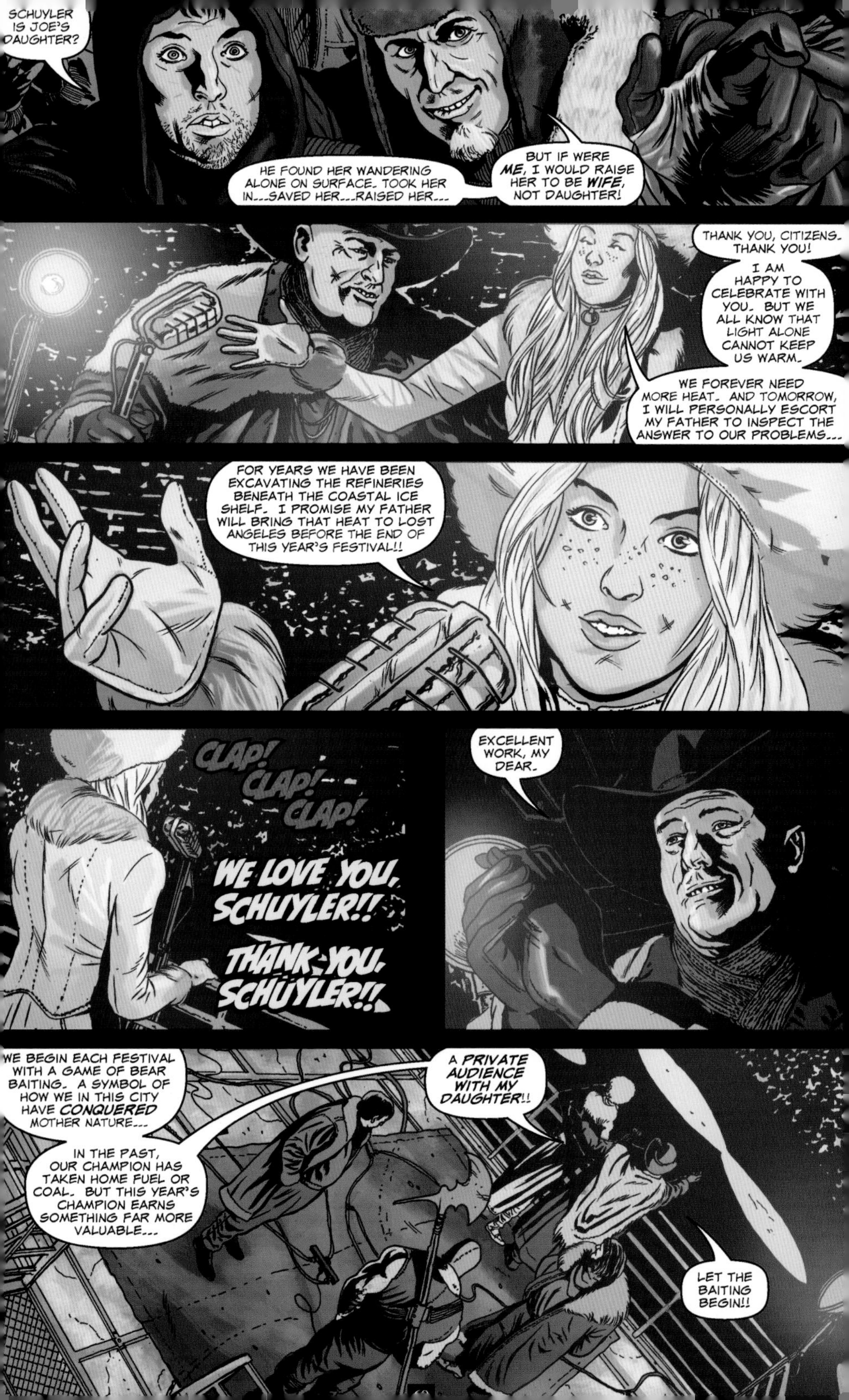
SCHUYLER IS JOE'S DAUGHTER?
HE FOUND HER WANDERING ALONE ON SURFACE. TOOK HER IN...SAVED HER...RAISED HER...
BUT IF WERE *ME*, I WOULD RAISE HER TO BE *WIFE*, NOT DAUGHTER!
THANK YOU, CITIZENS. THANK YOU!
I AM HAPPY TO CELEBRATE WITH YOU. BUT WE ALL KNOW THAT LIGHT ALONE CANNOT KEEP US WARM.
WE FOREVER NEED MORE HEAT. AND TOMORROW, I WILL PERSONALLY ESCORT MY FATHER TO INSPECT THE ANSWER TO OUR PROBLEMS...
FOR YEARS WE HAVE BEEN EXCAVATING THE REFINERIES BENEATH THE COASTAL ICE SHELF. I PROMISE MY FATHER WILL BRING THAT HEAT TO LOST ANGELES BEFORE THE END OF THIS YEAR'S FESTIVAL!!
CLAP! CLAP! CLAP!
WE LOVE YOU, SCHUYLER!!
THANK YOU, SCHUYLER!!
EXCELLENT WORK, MY DEAR.
WE BEGIN EACH FESTIVAL WITH A GAME OF BEAR BAITING. A SYMBOL OF HOW WE IN THIS CITY HAVE *CONQUERED* MOTHER NATURE...
IN THE PAST, OUR CHAMPION HAS TAKEN HOME FUEL OR COAL. BUT THIS YEAR'S CHAMPION EARNS SOMETHING FAR MORE VALUABLE...
A *PRIVATE AUDIENCE WITH MY DAUGHTER*!!
LET THE BAITING BEGIN!!

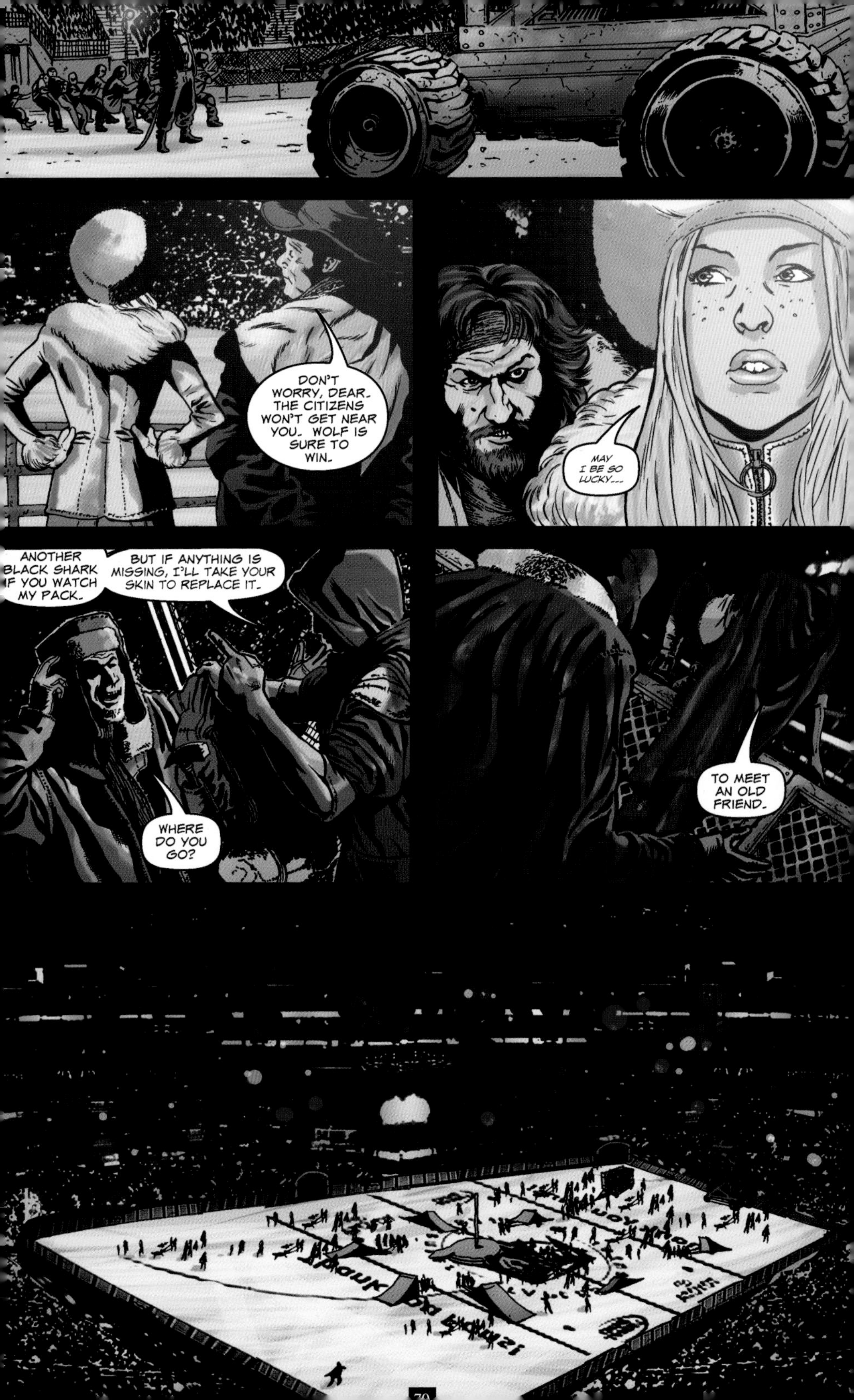

DON'T WORRY, DEAR. THE CITIZENS WON'T GET NEAR YOU. WOLF IS SURE TO WIN.
MAY I BE SO LUCKY...
ANOTHER BLACK SHARK IF YOU WATCH MY PACK.
BUT IF ANYTHING IS MISSING, I'LL TAKE YOUR SKIN TO REPLACE IT.
WHERE DO YOU GO?
TO MEET AN OLD FRIEND.

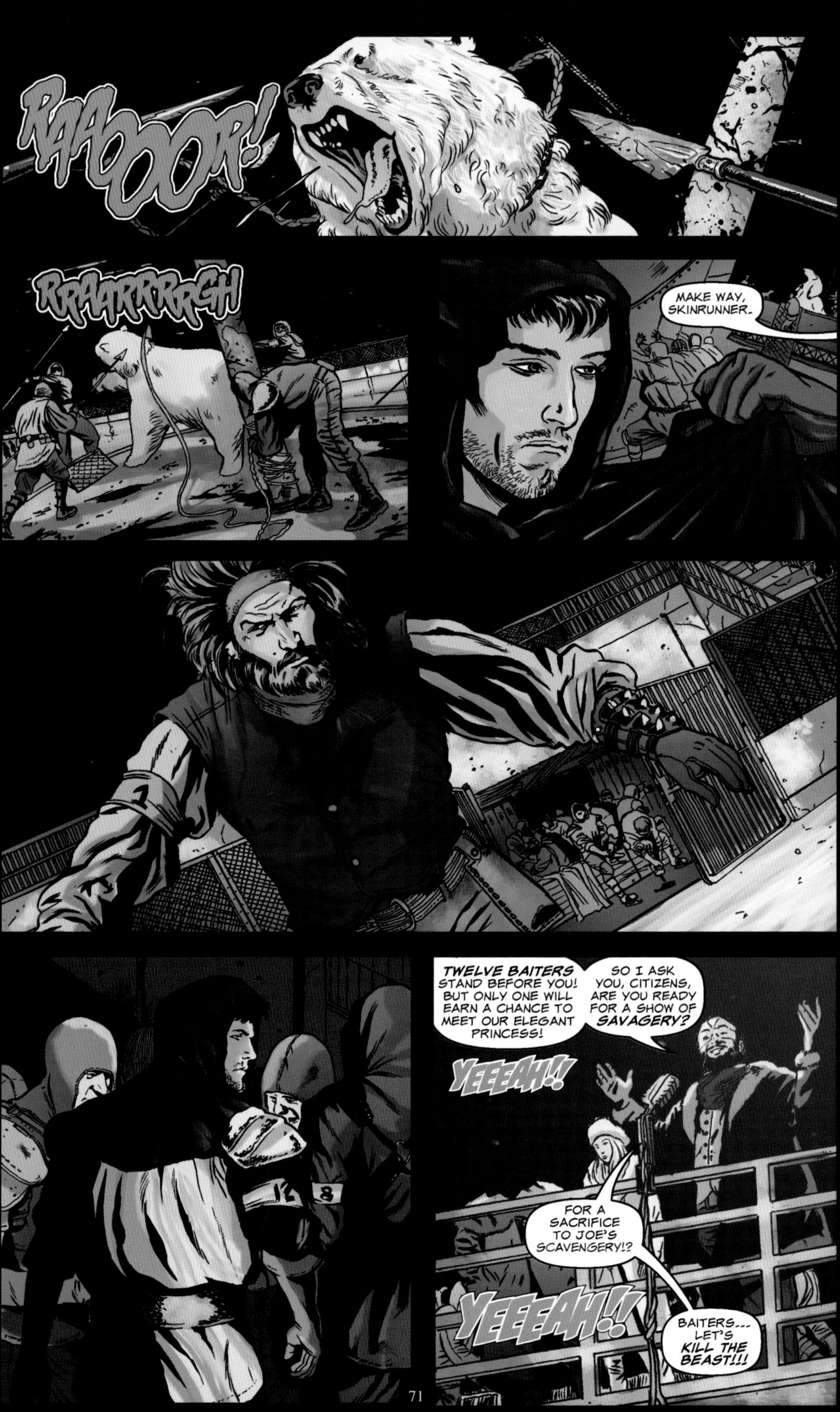
RAAOOOR!
RRRAARRRRGH
MAKE WAY, SKINRUNNER.
TWELVE BAITERS STAND BEFORE YOU! BUT ONLY ONE WILL EARN A CHANCE TO MEET OUR ELEGANT PRINCESS!
SO I ASK YOU, CITIZENS, ARE YOU READY FOR A SHOW OF SAVAGERY?
YEEEAH!!
FOR A SACRIFICE TO JOE'S SCAVENGERY!?
YEEEAH!!
BAITERS... LET'S KILL THE BEAST!!!

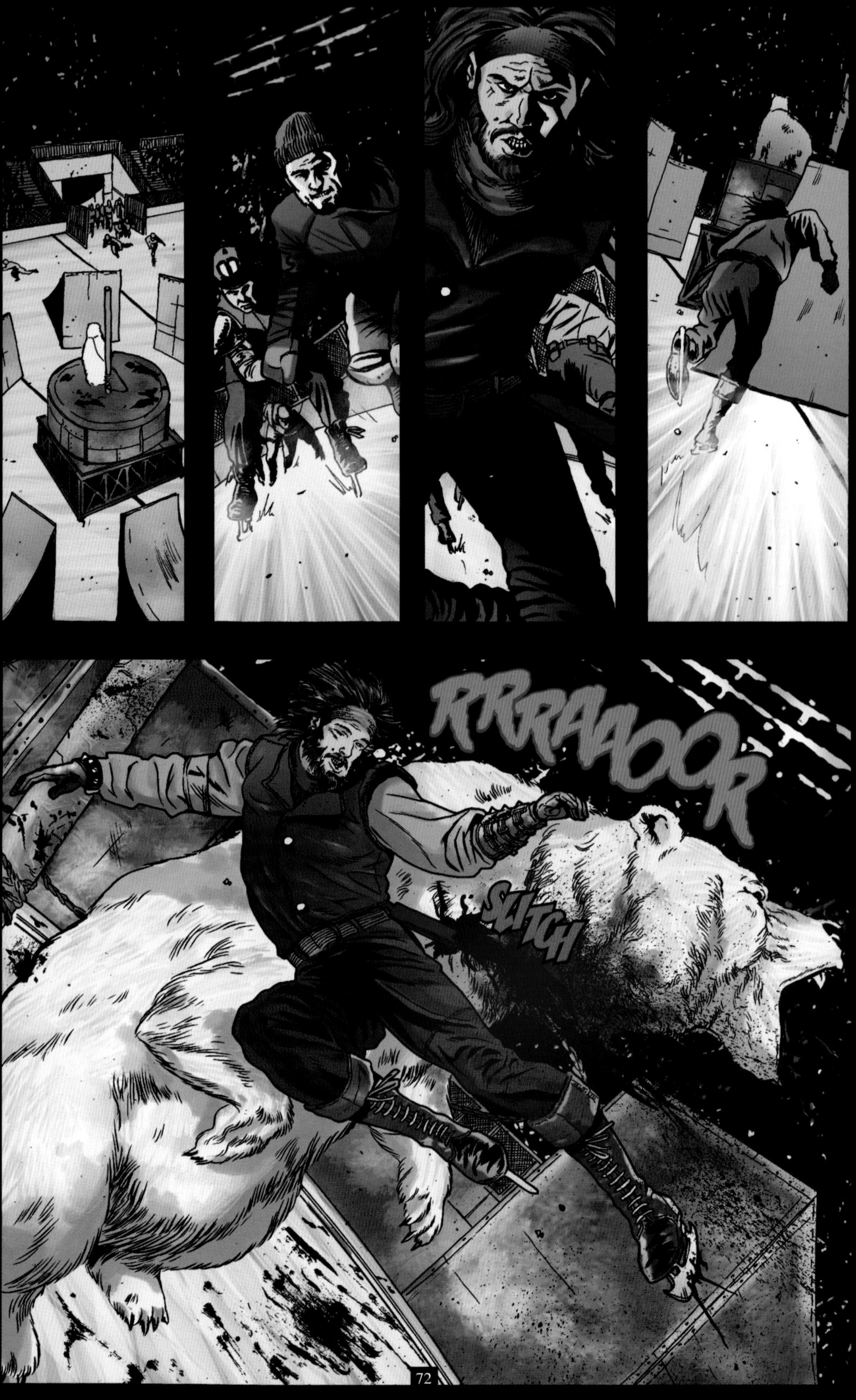
RRRAAAOOR
SLITCH

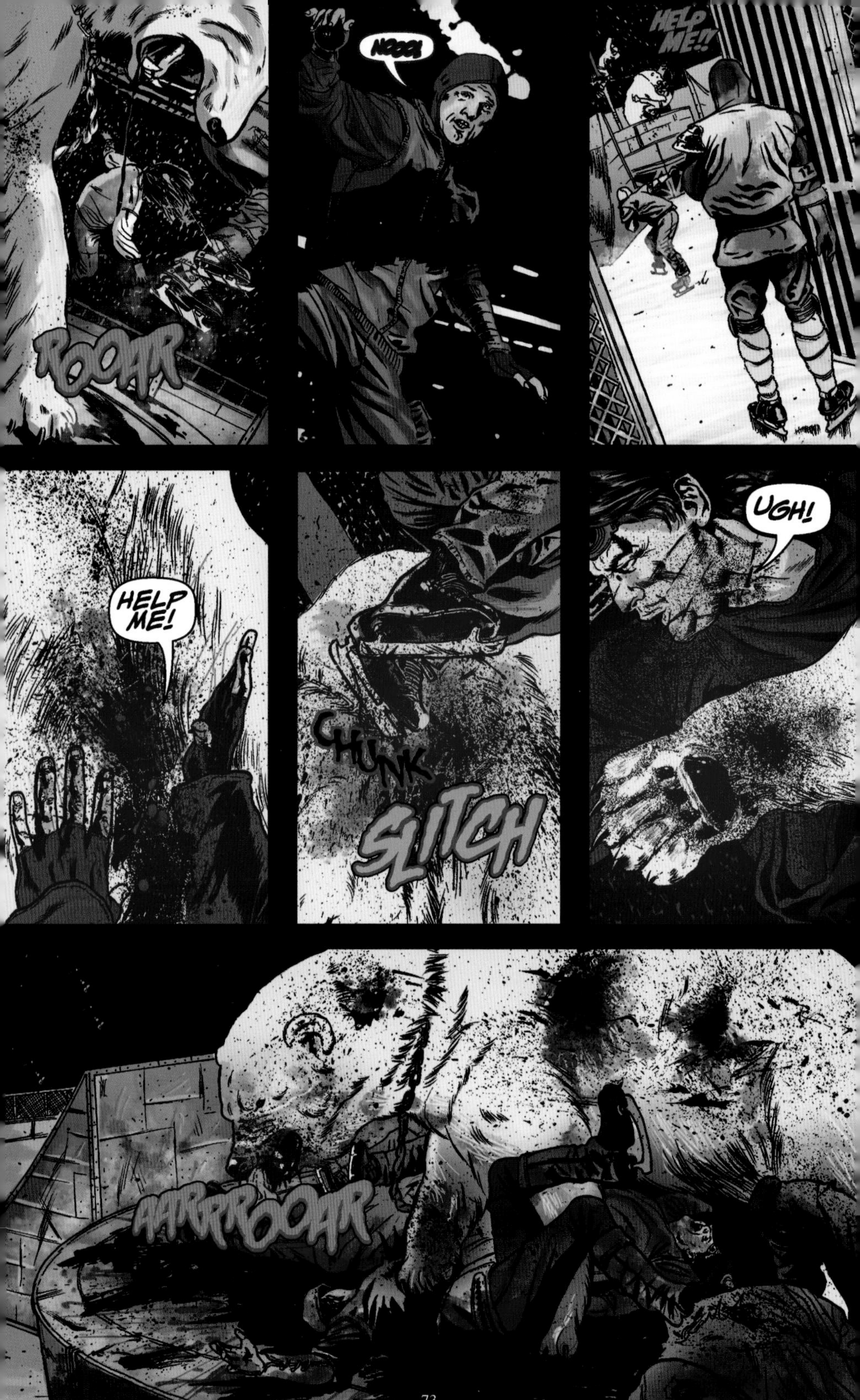
ROOAR
NOOO!
HELP ME!!
HELP ME!
CHUNK
SLITCH
UGH!
AARRROOAR

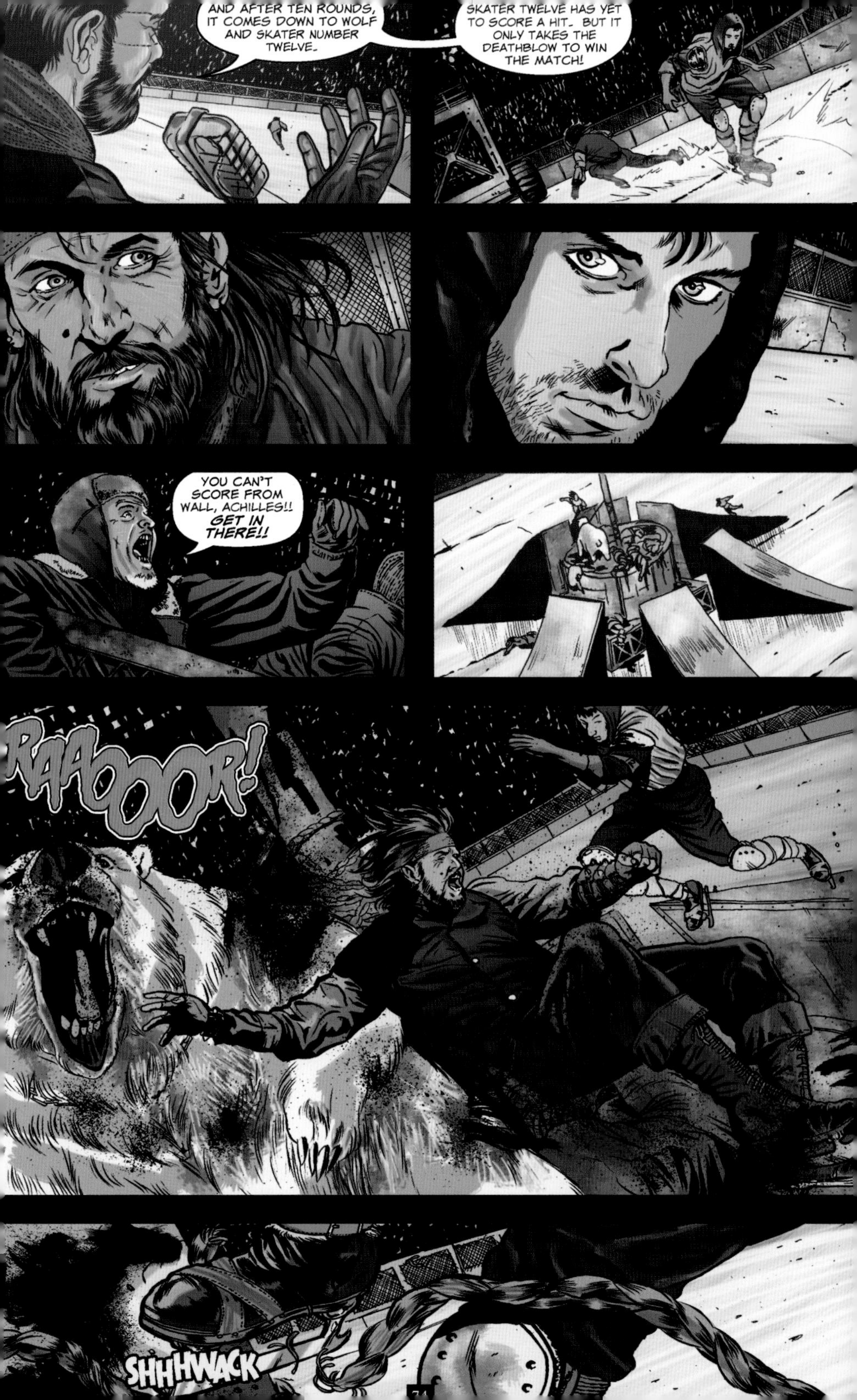
AND AFTER TEN ROUNDS, IT COMES DOWN TO WOLF AND SKATER NUMBER TWELVE.
SKATER TWELVE HAS YET TO SCORE A HIT. BUT IT ONLY TAKES THE DEATHBLOW TO WIN THE MATCH!
YOU CAN'T SCORE FROM WALL, ACHILLES!! GET IN THERE!!
RAAOOOR!
SHHHWACK

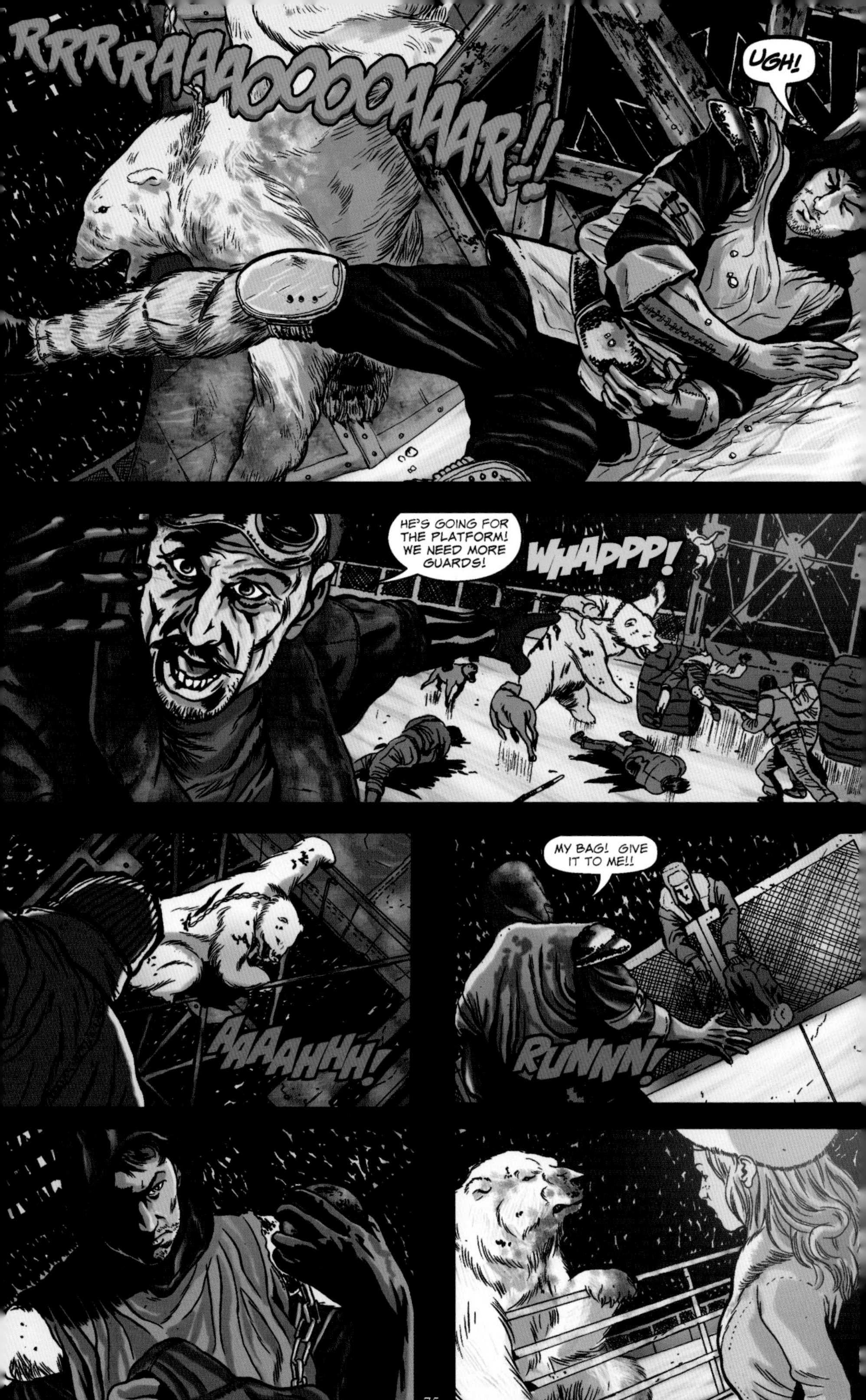
RRRRAAAOOOOOAAAR!!
UGH!
HE'S GOING FOR THE PLATFORM! WE NEED MORE GUARDS!
WHAPPP!
AAAAHHH!
MY BAG! GIVE IT TO ME!!
RUNNN!

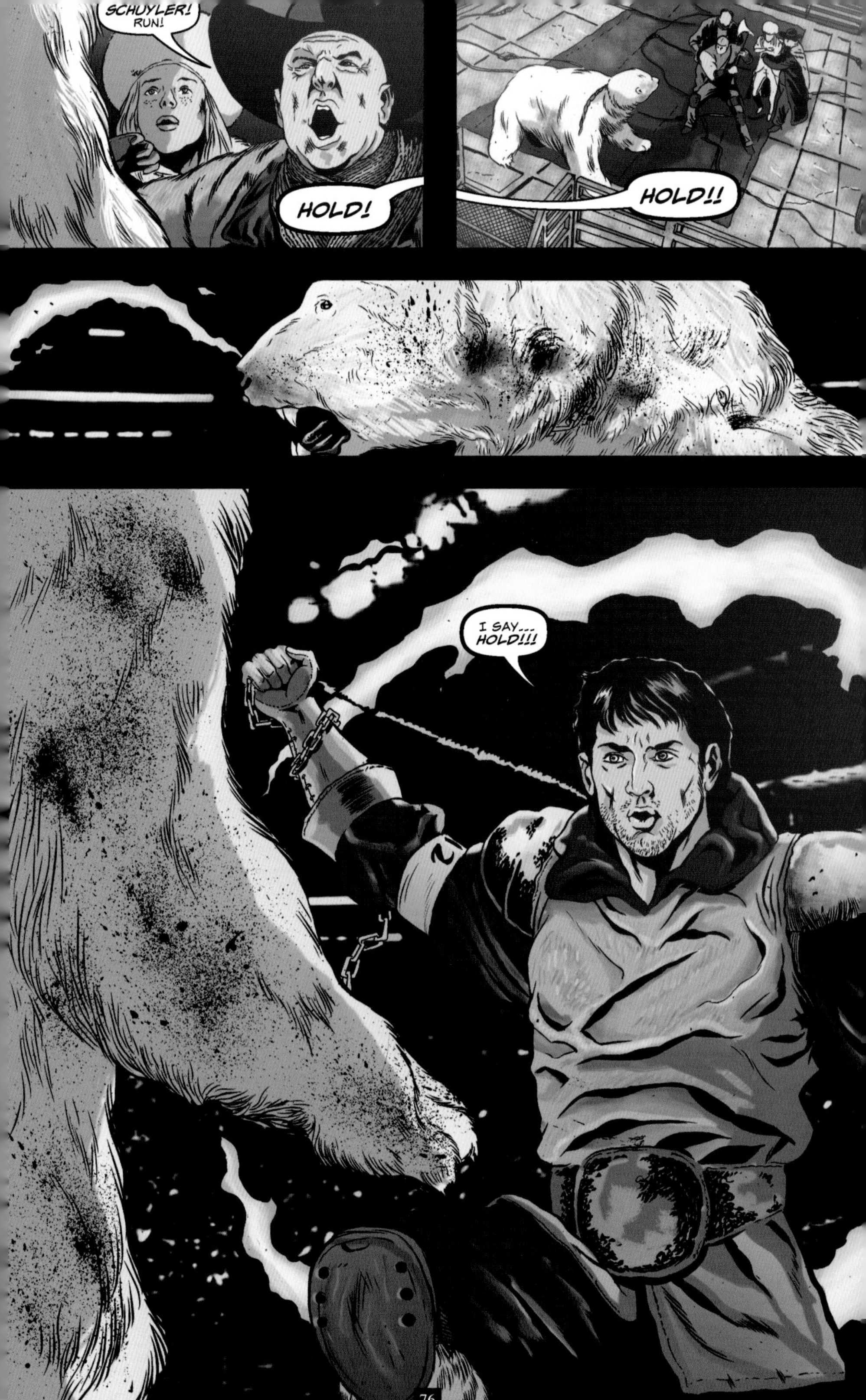
SCHUYLER! RUN!
HOLD!
HOLD!!
I SAY... HOLD!!!

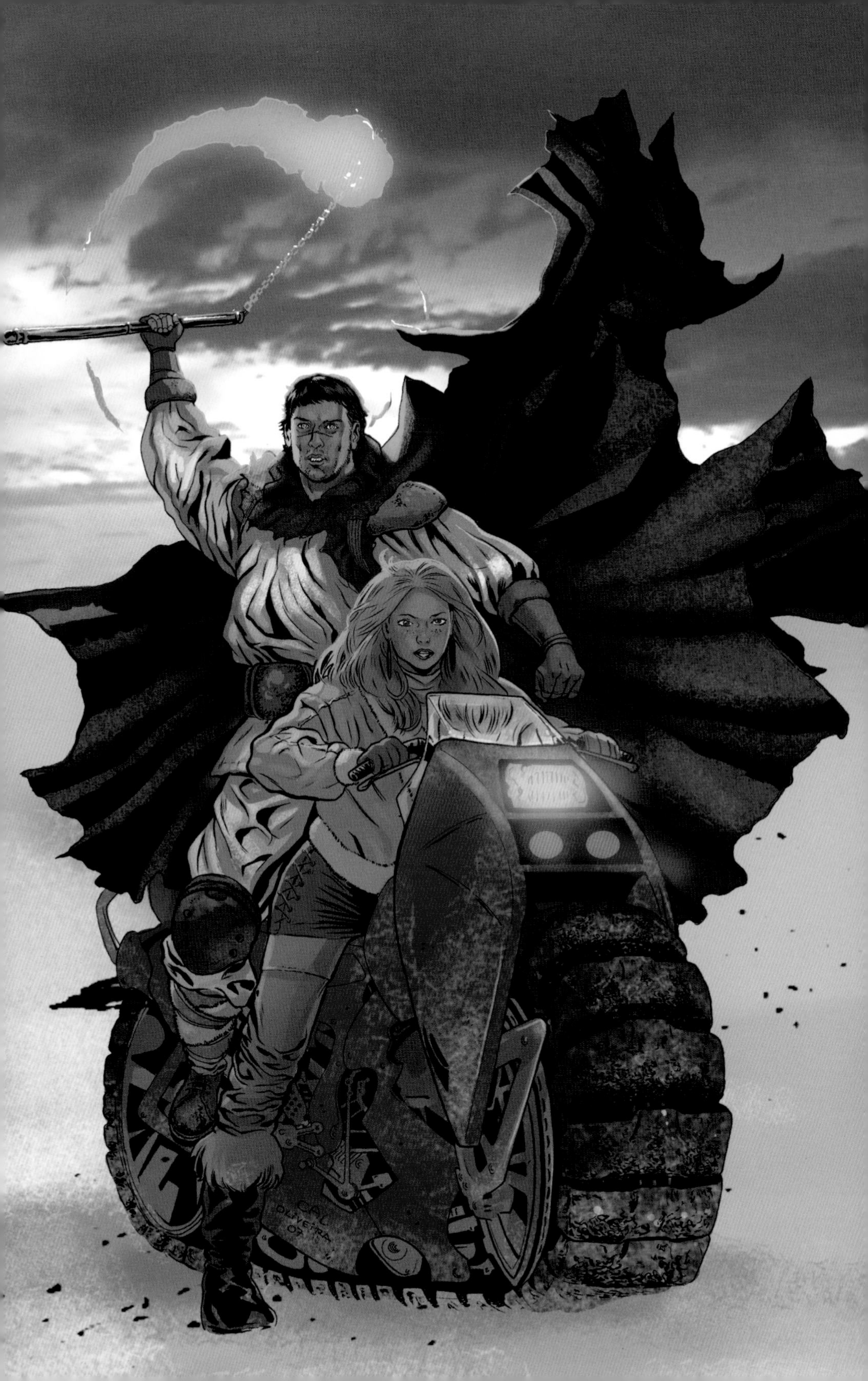

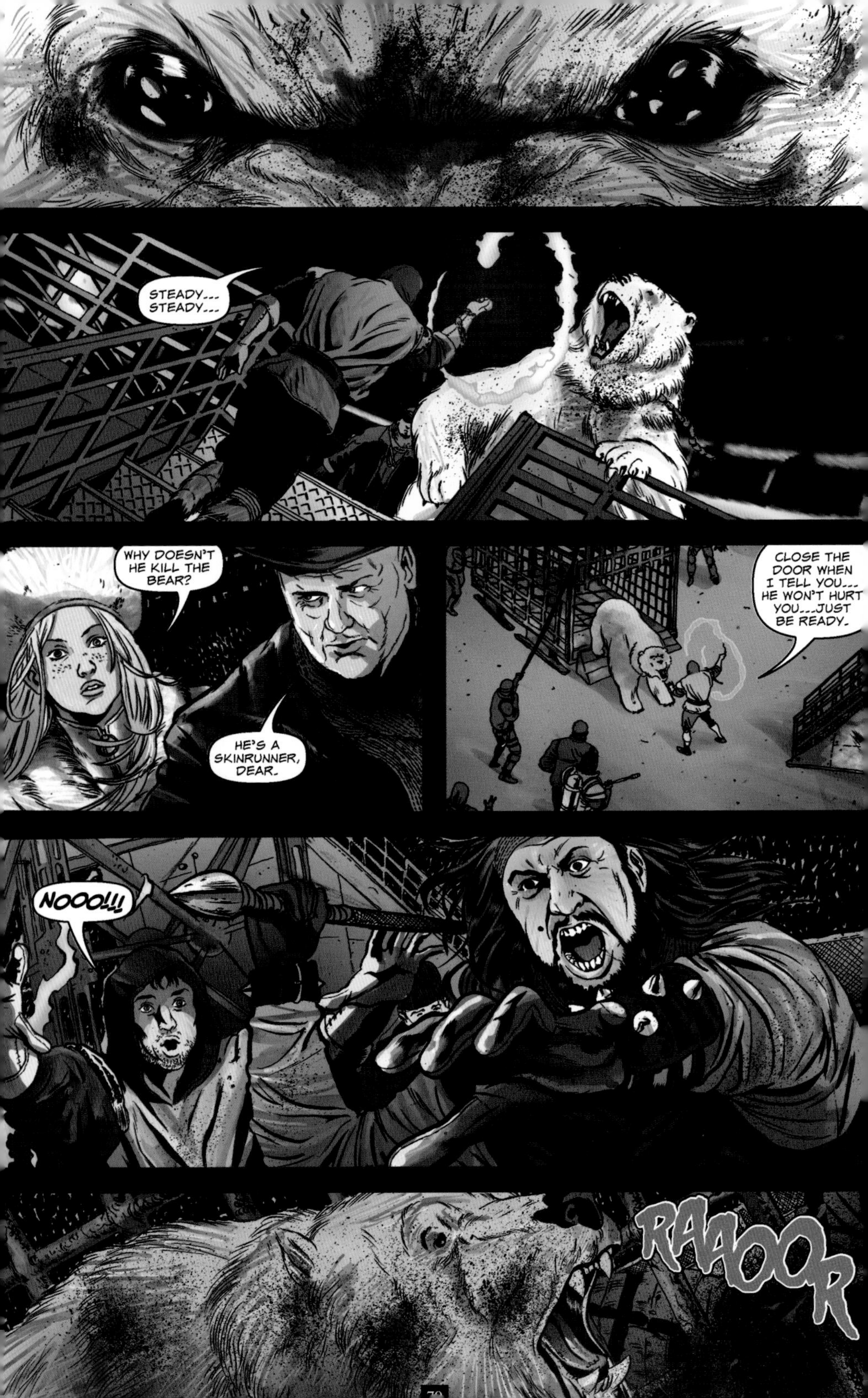
STEADY...
STEADY...
WHY DOESN'T HE KILL THE BEAR?
HE'S A SKINRUNNER, DEAR.
CLOSE THE DOOR WHEN I TELL YOU... HE WON'T HURT YOU...JUST BE READY.
NOOO!!!
RAAOOR

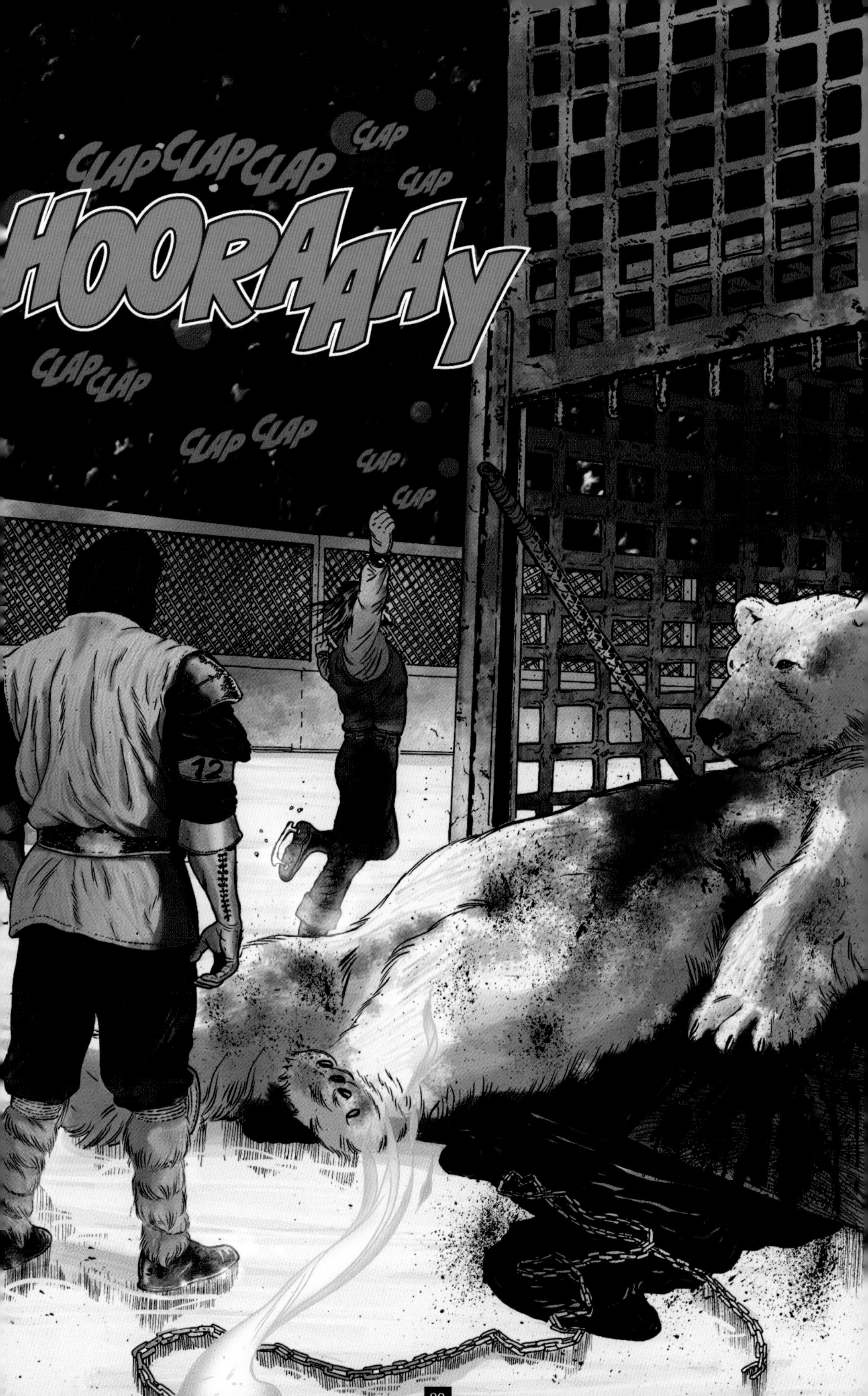
CLAP CLAP CLAP
CLAP
CLAP
HOORAAAAY
CLAP CLAP
CLAP CLAP
CLAP
CLAP

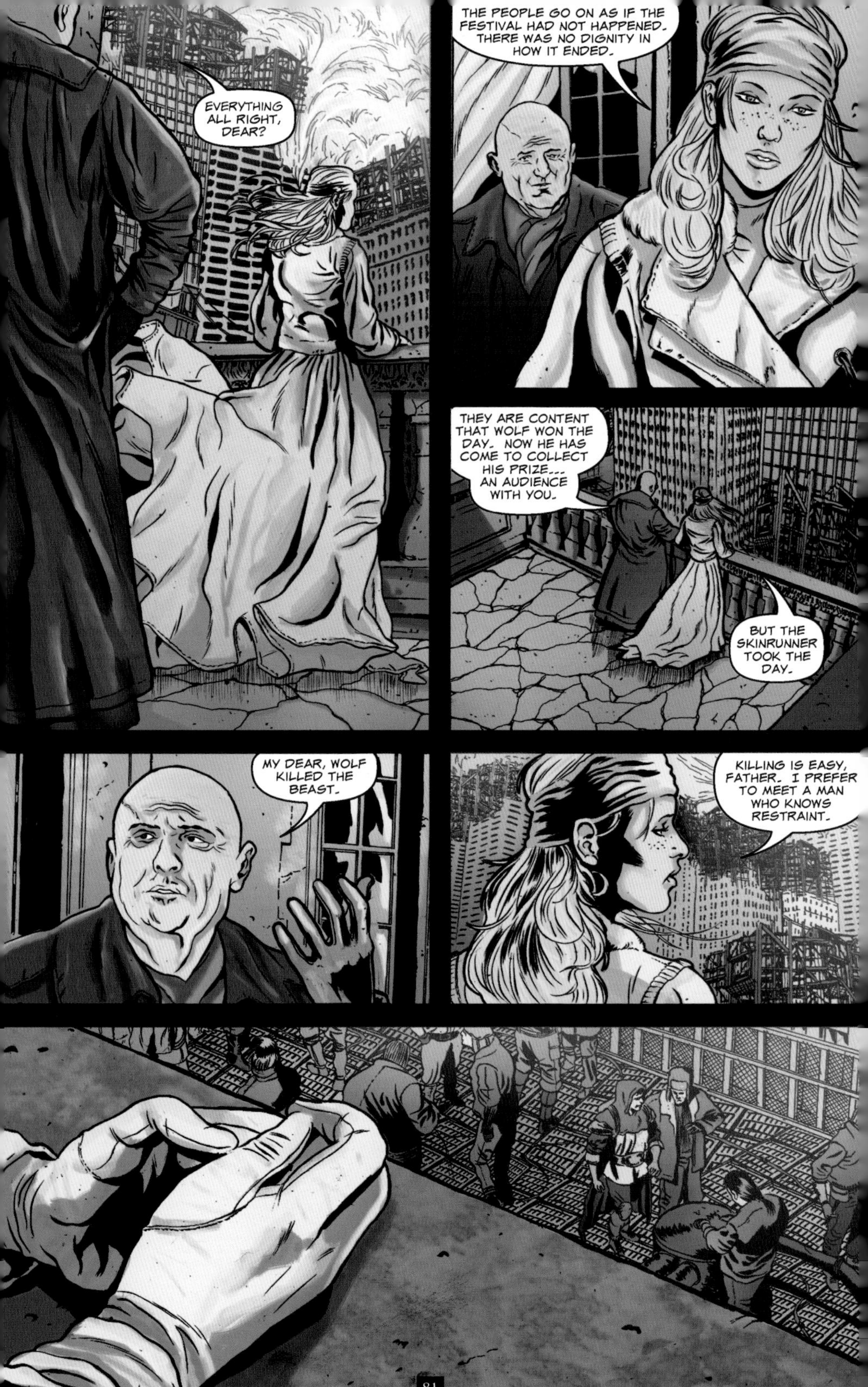
EVERYTHING ALL RIGHT, DEAR?
THE PEOPLE GO ON AS IF THE FESTIVAL HAD NOT HAPPENED. THERE WAS NO DIGNITY IN HOW IT ENDED.
THEY ARE CONTENT THAT WOLF WON THE DAY. NOW HE HAS COME TO COLLECT HIS PRIZE... AN AUDIENCE WITH YOU.
BUT THE SKINRUNNER TOOK THE DAY.
MY DEAR, WOLF KILLED THE BEAST.
KILLING IS EASY, FATHER. I PREFER TO MEET A MAN WHO KNOWS RESTRAINT.

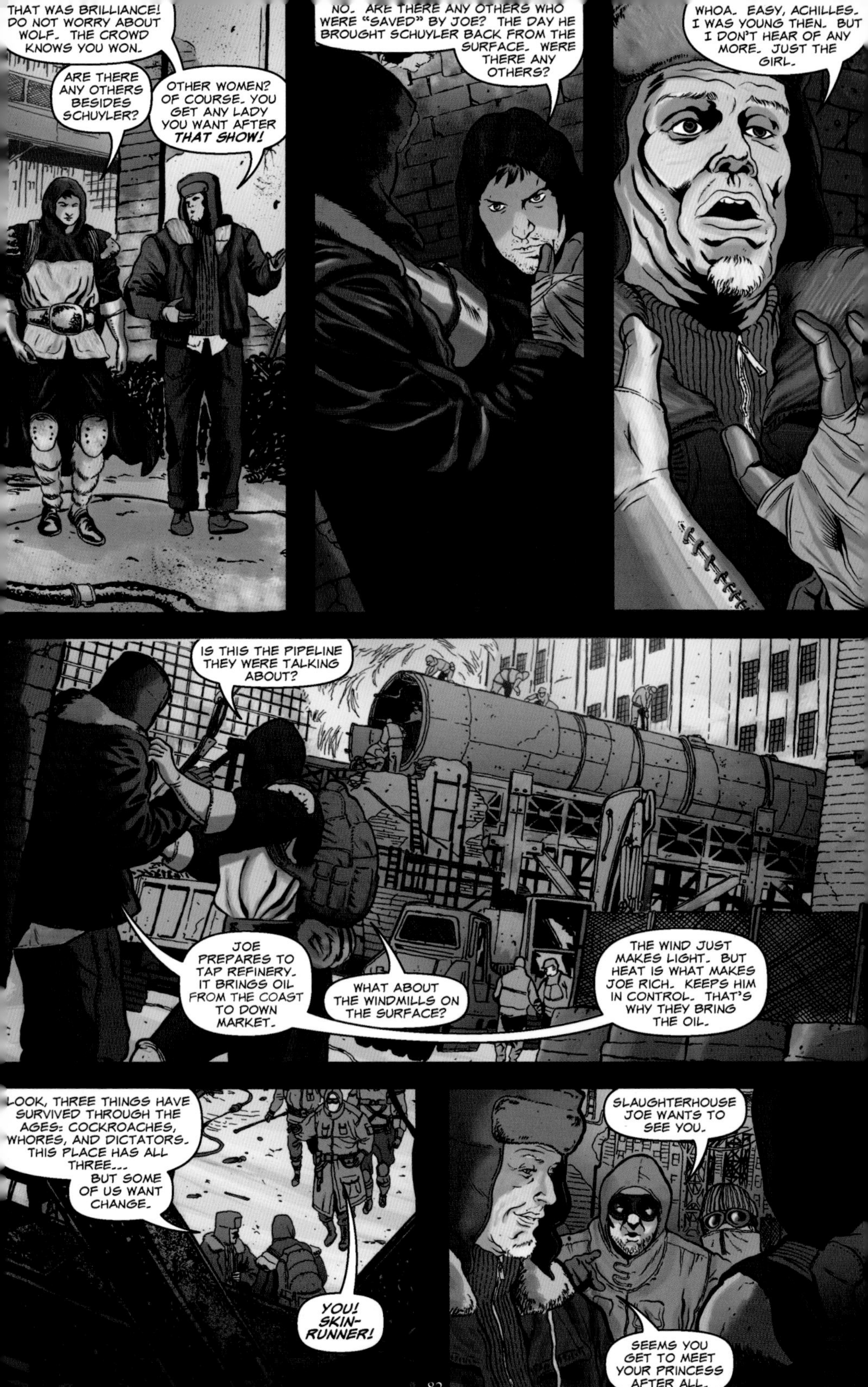
THAT WAS BRILLIANCE! DO NOT WORRY ABOUT WOLF. THE CROWD KNOWS YOU WON.
ARE THERE ANY OTHERS BESIDES SCHUYLER?
OTHER WOMEN? OF COURSE. YOU GET ANY LADY YOU WANT AFTER THAT SHOW!
NO. ARE THERE ANY OTHERS WHO WERE "SAVED" BY JOE? THE DAY HE BROUGHT SCHUYLER BACK FROM THE SURFACE. WERE THERE ANY OTHERS?
WHOA. EASY, ACHILLES. I WAS YOUNG THEN. BUT I DON'T HEAR OF ANY MORE. JUST THE GIRL.
IS THIS THE PIPELINE THEY WERE TALKING ABOUT?
JOE PREPARES TO TAP REFINERY. IT BRINGS OIL FROM THE COAST TO DOWN MARKET.
WHAT ABOUT THE WINDMILLS ON THE SURFACE?
THE WIND JUST MAKES LIGHT. BUT HEAT IS WHAT MAKES JOE RICH. KEEPS HIM IN CONTROL. THAT'S WHY THEY BRING THE OIL.
LOOK, THREE THINGS HAVE SURVIVED THROUGH THE AGES: COCKROACHES, WHORES, AND DICTATORS. THIS PLACE HAS ALL THREE...
BUT SOME OF US WANT CHANGE.
YOU! SKIN-RUNNER!
SLAUGHTERHOUSE JOE WANTS TO SEE YOU.
SEEMS YOU GET TO MEET YOUR PRINCESS AFTER ALL.

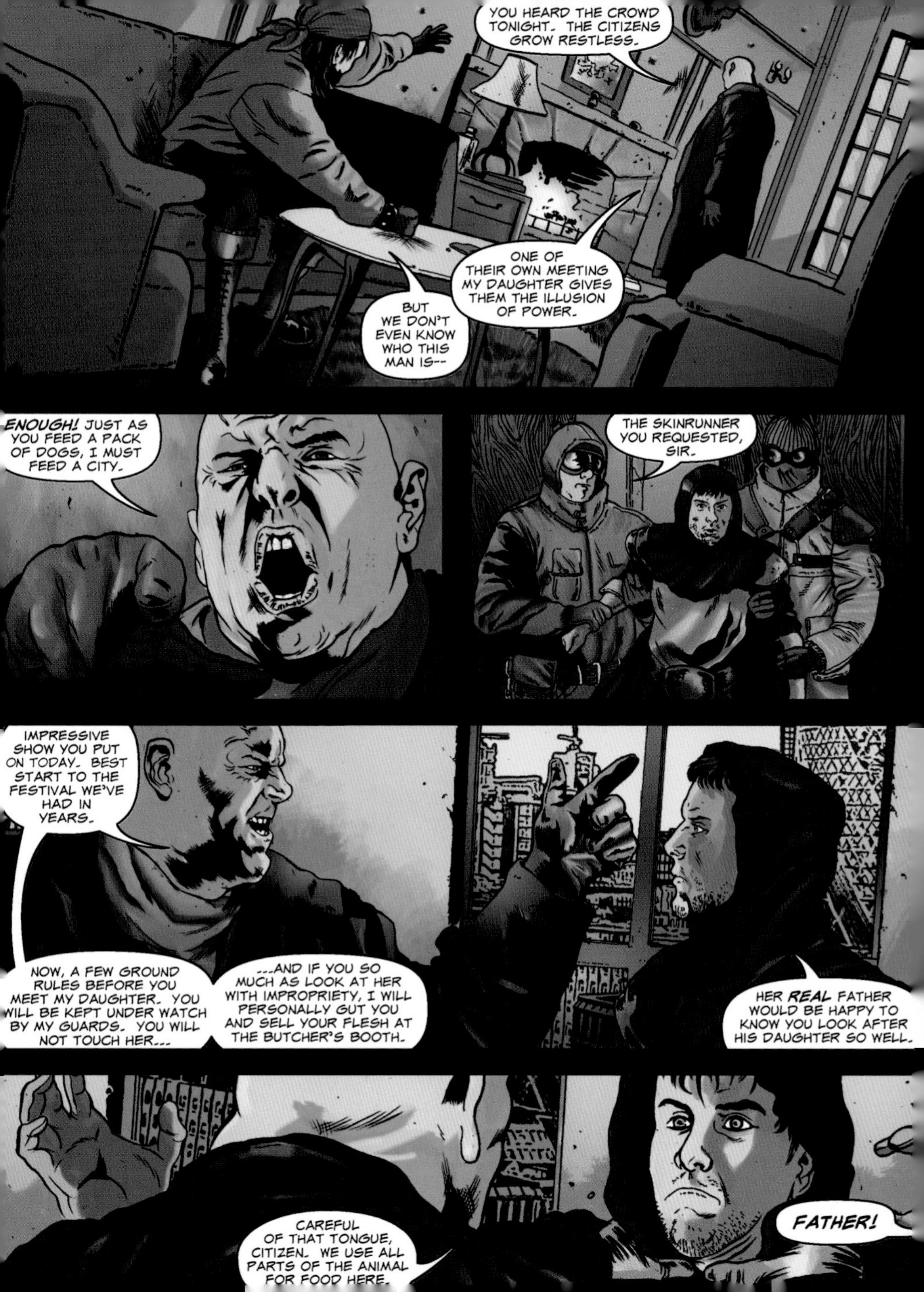
YOU HEARD THE CROWD TONIGHT. THE CITIZENS GROW RESTLESS.
ONE OF THEIR OWN MEETING MY DAUGHTER GIVES THEM THE ILLUSION OF POWER.
BUT WE DON'T EVEN KNOW WHO THIS MAN IS--
ENOUGH! JUST AS YOU FEED A PACK OF DOGS, I MUST FEED A CITY.
THE SKINRUNNER YOU REQUESTED, SIR.
IMPRESSIVE SHOW YOU PUT ON TODAY. BEST START TO THE FESTIVAL WE'VE HAD IN YEARS.
NOW, A FEW GROUND RULES BEFORE YOU MEET MY DAUGHTER. YOU WILL BE KEPT UNDER WATCH BY MY GUARDS. YOU WILL NOT TOUCH HER...
...AND IF YOU SO MUCH AS LOOK AT HER WITH IMPROPRIETY, I WILL PERSONALLY GUT YOU AND SELL YOUR FLESH AT THE BUTCHER'S BOOTH.
HER REAL FATHER WOULD BE HAPPY TO KNOW YOU LOOK AFTER HIS DAUGHTER SO WELL.
FATHER!
CAREFUL OF THAT TONGUE, CITIZEN. WE USE ALL PARTS OF THE ANIMAL FOR FOOD HERE.

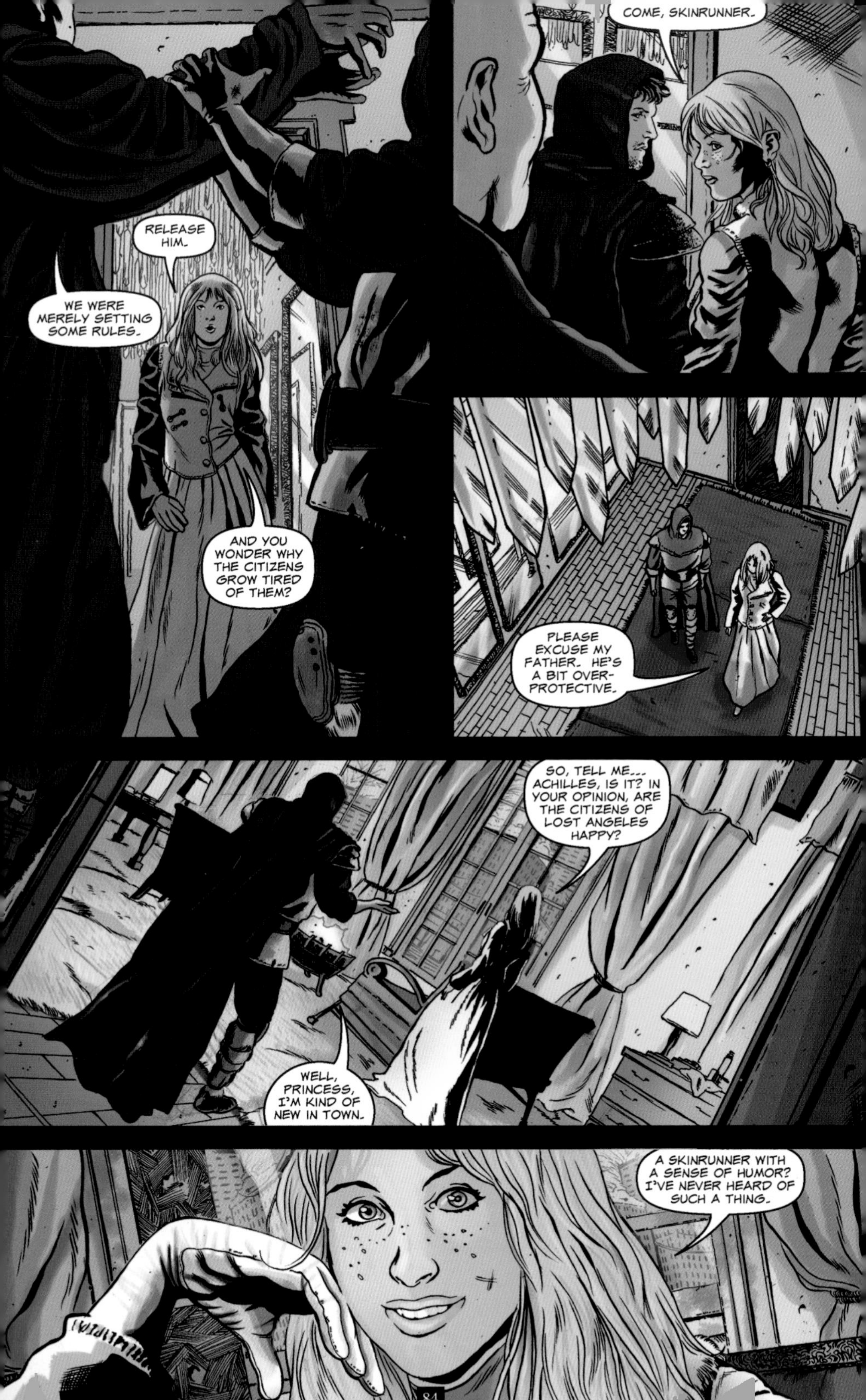

RELEASE HIM.
WE WERE MERELY SETTING SOME RULES.
AND YOU WONDER WHY THE CITIZENS GROW TIRED OF THEM?
COME, SKINRUNNER.
PLEASE EXCUSE MY FATHER. HE'S A BIT OVER-PROTECTIVE.
SO, TELL ME... ACHILLES, IS IT? IN YOUR OPINION, ARE THE CITIZENS OF LOST ANGELES HAPPY?
WELL, PRINCESS, I'M KIND OF NEW IN TOWN.
A SKINRUNNER WITH A SENSE OF HUMOR? I'VE NEVER HEARD OF SUCH A THING.

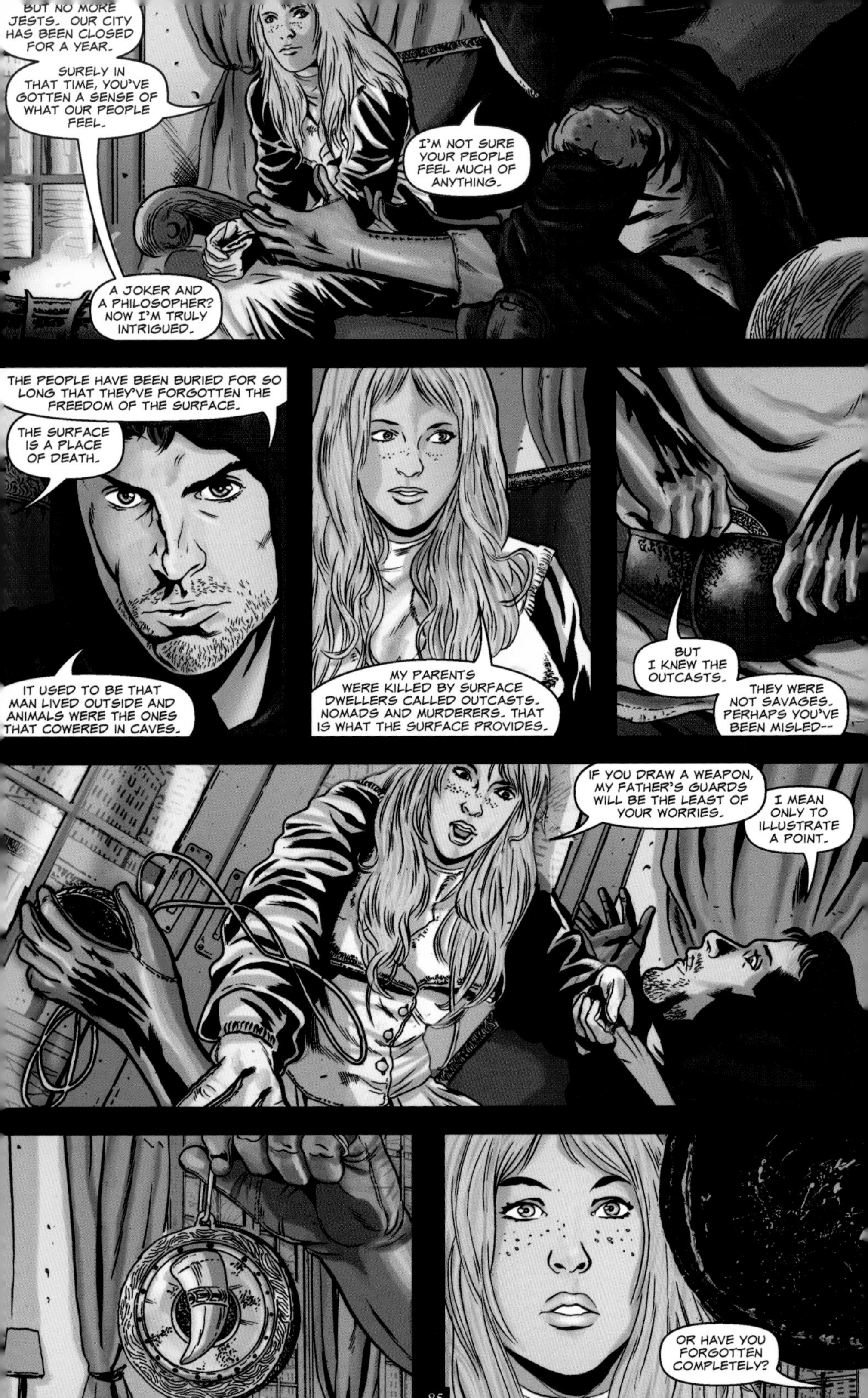
BUT NO MORE JESTS. OUR CITY HAS BEEN CLOSED FOR A YEAR.
SURELY IN THAT TIME, YOU'VE GOTTEN A SENSE OF WHAT OUR PEOPLE FEEL.
I'M NOT SURE YOUR PEOPLE FEEL MUCH OF ANYTHING.
A JOKER AND A PHILOSOPHER? NOW I'M TRULY INTRIGUED.
THE PEOPLE HAVE BEEN BURIED FOR SO LONG THAT THEY'VE FORGOTTEN THE FREEDOM OF THE SURFACE.
THE SURFACE IS A PLACE OF DEATH.
IT USED TO BE THAT MAN LIVED OUTSIDE AND ANIMALS WERE THE ONES THAT COWERED IN CAVES.
MY PARENTS WERE KILLED BY SURFACE DWELLERS CALLED OUTCASTS. NOMADS AND MURDERERS. THAT IS WHAT THE SURFACE PROVIDES.
BUT I KNEW THE OUTCASTS.
THEY WERE NOT SAVAGES. PERHAPS YOU'VE BEEN MISLED--
IF YOU DRAW A WEAPON, MY FATHER'S GUARDS WILL BE THE LEAST OF YOUR WORRIES.
I MEAN ONLY TO ILLUSTRATE A POINT.
OR HAVE YOU FORGOTTEN COMPLETELY?

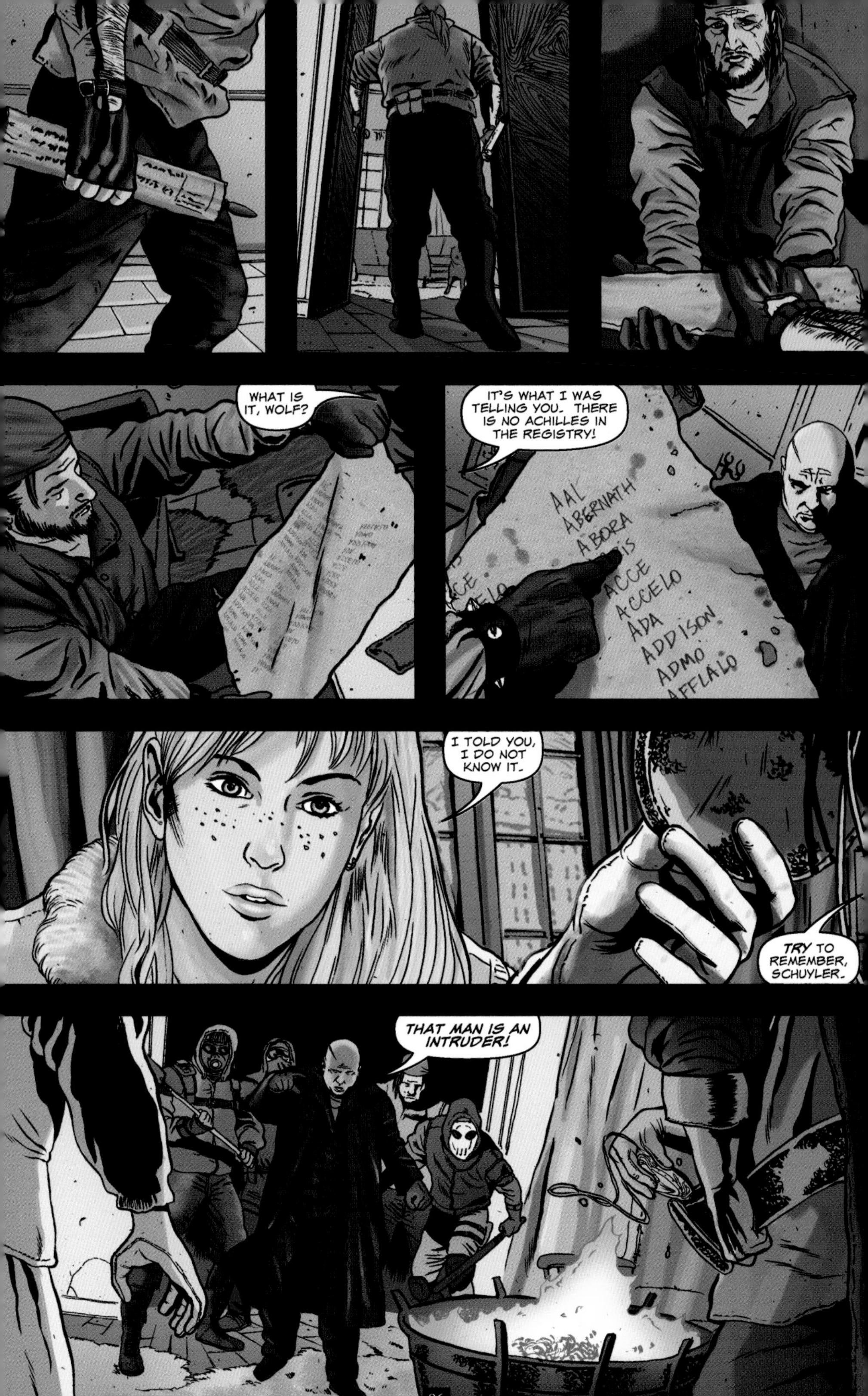
WHAT IS IT, WOLF?
IT'S WHAT I WAS TELLING YOU. THERE IS NO ACHILLES IN THE REGISTRY!
AAL
ABERNATH
ABORA
ACCE
ACCELO
ADA
ADDISON
ADMO
AFFLALO
I TOLD YOU, I DO NOT KNOW IT.
TRY TO REMEMBER, SCHUYLER.
THAT MAN IS AN INTRUDER!

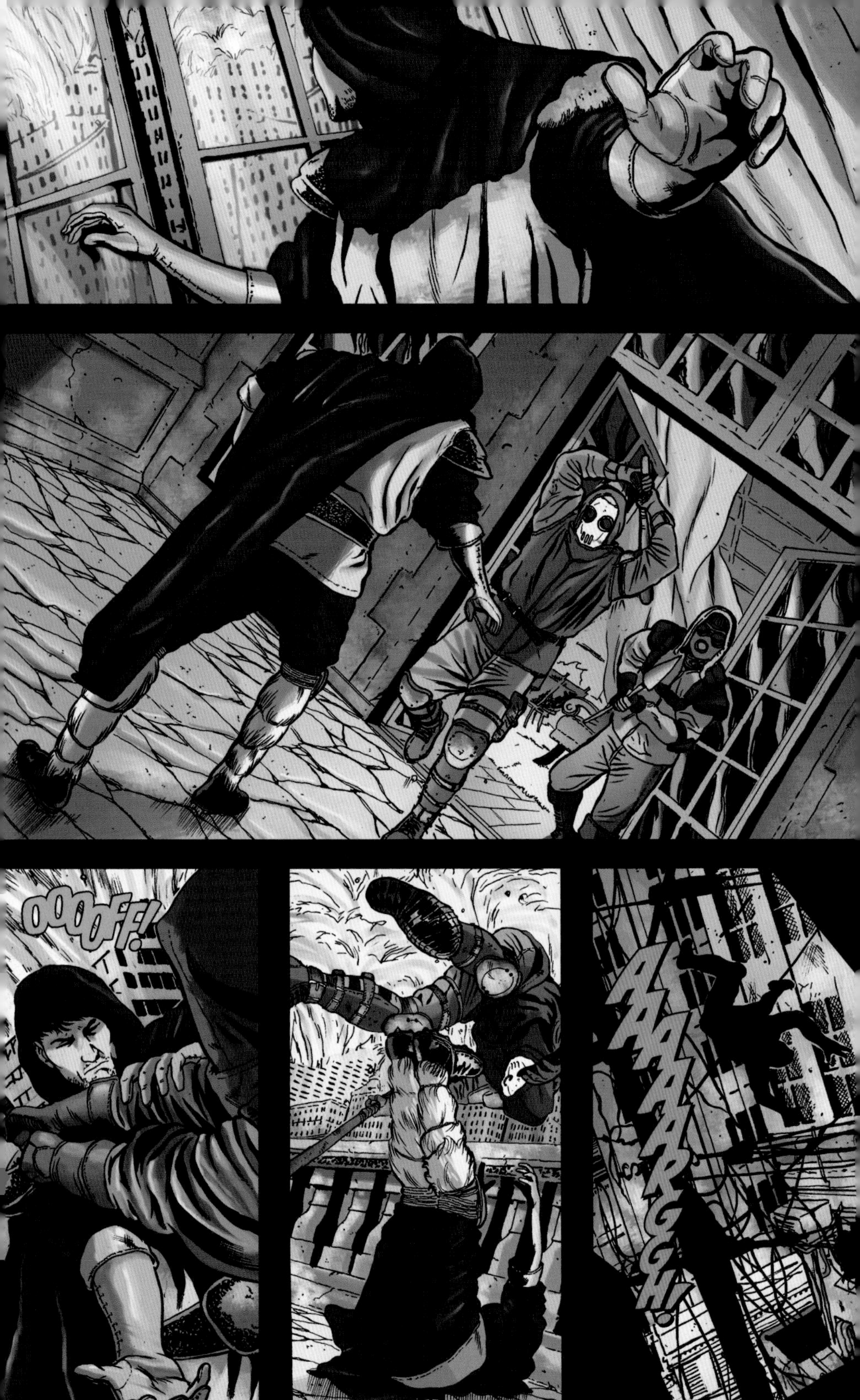
OOOOFF!
AAARRGGH!

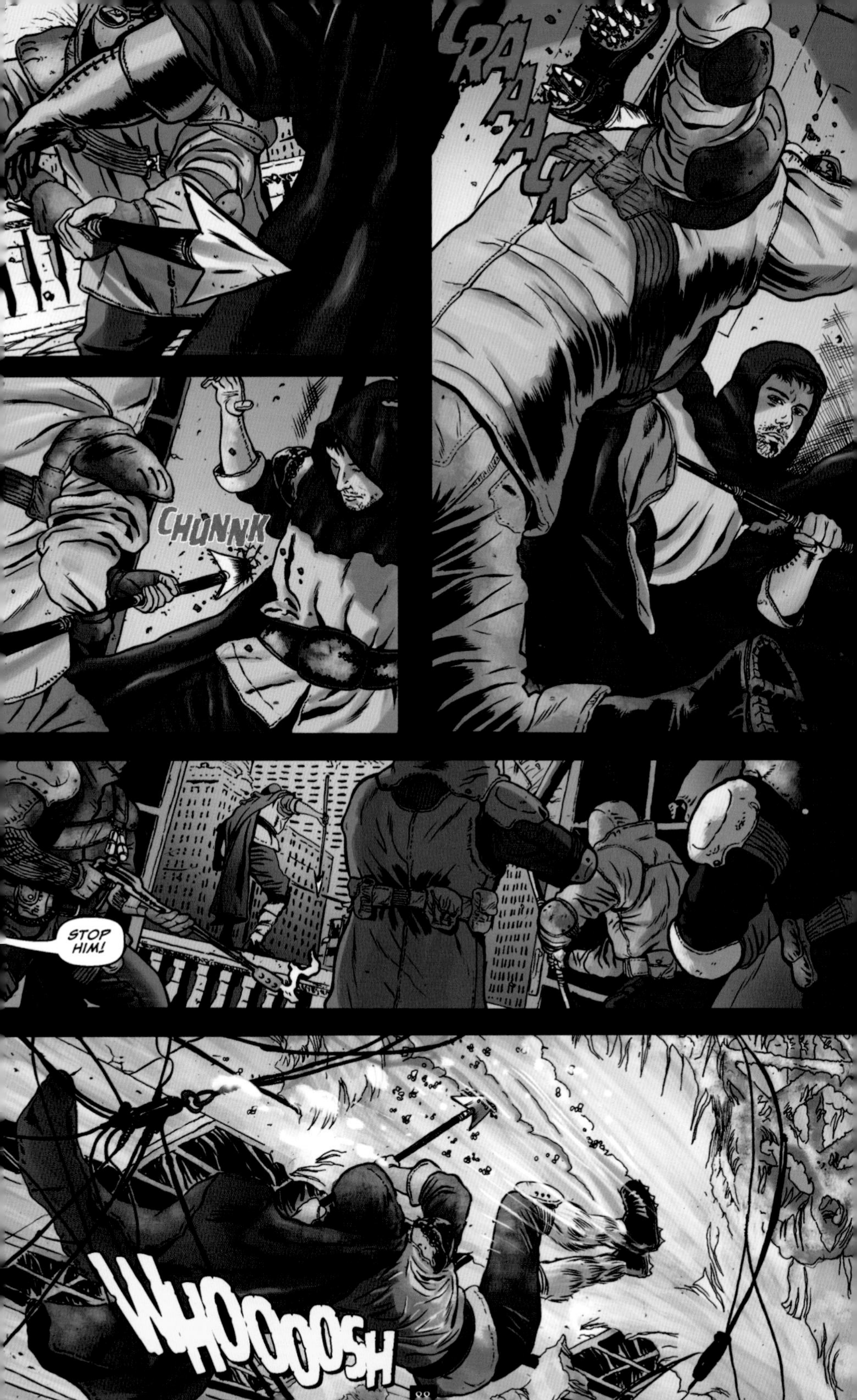
CRAAACK
CHUNNK
STOP HIM!
WHOOOOSH

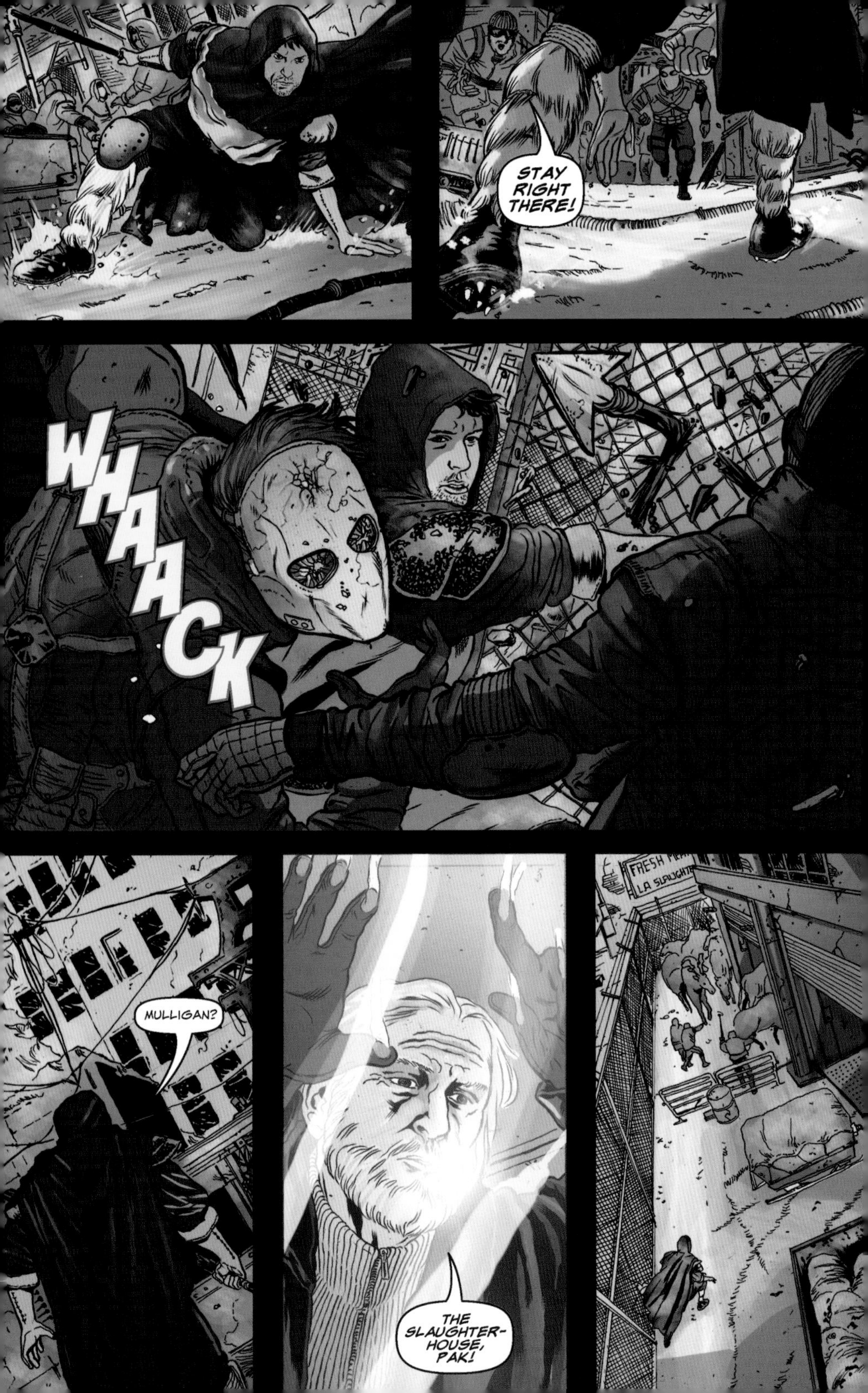
STAY RIGHT THERE!
WHAAACK
MULLIGAN?
THE SLAUGHTER-HOUSE, PAK!
FRESH MEA
LA SLAUGHT

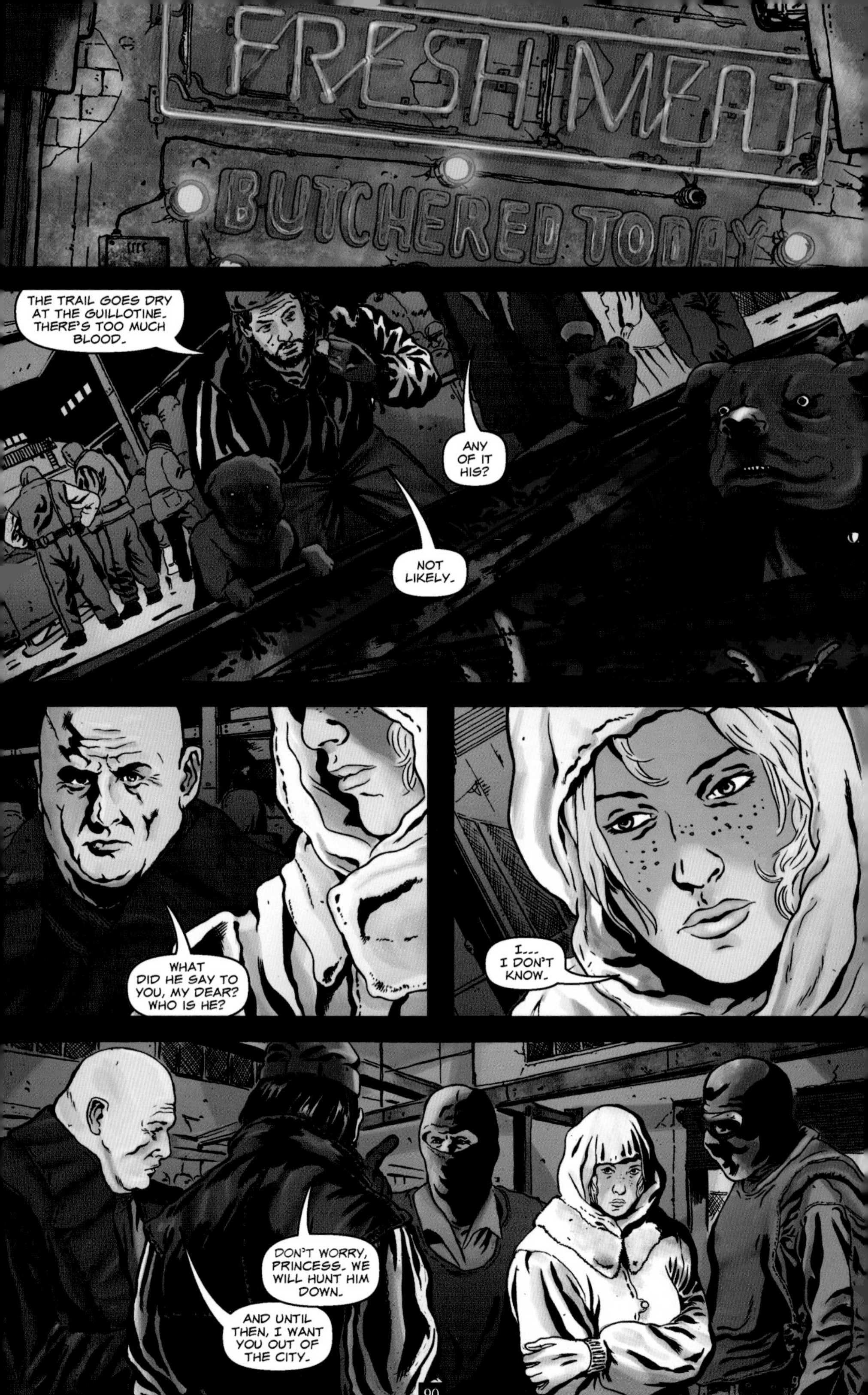
FRESH MEAT
BUTCHERED TODAY
THE TRAIL GOES DRY AT THE GUILLOTINE. THERE'S TOO MUCH BLOOD.
ANY OF IT HIS?
NOT LIKELY.
WHAT DID HE SAY TO YOU, MY DEAR? WHO IS HE?
I... I DON'T KNOW.
DON'T WORRY, PRINCESS. WE WILL HUNT HIM DOWN.
AND UNTIL THEN, I WANT YOU OUT OF THE CITY.

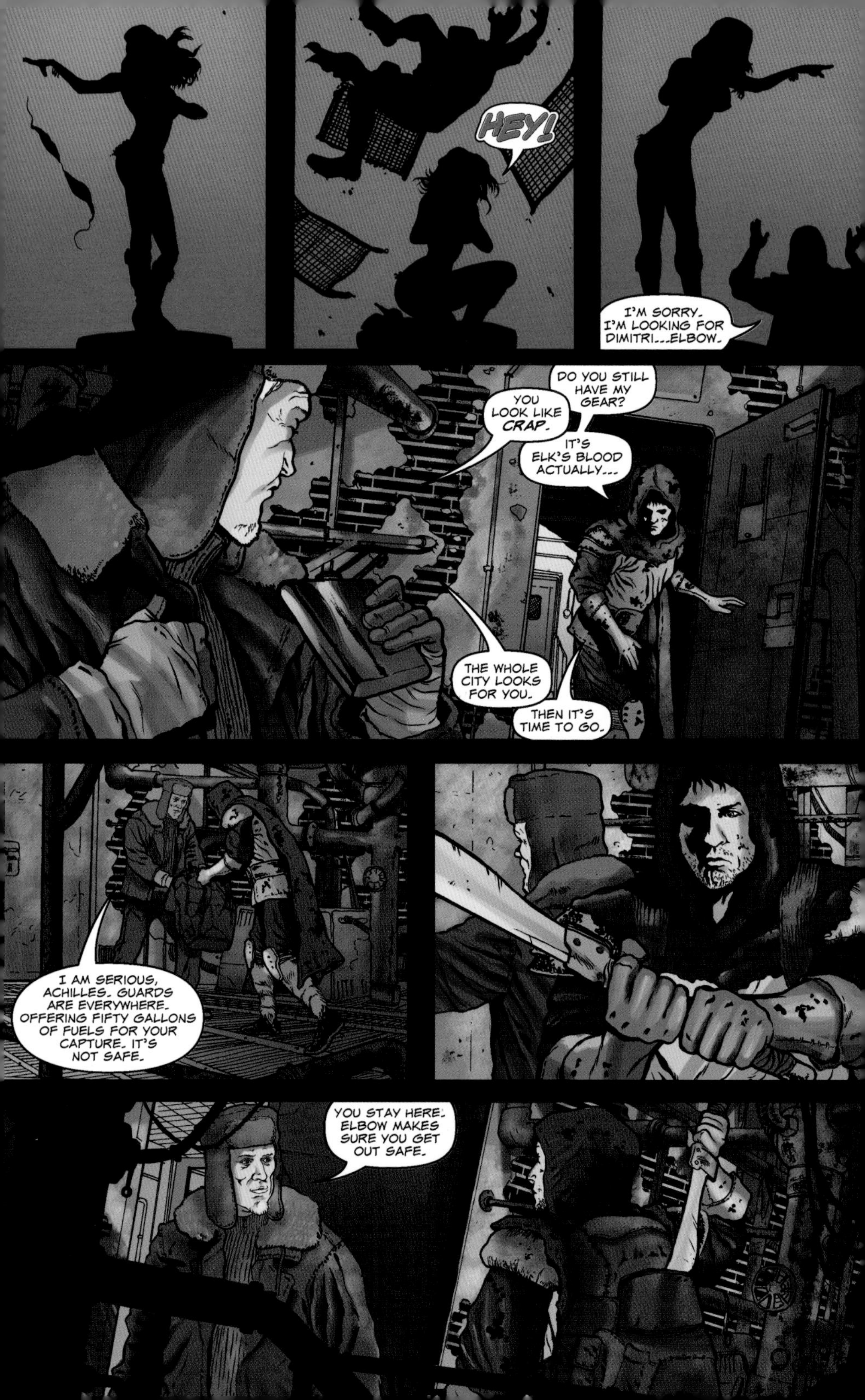
HEY!
I'M SORRY. I'M LOOKING FOR DIMITRI...ELBOW.
YOU LOOK LIKE CRAP.
DO YOU STILL HAVE MY GEAR?
IT'S ELK'S BLOOD ACTUALLY...
THE WHOLE CITY LOOKS FOR YOU.
THEN IT'S TIME TO GO.
I AM SERIOUS, ACHILLES. GUARDS ARE EVERYWHERE. OFFERING FIFTY GALLONS OF FUELS FOR YOUR CAPTURE. IT'S NOT SAFE.
YOU STAY HERE. ELBOW MAKES SURE YOU GET OUT SAFE.

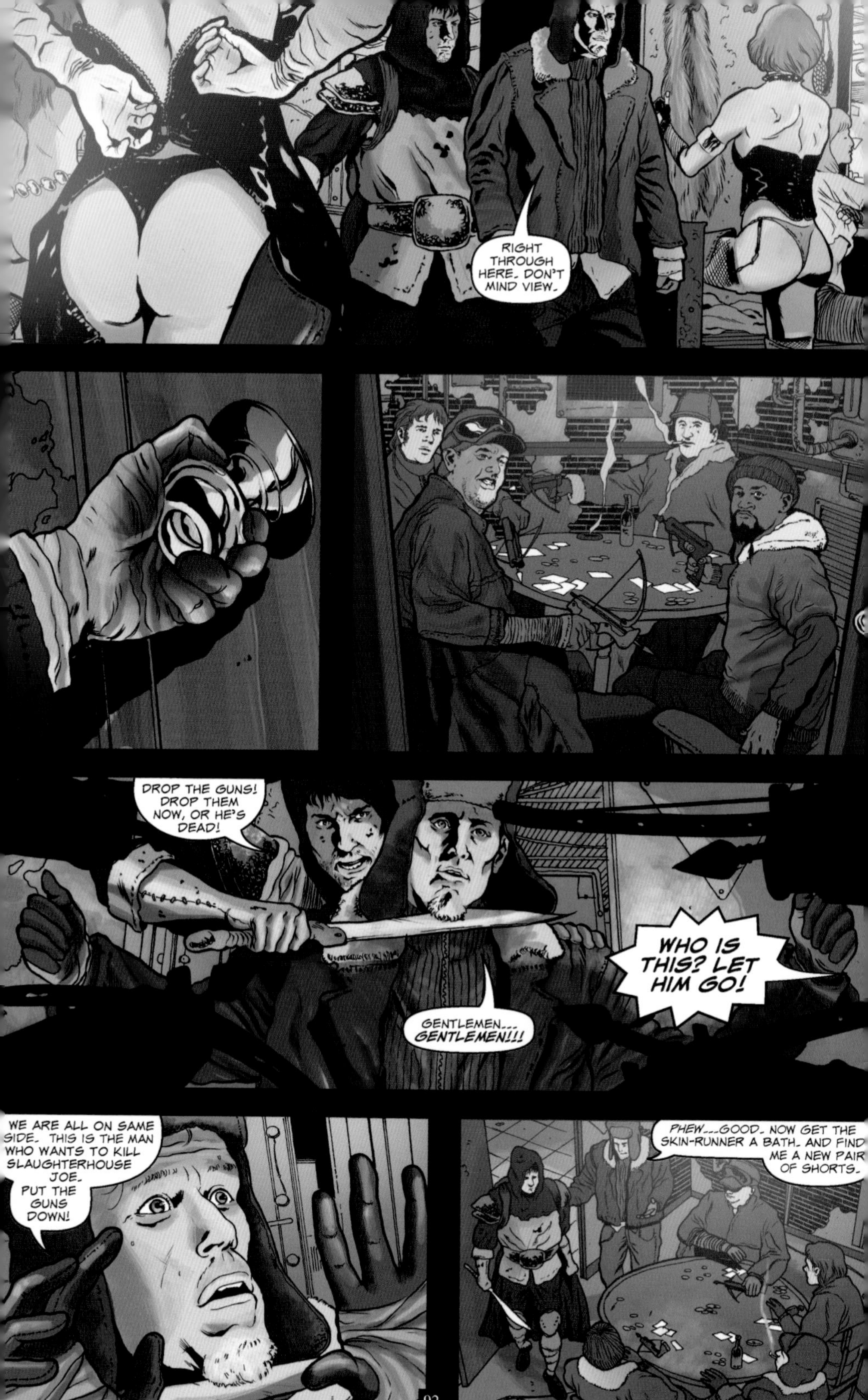
RIGHT THROUGH HERE. DON'T MIND VIEW.
DROP THE GUNS! DROP THEM NOW, OR HE'S DEAD!
WHO IS THIS? LET HIM GO!
GENTLEMEN... GENTLEMEN!!!
WE ARE ALL ON SAME SIDE. THIS IS THE MAN WHO WANTS TO KILL SLAUGHTERHOUSE JOE. PUT THE GUNS DOWN!
PHEW...GOOD. NOW GET THE SKIN-RUNNER A BATH. AND FIND ME A NEW PAIR OF SHORTS.

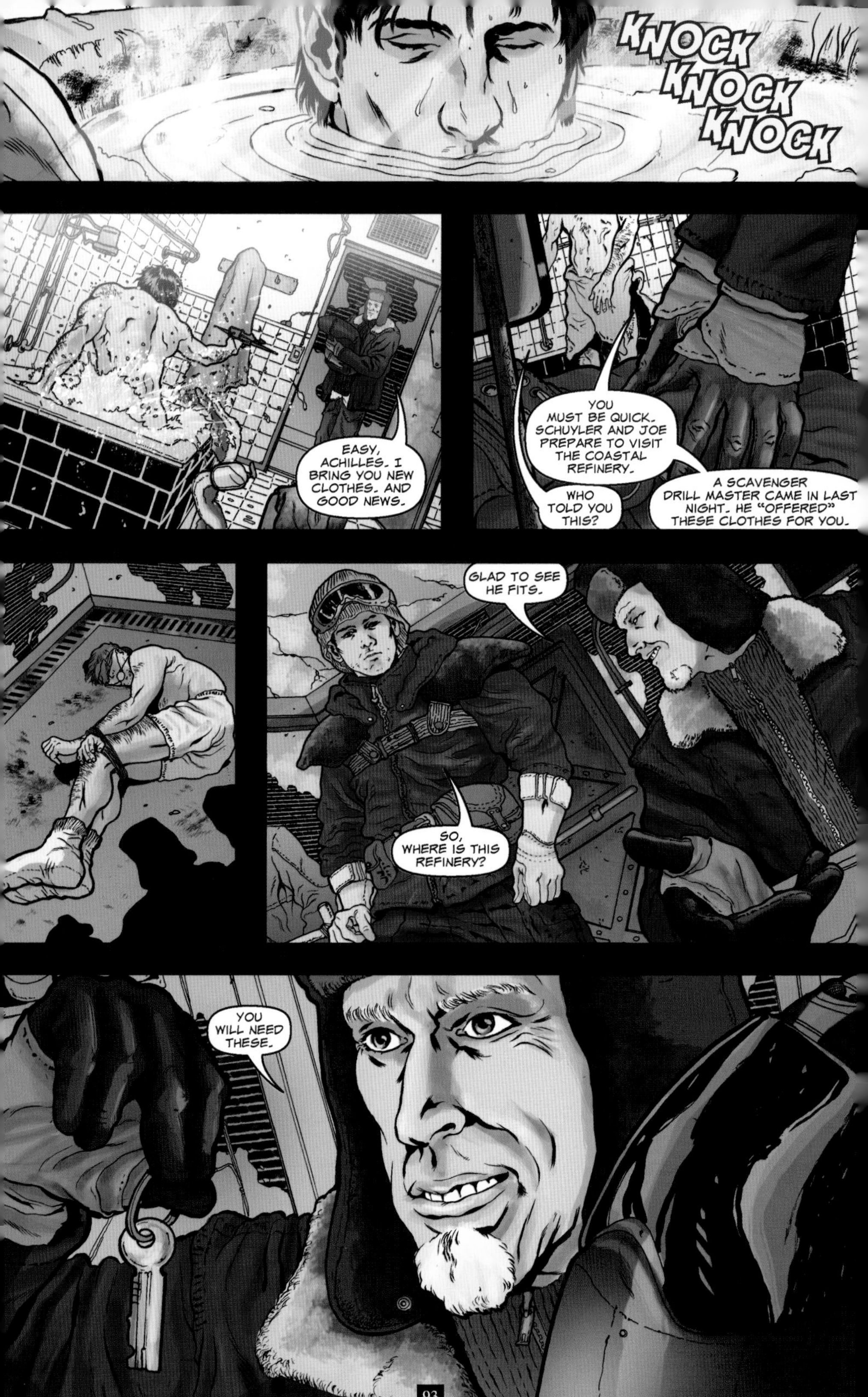
KNOCK KNOCK KNOCK
EASY, ACHILLES. I BRING YOU NEW CLOTHES. AND GOOD NEWS.
YOU MUST BE QUICK. SCHUYLER AND JOE PREPARE TO VISIT THE COASTAL REFINERY.
WHO TOLD YOU THIS?
A SCAVENGER DRILL MASTER CAME IN LAST NIGHT. HE "OFFERED" THESE CLOTHES FOR YOU.
GLAD TO SEE HE FITS.
SO, WHERE IS THIS REFINERY?
YOU WILL NEED THESE.

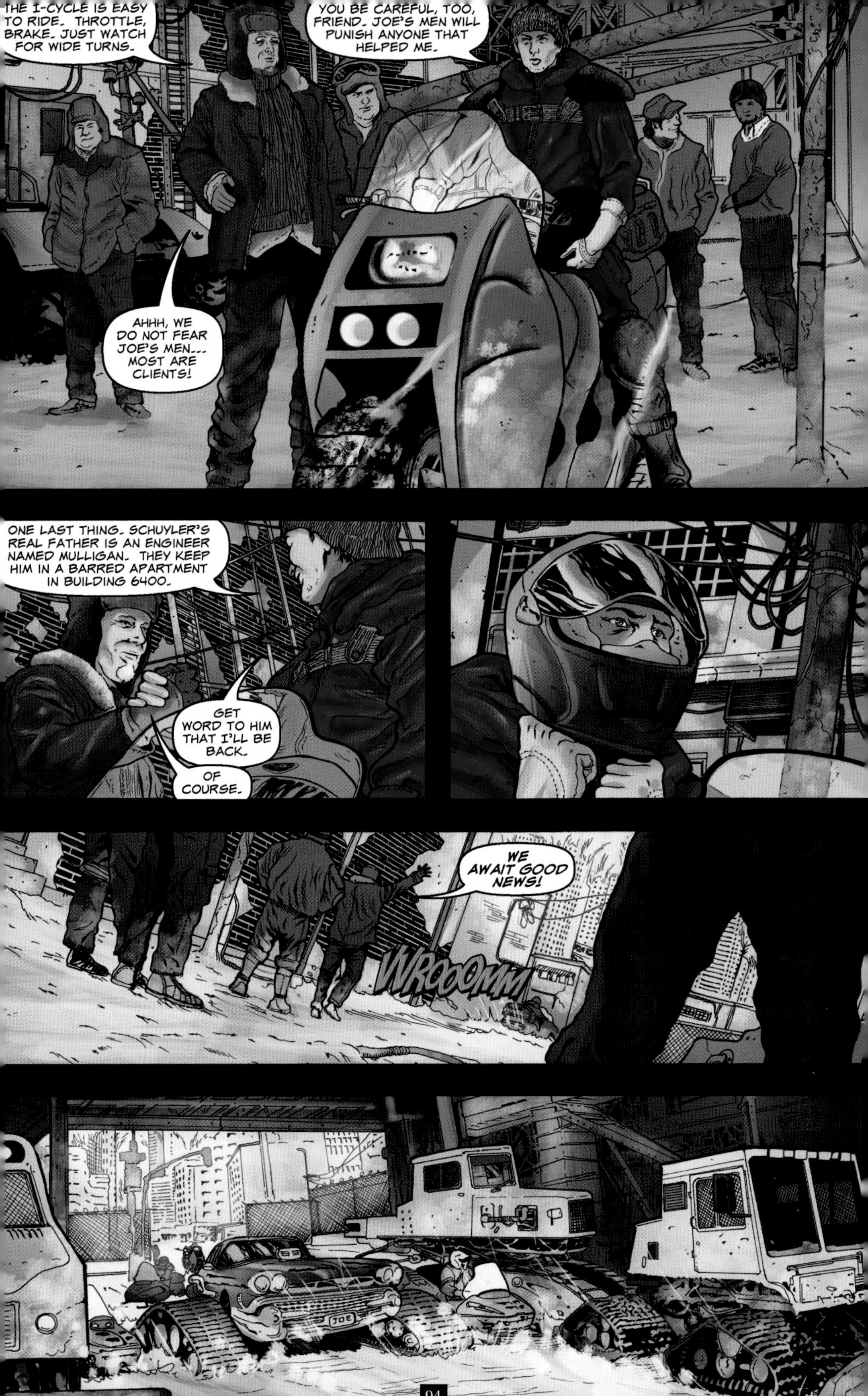
THE I-CYCLE IS EASY TO RIDE. THROTTLE, BRAKE. JUST WATCH FOR WIDE TURNS.
YOU BE CAREFUL, TOO, FRIEND. JOE'S MEN WILL PUNISH ANYONE THAT HELPED ME.
AHHH, WE DO NOT FEAR JOE'S MEN... MOST ARE CLIENTS!
ONE LAST THING. SCHUYLER'S REAL FATHER IS AN ENGINEER NAMED MULLIGAN. THEY KEEP HIM IN A BARRED APARTMENT IN BUILDING 6400.
GET WORD TO HIM THAT I'LL BE BACK.
OF COURSE.
WE AWAIT GOOD NEWS!
VVROOOMM
JOE

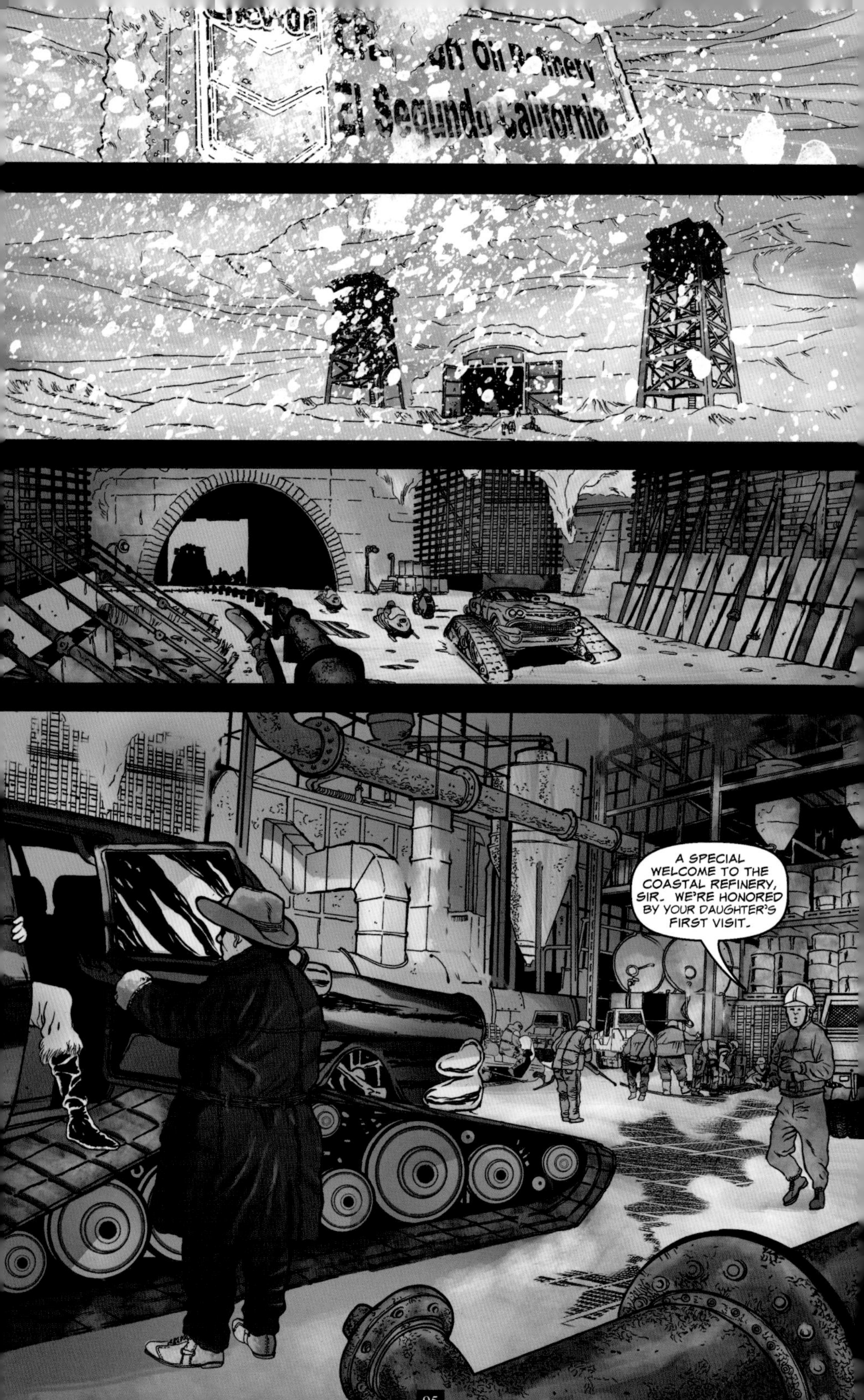
El Segundo California
A SPECIAL WELCOME TO THE COASTAL REFINERY, SIR. WE'RE HONORED BY YOUR DAUGHTER'S FIRST VISIT.

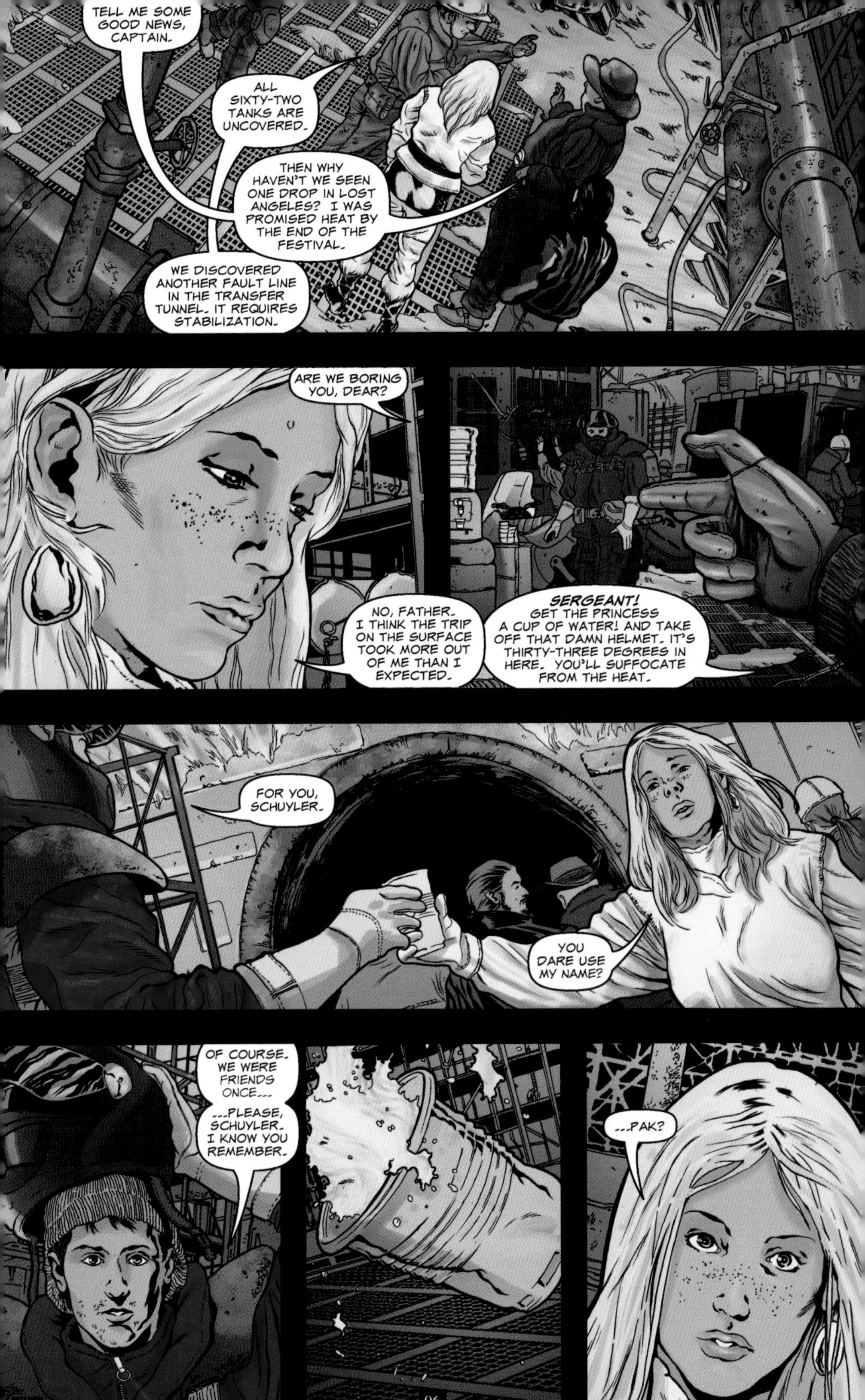
TELL ME SOME GOOD NEWS, CAPTAIN.
ALL SIXTY-TWO TANKS ARE UNCOVERED.
THEN WHY HAVEN'T WE SEEN ONE DROP IN LOST ANGELES? I WAS PROMISED HEAT BY THE END OF THE FESTIVAL.
WE DISCOVERED ANOTHER FAULT LINE IN THE TRANSFER TUNNEL. IT REQUIRES STABILIZATION.
ARE WE BORING YOU, DEAR?
NO, FATHER. I THINK THE TRIP ON THE SURFACE TOOK MORE OUT OF ME THAN I EXPECTED.
SERGEANT! GET THE PRINCESS A CUP OF WATER! AND TAKE OFF THAT DAMN HELMET. IT'S THIRTY-THREE DEGREES IN HERE. YOU'LL SUFFOCATE FROM THE HEAT.
FOR YOU, SCHUYLER.
YOU DARE USE MY NAME?
OF COURSE. WE WERE FRIENDS ONCE...
...PLEASE, SCHUYLER. I KNOW YOU REMEMBER.
...PAK?

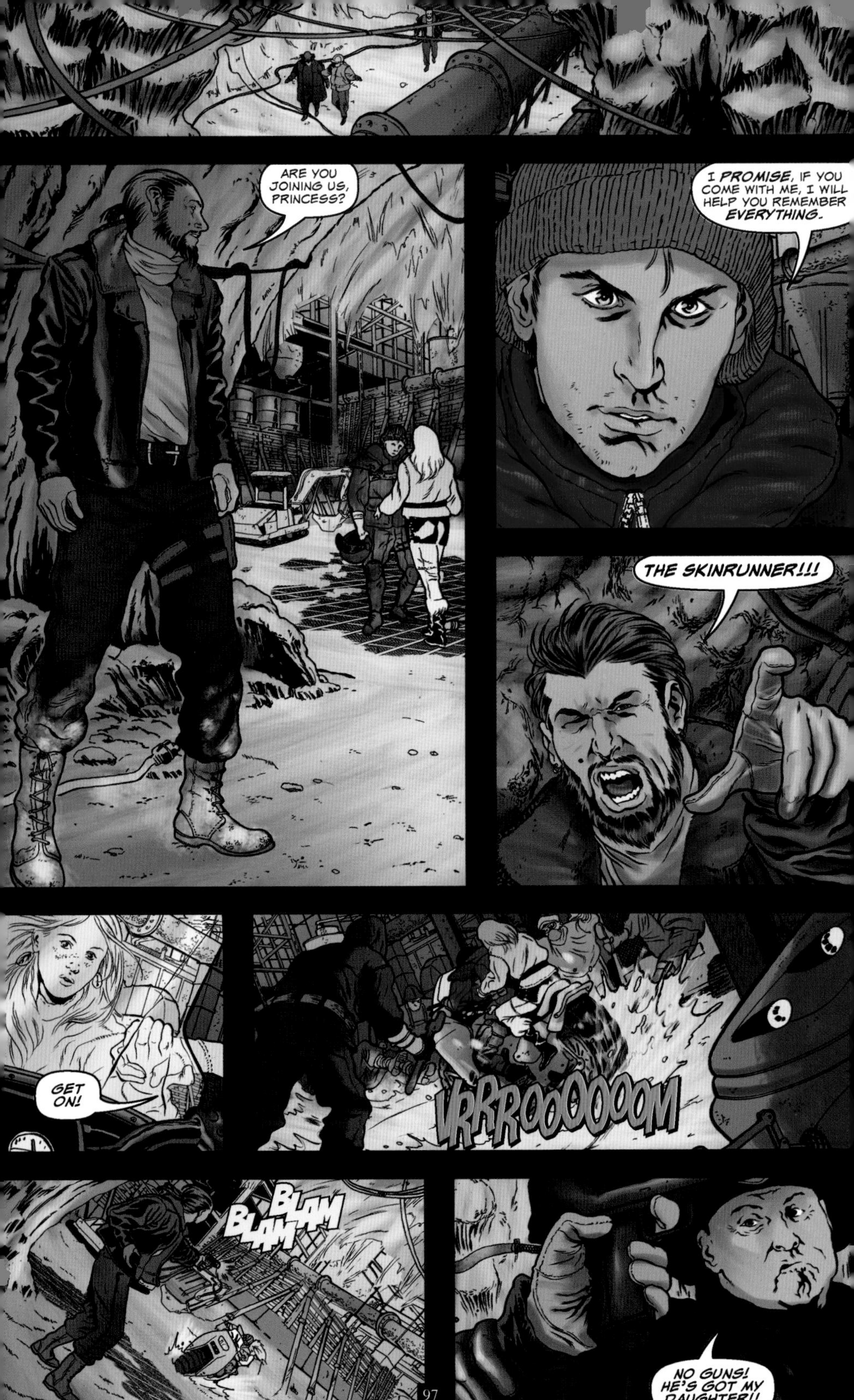
ARE YOU JOINING US, PRINCESS?
I PROMISE, IF YOU COME WITH ME, I WILL HELP YOU REMEMBER EVERYTHING.
THE SKINRUNNER!!!
GET ON!
VRRROOOOOOM
BLAM BLAM BLAM
NO GUNS! HE'S GOT MY DAUGHTER!!

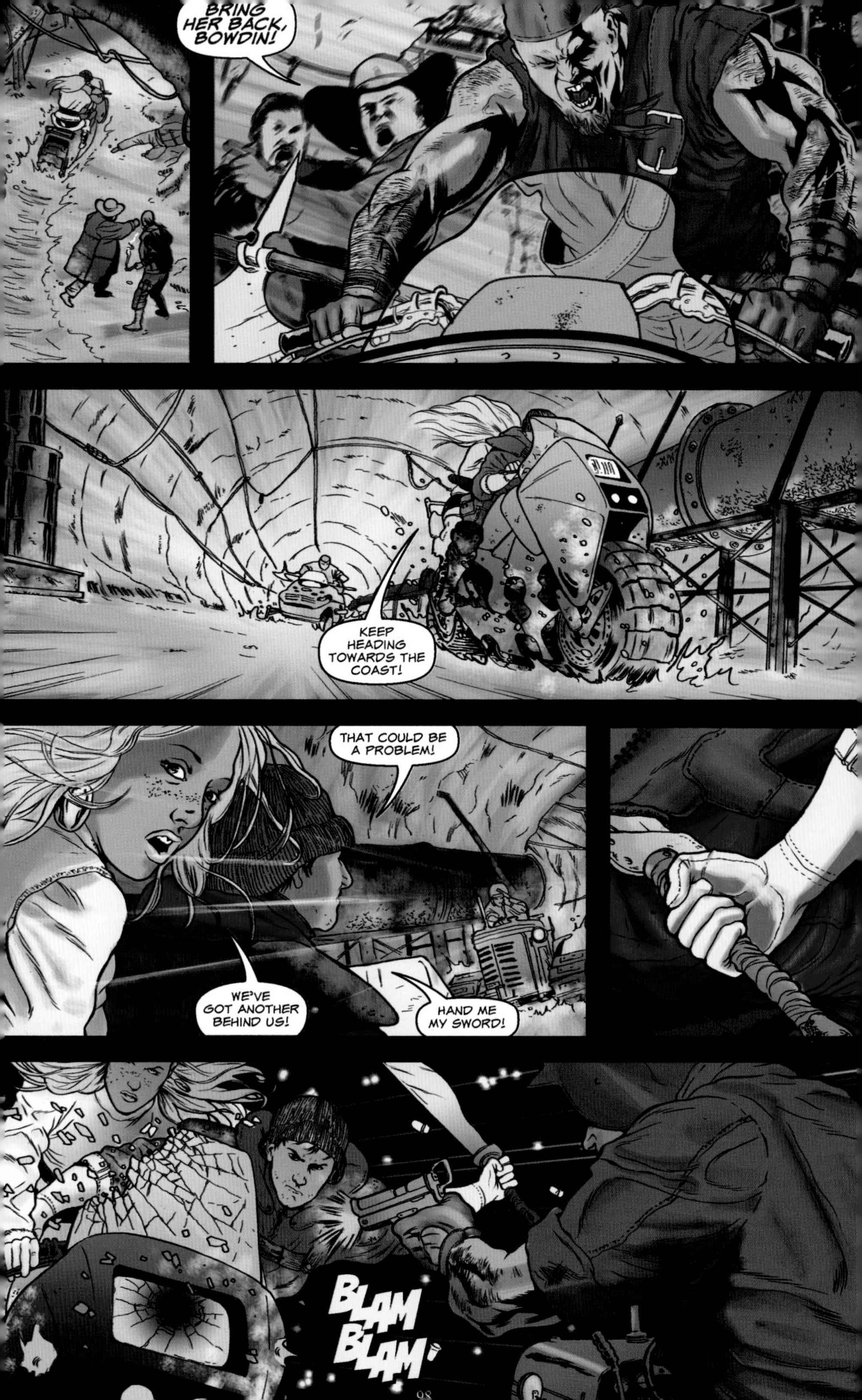
BRING HER BACK, BOWDIN!
KEEP HEADING TOWARDS THE COAST!
THAT COULD BE A PROBLEM!
WE'VE GOT ANOTHER BEHIND US!
HAND ME MY SWORD!
BLAM BLAM

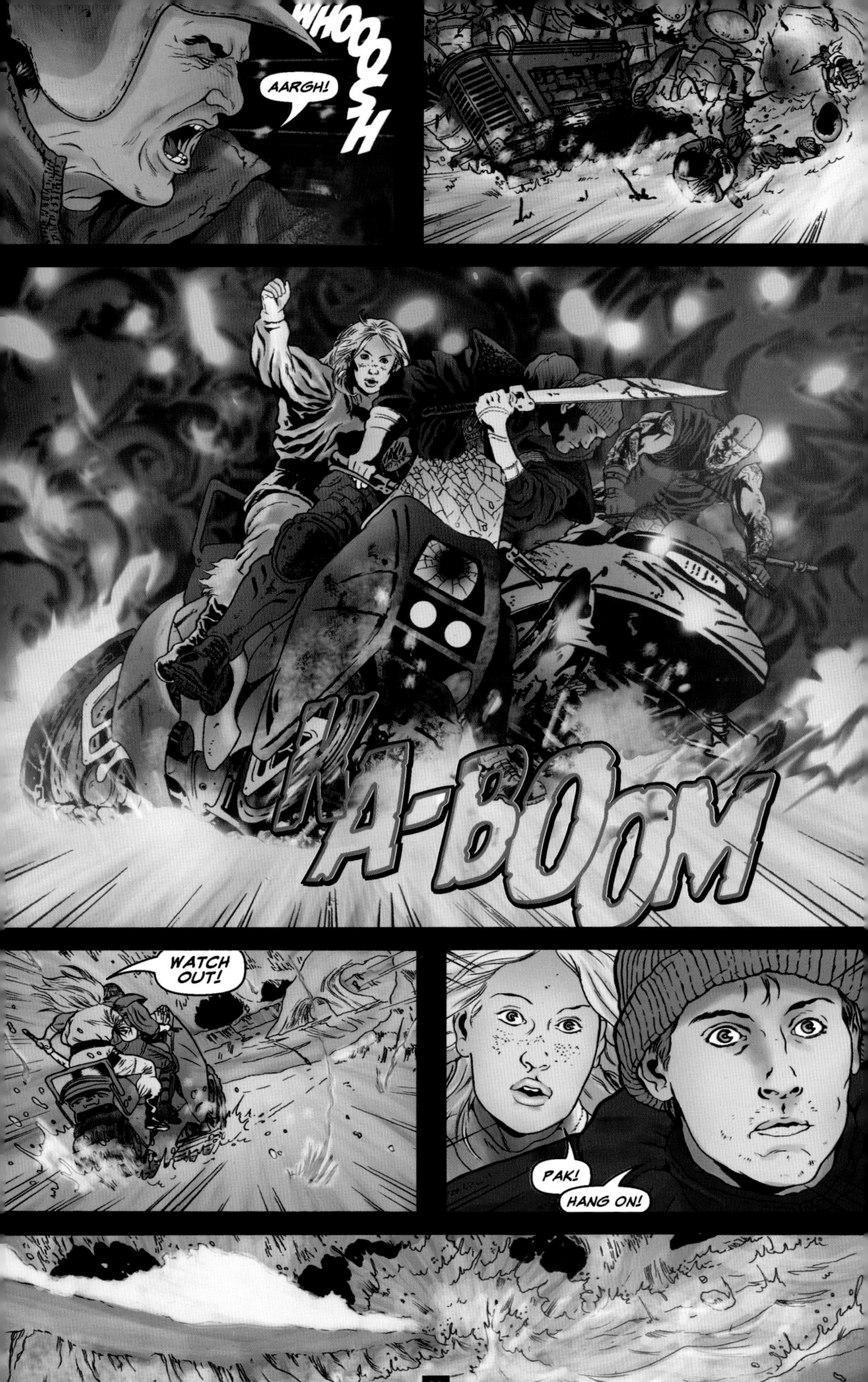
WHOOOSH
AARGH!
KA-BOOM
WATCH OUT!
PAK!
HANG ON!

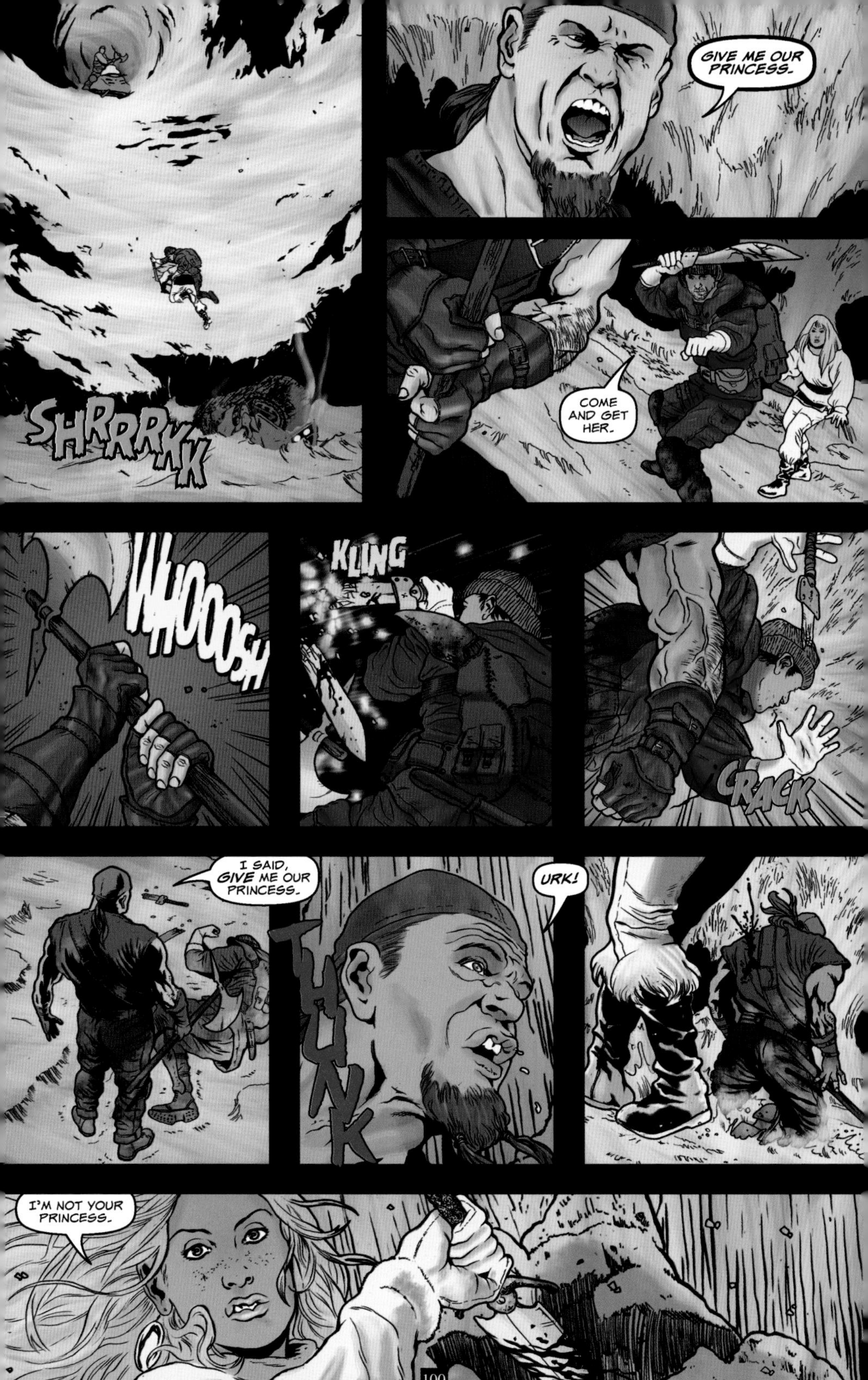
SHRRRKK
GIVE ME OUR PRINCESS.
COME AND GET HER.
WHOOOSH
KLING
CRACK
I SAID, GIVE ME OUR PRINCESS.
THUNK
URK!
I'M NOT YOUR PRINCESS.

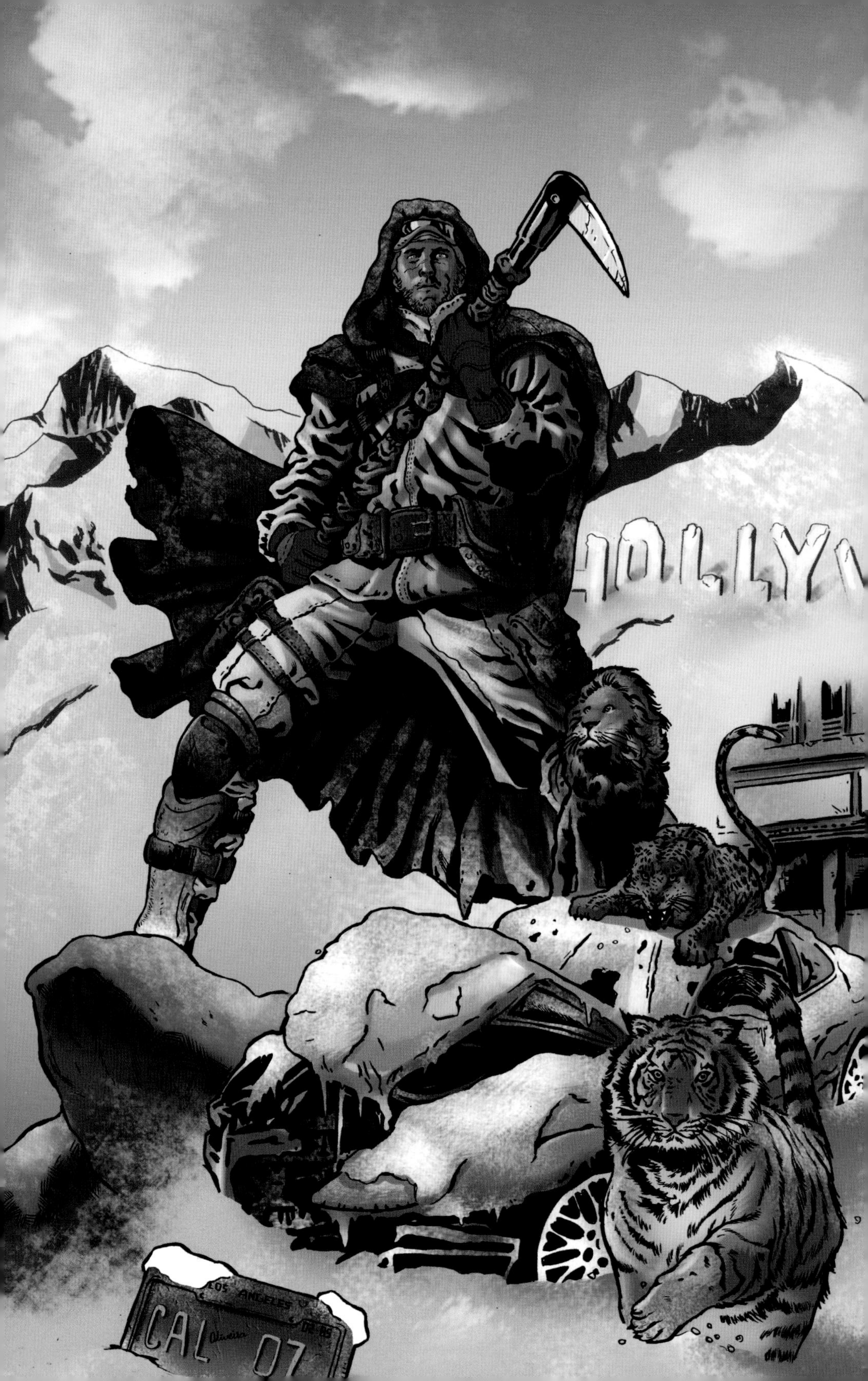
LOS ANGELES
CAL 07

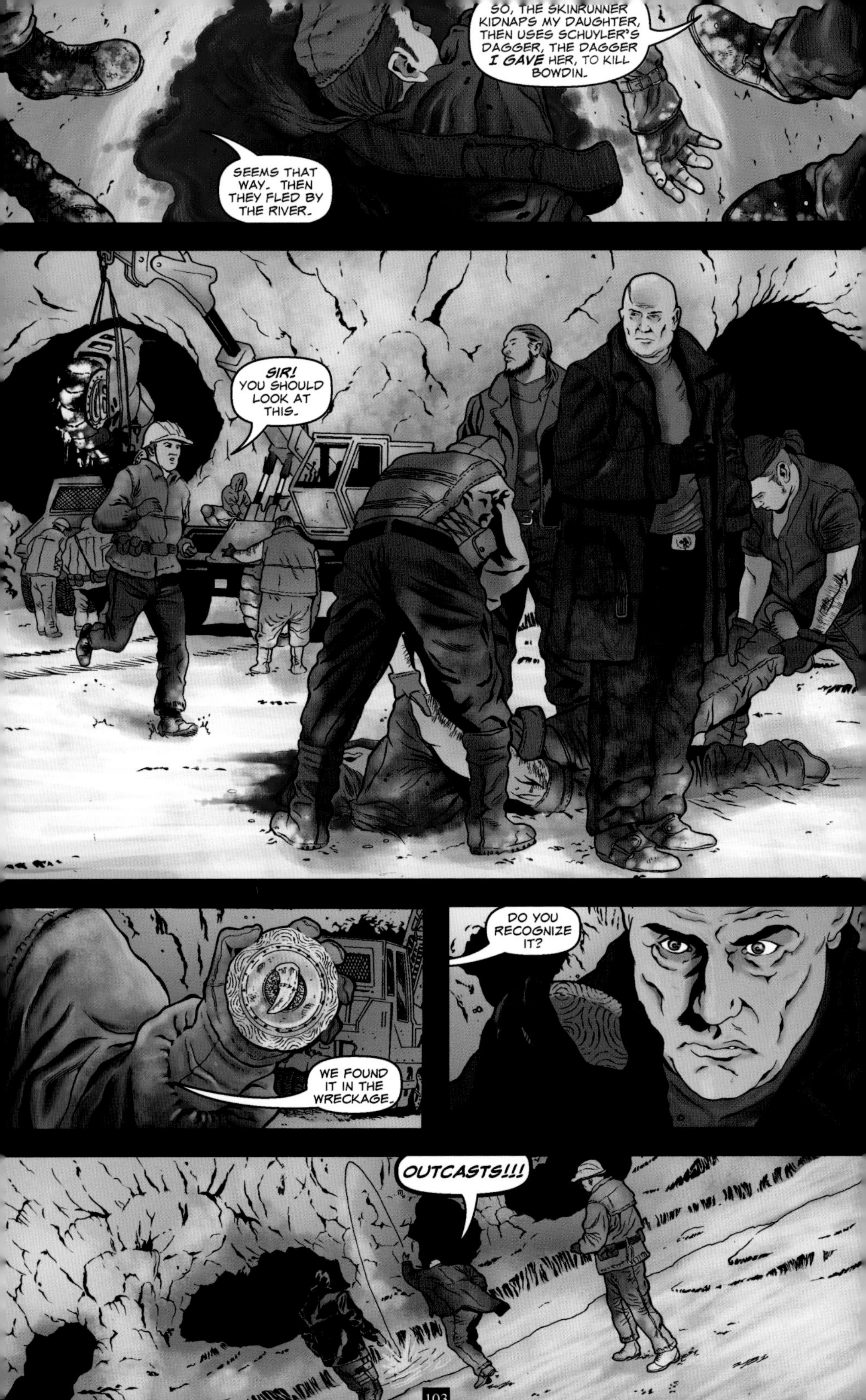
SO, THE SKINRUNNER KIDNAPS MY DAUGHTER, THEN USES SCHUYLER'S DAGGER, THE DAGGER **I GAVE** HER, TO KILL BOWDIN.
SEEMS THAT WAY. THEN THEY FLED BY THE RIVER.
SIR! YOU SHOULD LOOK AT THIS.
WE FOUND IT IN THE WRECKAGE.
DO YOU RECOGNIZE IT?
OUTCASTS!!!

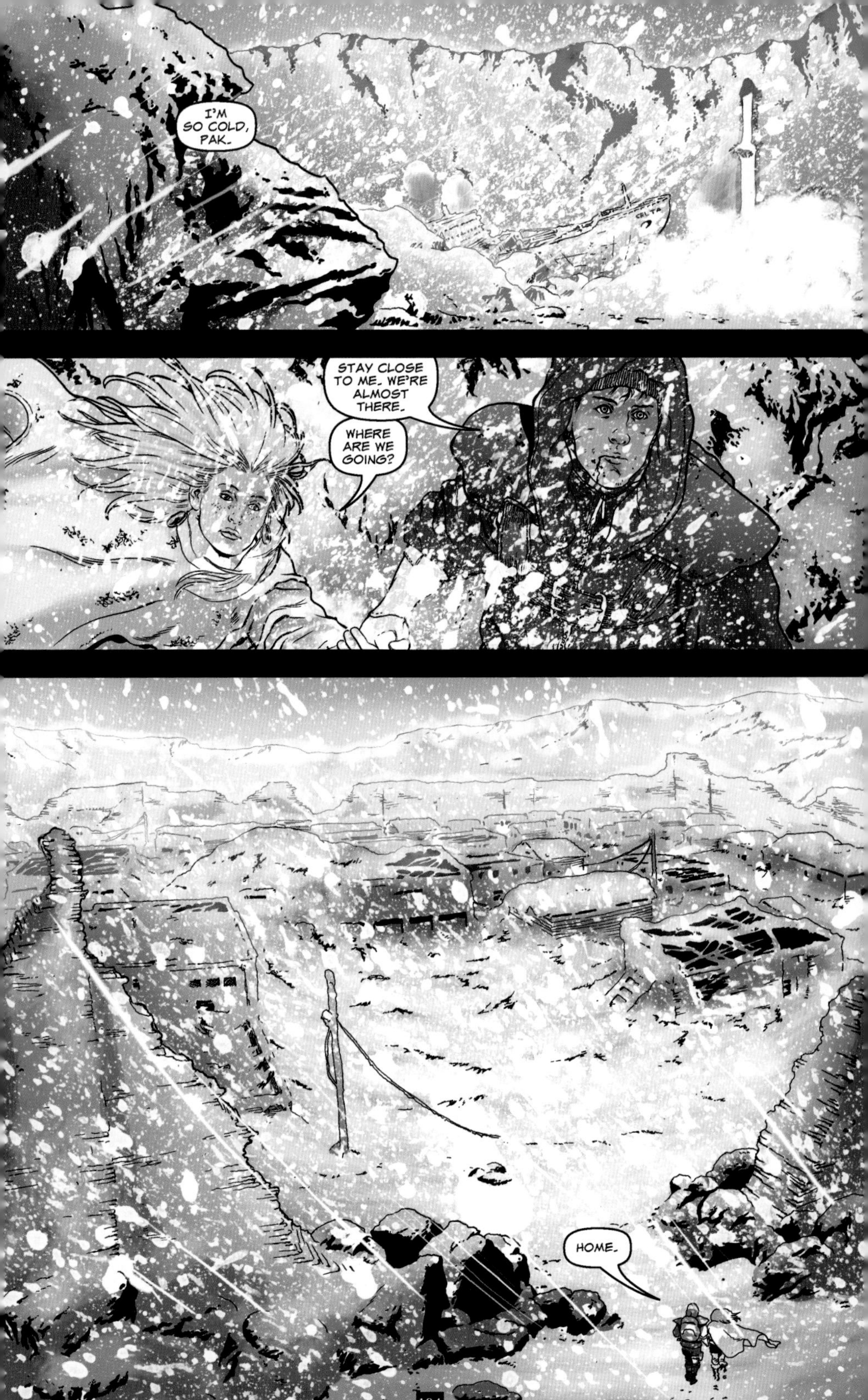
I'M SO COLD, PAK.
CELTA
STAY CLOSE TO ME. WE'RE ALMOST THERE.
WHERE ARE WE GOING?
HOME.

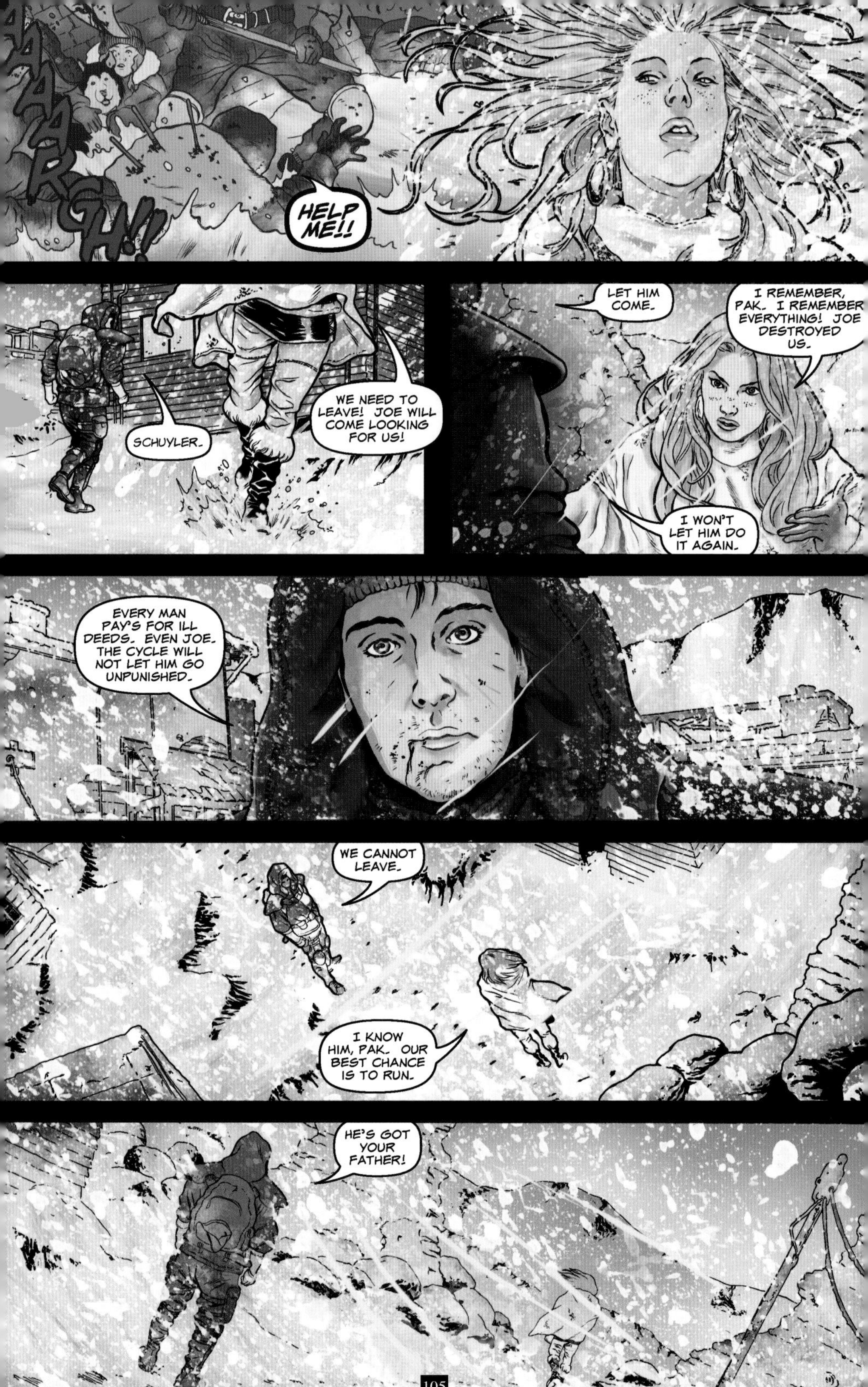
AAAARGH!!
HELP ME!!
SCHUYLER.
WE NEED TO LEAVE! JOE WILL COME LOOKING FOR US!
LET HIM COME.
I REMEMBER, PAK. I REMEMBER EVERYTHING! JOE DESTROYED US.
I WON'T LET HIM DO IT AGAIN.
EVERY MAN PAY'S FOR ILL DEEDS. EVEN JOE. THE CYCLE WILL NOT LET HIM GO UNPUNISHED.
WE CANNOT LEAVE.
I KNOW HIM, PAK. OUR BEST CHANCE IS TO RUN.
HE'S GOT YOUR FATHER!

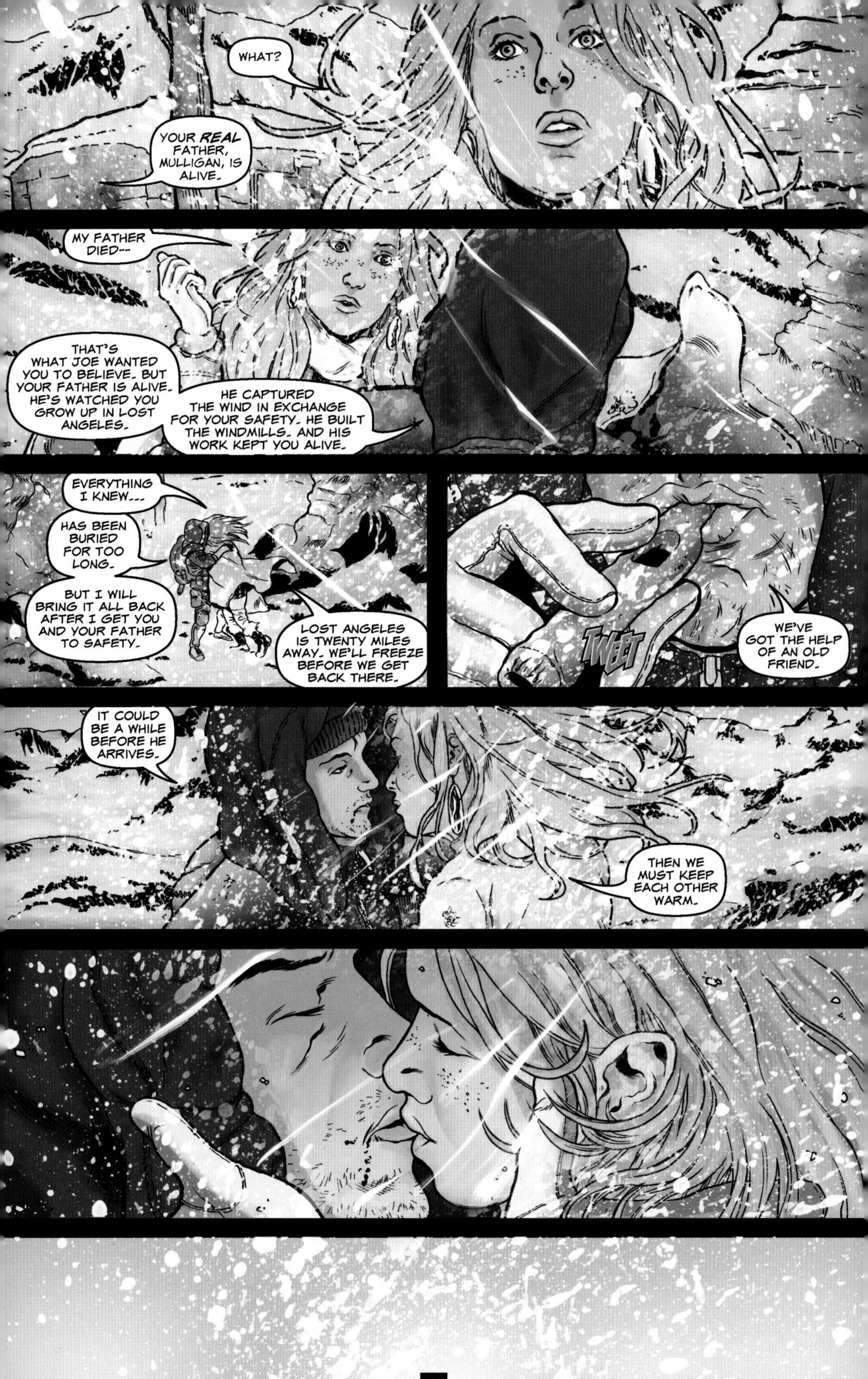
WHAT?
YOUR REAL FATHER, MULLIGAN, IS ALIVE.
MY FATHER DIED--
THAT'S WHAT JOE WANTED YOU TO BELIEVE. BUT YOUR FATHER IS ALIVE. HE'S WATCHED YOU GROW UP IN LOST ANGELES.
HE CAPTURED THE WIND IN EXCHANGE FOR YOUR SAFETY. HE BUILT THE WINDMILLS. AND HIS WORK KEPT YOU ALIVE.
EVERYTHING I KNEW...
HAS BEEN BURIED FOR TOO LONG.
BUT I WILL BRING IT ALL BACK AFTER I GET YOU AND YOUR FATHER TO SAFETY.
LOST ANGELES IS TWENTY MILES AWAY. WE'LL FREEZE BEFORE WE GET BACK THERE.
TWEET
WE'VE GOT THE HELP OF AN OLD FRIEND.
IT COULD BE A WHILE BEFORE HE ARRIVES.
THEN WE MUST KEEP EACH OTHER WARM.

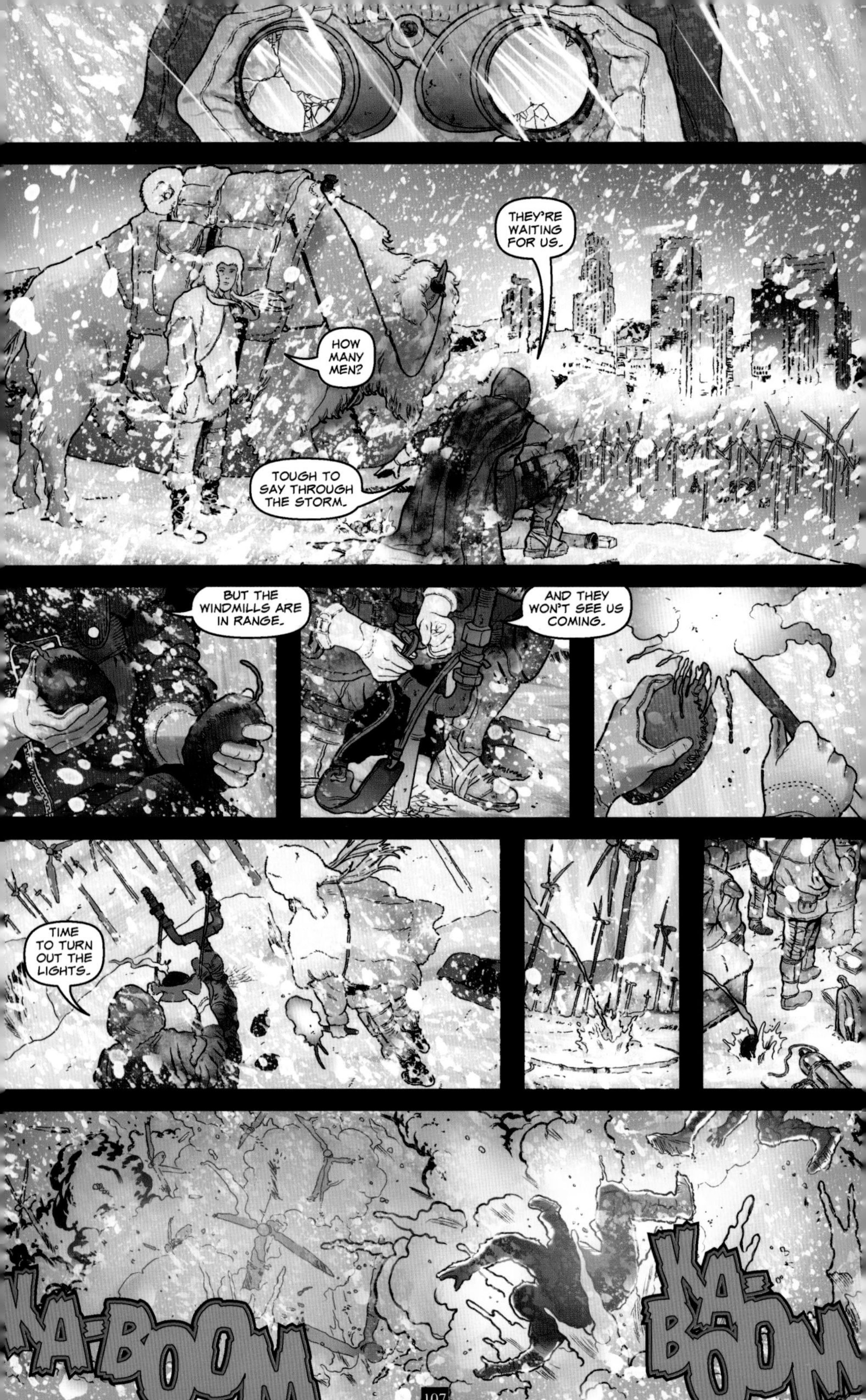
HOW MANY MEN?
THEY'RE WAITING FOR US.
TOUGH TO SAY THROUGH THE STORM.
BUT THE WINDMILLS ARE IN RANGE.
AND THEY WON'T SEE US COMING.
TIME TO TURN OUT THE LIGHTS.
KA-BOOM
KA-BOOM

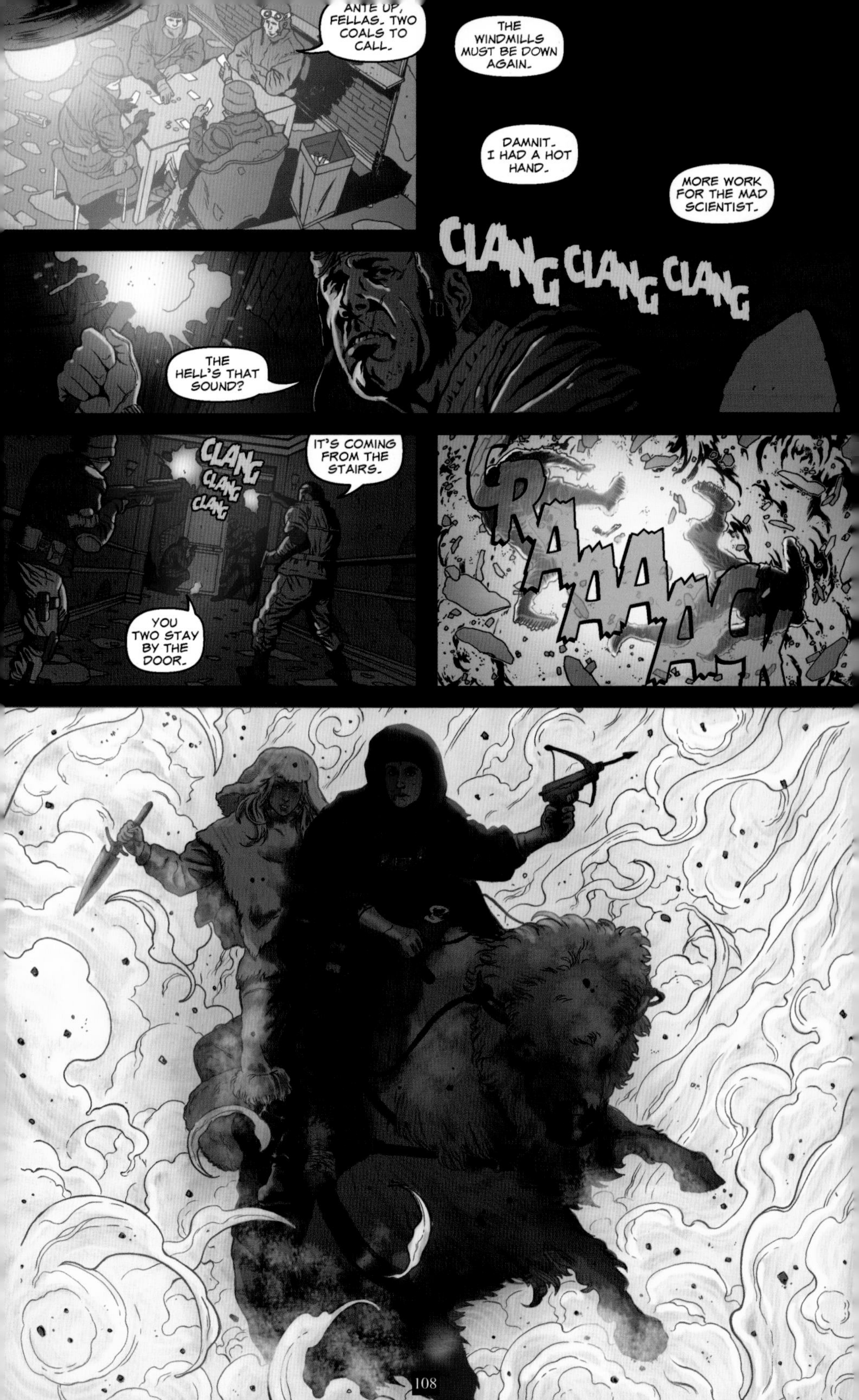
ANTE UP, FELLAS. TWO COALS TO CALL.
THE WINDMILLS MUST BE DOWN AGAIN.
DAMNIT. I HAD A HOT HAND.
MORE WORK FOR THE MAD SCIENTIST.
CLANG CLANG CLANG
THE HELL'S THAT SOUND?
CLANG CLANG CLANG
IT'S COMING FROM THE STAIRS.
YOU TWO STAY BY THE DOOR.

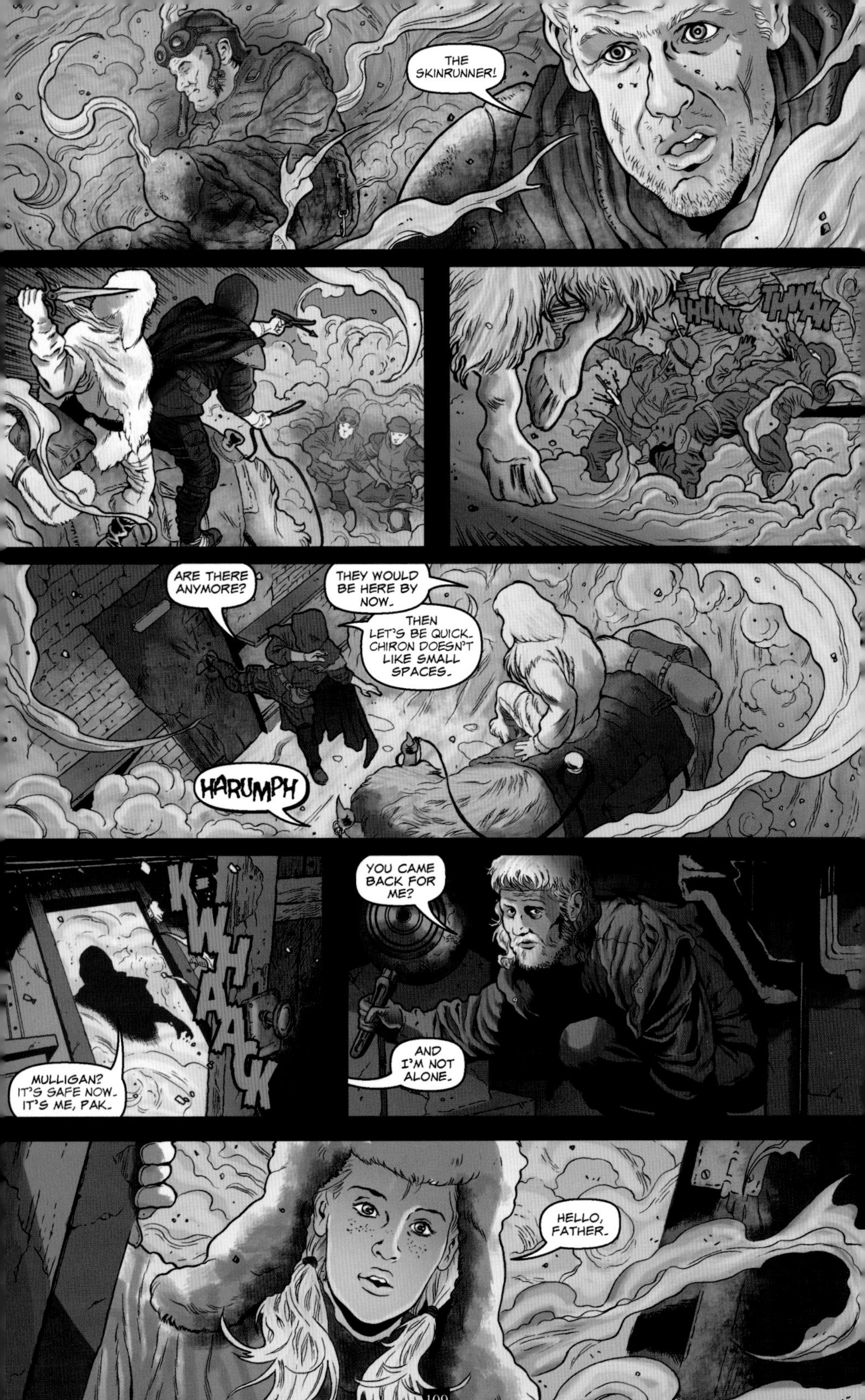
THE SKINRUNNER!
THUNK
THWAK
ARE THERE ANYMORE?
THEY WOULD BE HERE BY NOW.
THEN LET'S BE QUICK. CHIRON DOESN'T LIKE SMALL SPACES.
HARUMPH
KWHAAACK
MULLIGAN? IT'S SAFE NOW. IT'S ME, PAK.
YOU CAME BACK FOR ME?
AND I'M NOT ALONE.
HELLO, FATHER.

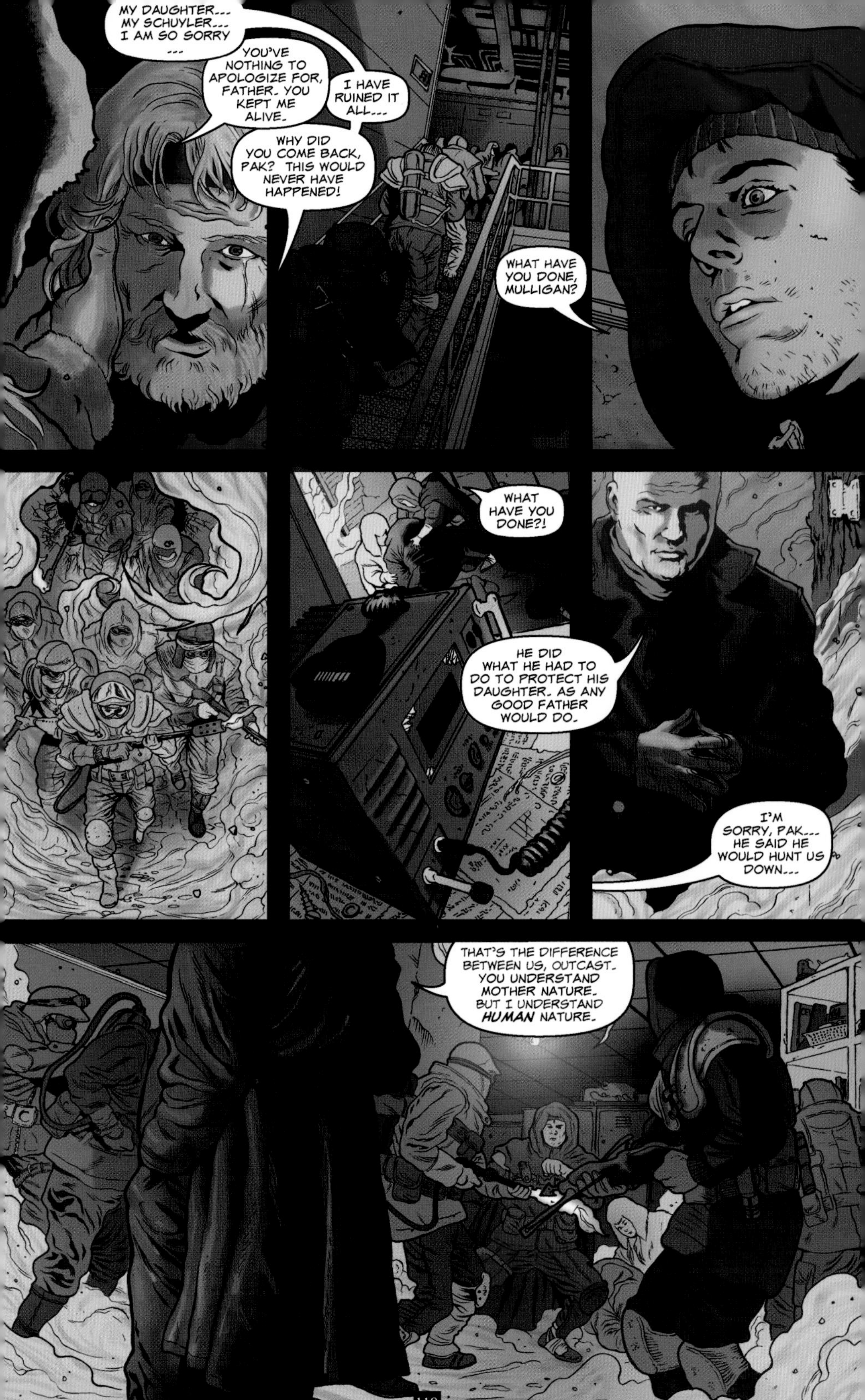
MY DAUGHTER... MY SCHUYLER... I AM SO SORRY ...
YOU'VE NOTHING TO APOLOGIZE FOR, FATHER. YOU KEPT ME ALIVE.
I HAVE RUINED IT ALL...
WHY DID YOU COME BACK, PAK? THIS WOULD NEVER HAVE HAPPENED!
WHAT HAVE YOU DONE, MULLIGAN?
WHAT HAVE YOU DONE?!
HE DID WHAT HE HAD TO DO TO PROTECT HIS DAUGHTER. AS ANY GOOD FATHER WOULD DO.
I'M SORRY, PAK... HE SAID HE WOULD HUNT US DOWN...
THAT'S THE DIFFERENCE BETWEEN US, OUTCAST. YOU UNDERSTAND MOTHER NATURE. BUT I UNDERSTAND ***HUMAN*** NATURE.

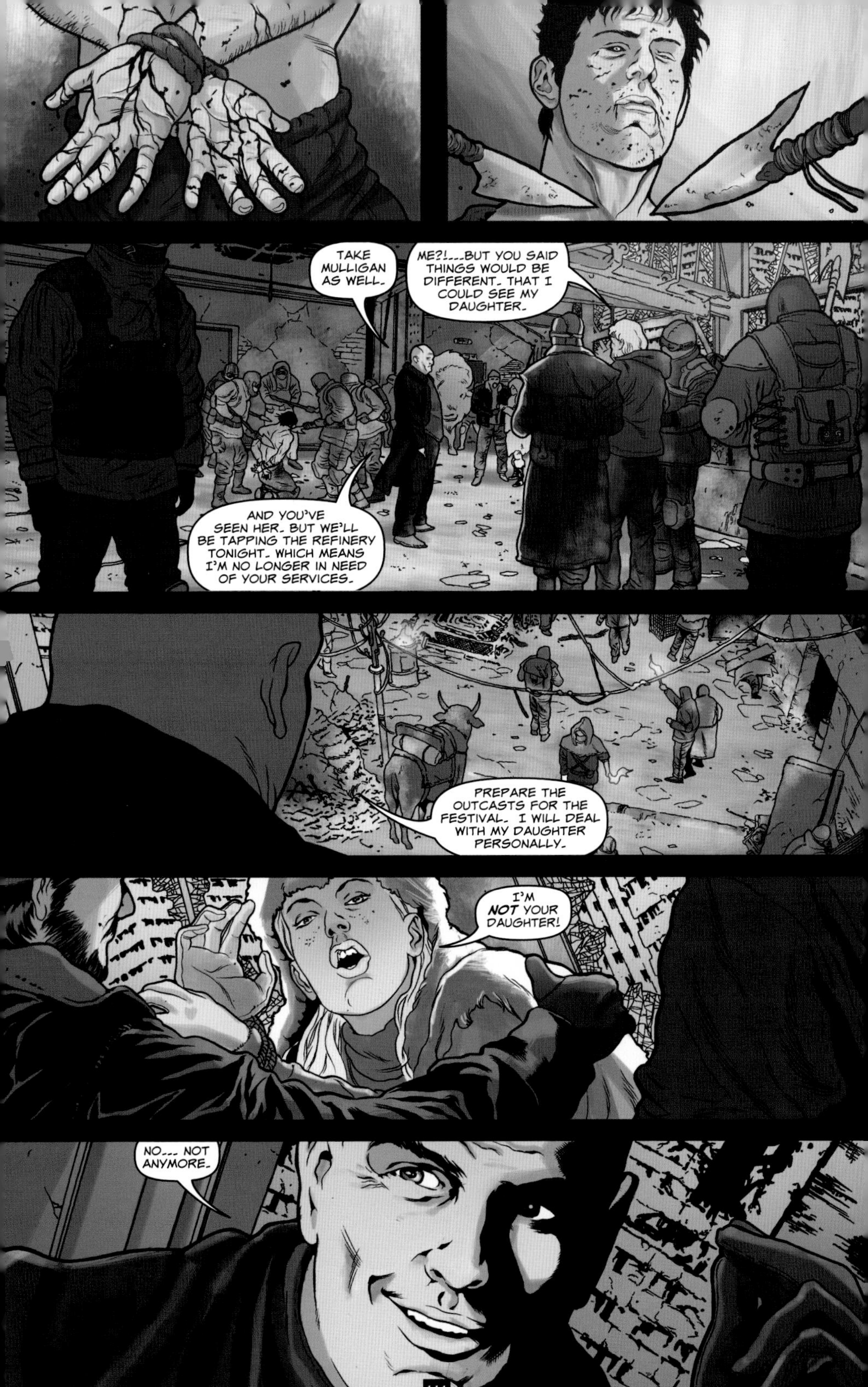
TAKE MULLIGAN AS WELL.
ME?!...BUT YOU SAID THINGS WOULD BE DIFFERENT. THAT I COULD SEE MY DAUGHTER.
AND YOU'VE SEEN HER. BUT WE'LL BE TAPPING THE REFINERY TONIGHT. WHICH MEANS I'M NO LONGER IN NEED OF YOUR SERVICES.
PREPARE THE OUTCASTS FOR THE FESTIVAL. I WILL DEAL WITH MY DAUGHTER PERSONALLY.
I'M ***NOT*** YOUR DAUGHTER!
NO... NOT ANYMORE.

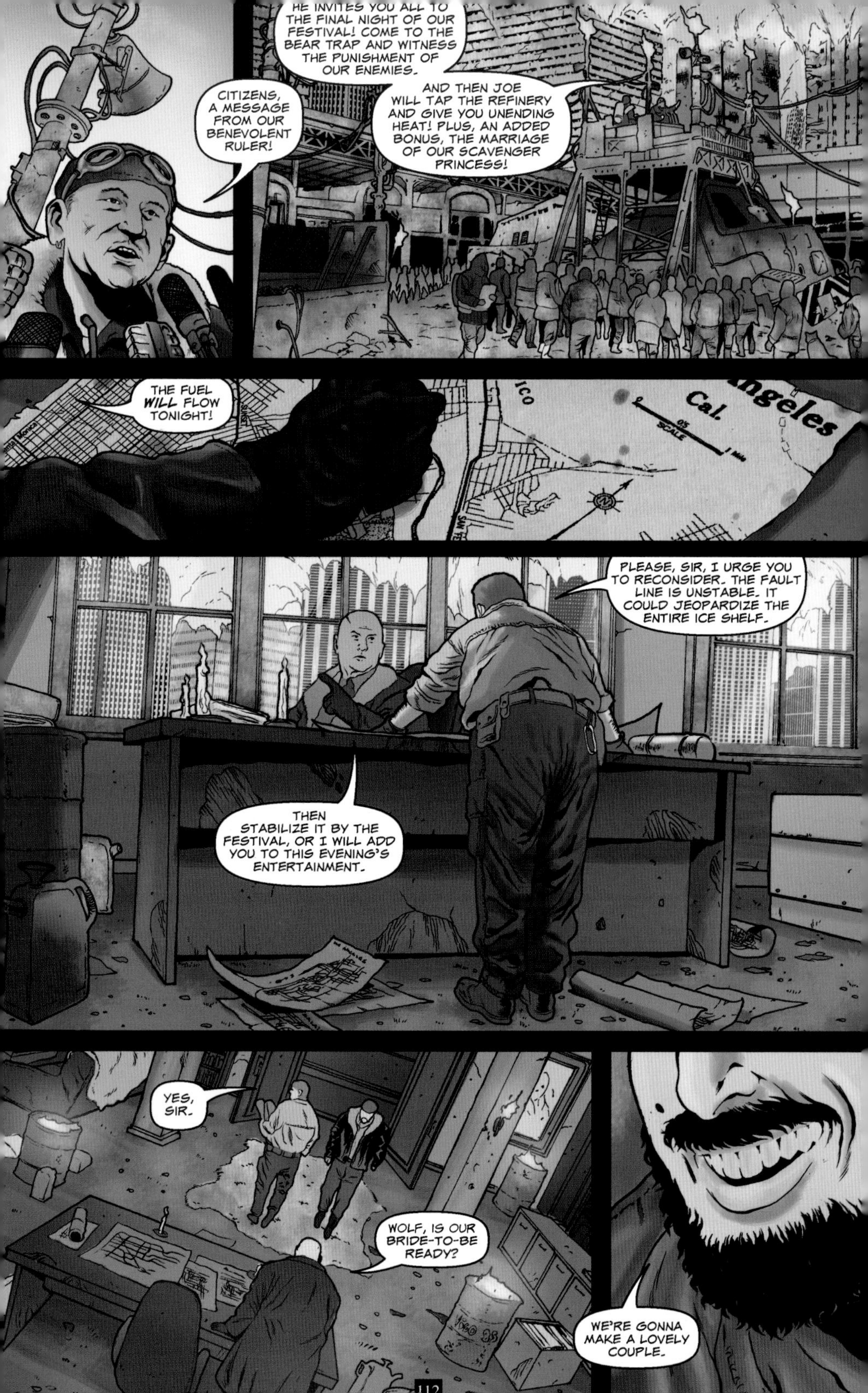
CITIZENS, A MESSAGE FROM OUR BENEVOLENT RULER!
HE INVITES YOU ALL TO THE FINAL NIGHT OF OUR FESTIVAL! COME TO THE BEAR TRAP AND WITNESS THE PUNISHMENT OF OUR ENEMIES.
AND THEN JOE WILL TAP THE REFINERY AND GIVE YOU UNENDING HEAT! PLUS, AN ADDED BONUS, THE MARRIAGE OF OUR SCAVENGER PRINCESS!
THE FUEL WILL FLOW TONIGHT!
Cal.
SCALE
PLEASE, SIR, I URGE YOU TO RECONSIDER. THE FAULT LINE IS UNSTABLE. IT COULD JEOPARDIZE THE ENTIRE ICE SHELF.
THEN STABILIZE IT BY THE FESTIVAL, OR I WILL ADD YOU TO THIS EVENING'S ENTERTAINMENT.
YES, SIR.
WOLF, IS OUR BRIDE-TO-BE READY?
WE'RE GONNA MAKE A LOVELY COUPLE.

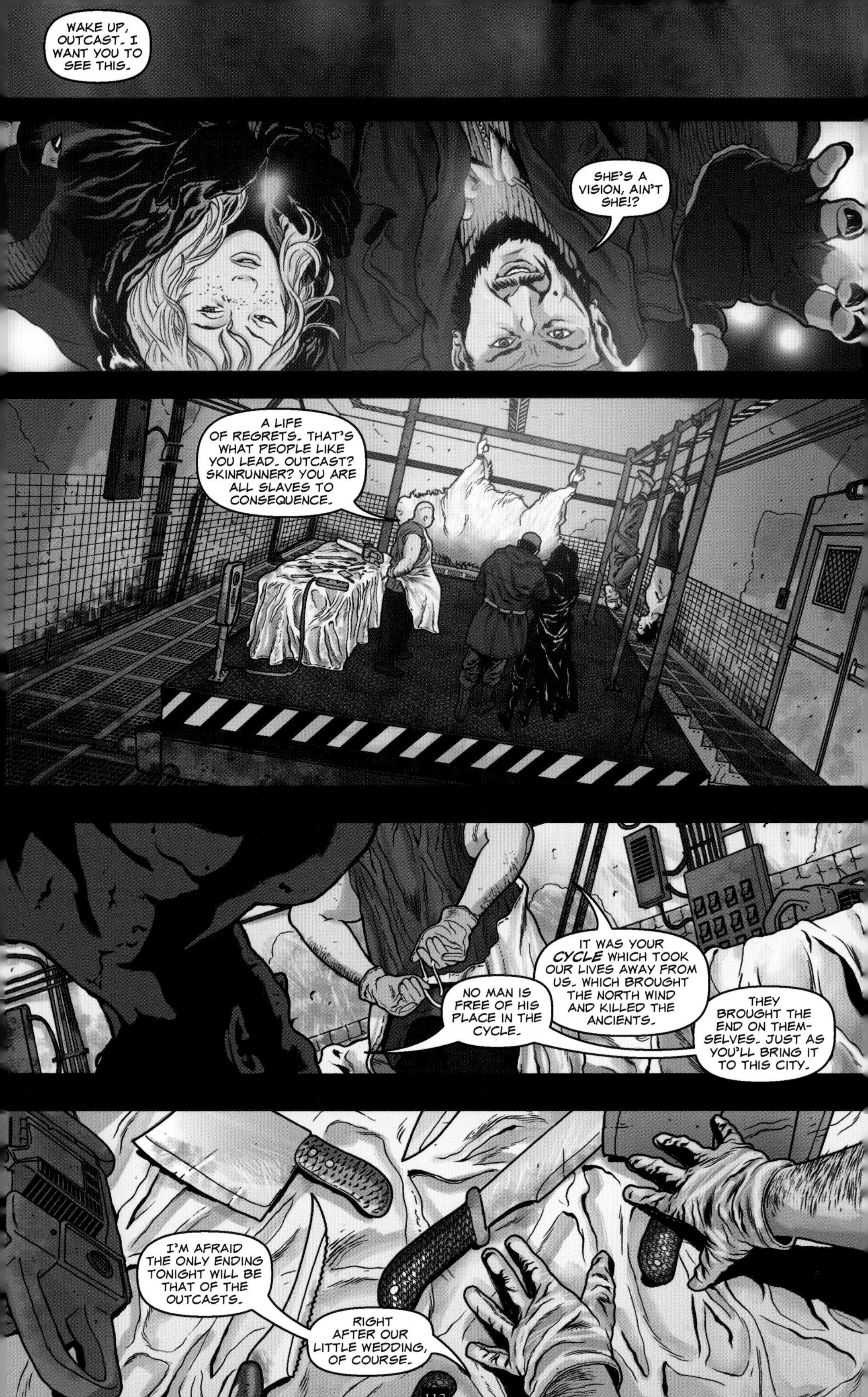
WAKE UP, OUTCAST. I WANT YOU TO SEE THIS.
SHE'S A VISION, AIN'T SHE!?
A LIFE OF REGRETS. THAT'S WHAT PEOPLE LIKE YOU LEAD. OUTCAST? SKINRUNNER? YOU ARE ALL SLAVES TO CONSEQUENCE.
IT WAS YOUR *CYCLE* WHICH TOOK OUR LIVES AWAY FROM US. WHICH BROUGHT THE NORTH WIND AND KILLED THE ANCIENTS.
NO MAN IS FREE OF HIS PLACE IN THE CYCLE.
THEY BROUGHT THE END ON THEMSELVES. JUST AS YOU'LL BRING IT TO THIS CITY.
I'M AFRAID THE ONLY ENDING TONIGHT WILL BE THAT OF THE OUTCASTS.
RIGHT AFTER OUR LITTLE WEDDING, OF COURSE.

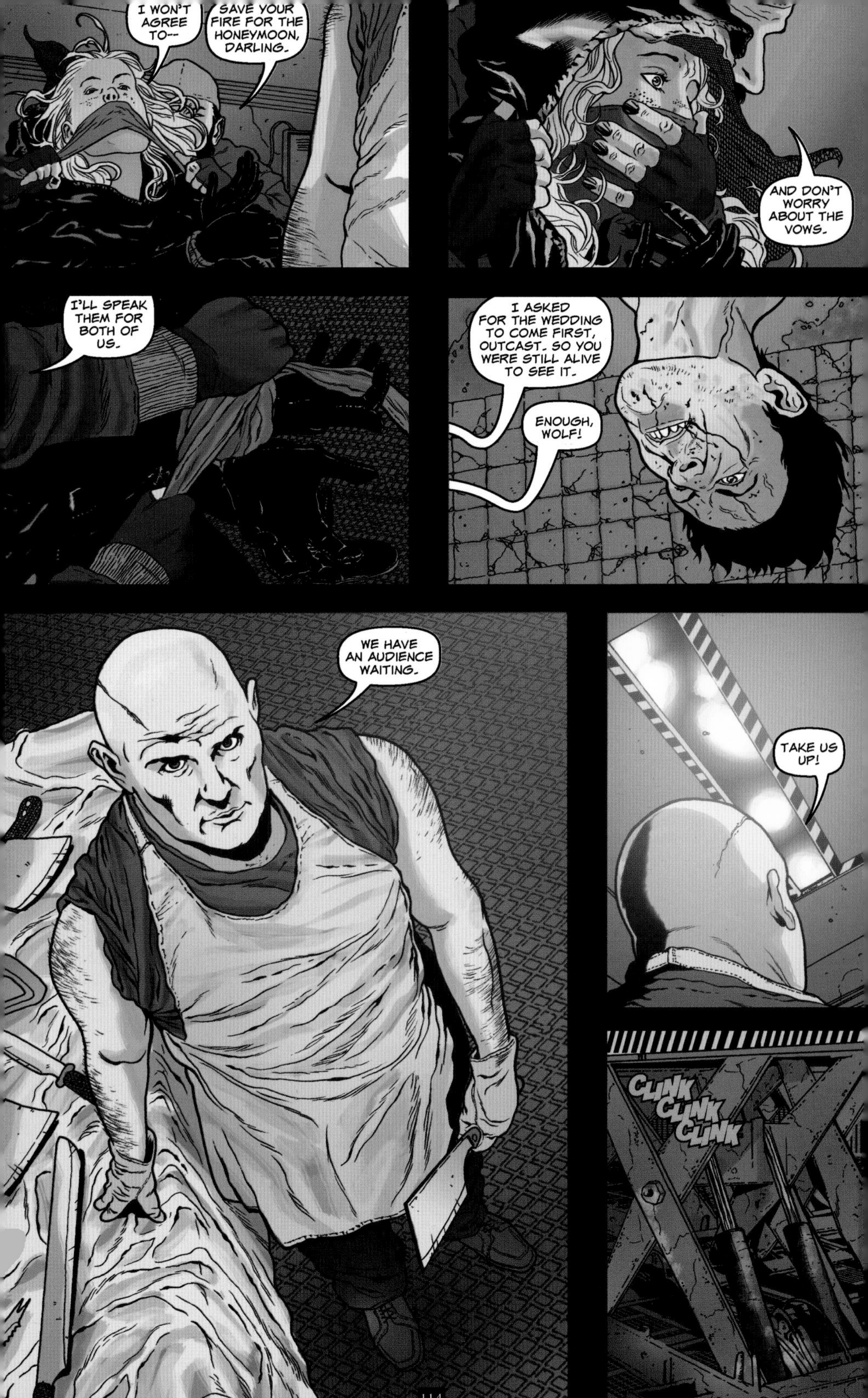
I WON'T AGREE TO--
SAVE YOUR FIRE FOR THE HONEYMOON, DARLING.
AND DON'T WORRY ABOUT THE VOWS.
I'LL SPEAK THEM FOR BOTH OF US.
I ASKED FOR THE WEDDING TO COME FIRST, OUTCAST. SO YOU WERE STILL ALIVE TO SEE IT.
ENOUGH, WOLF!
WE HAVE AN AUDIENCE WAITING.
TAKE US UP!
CLINK CLINK CLINK

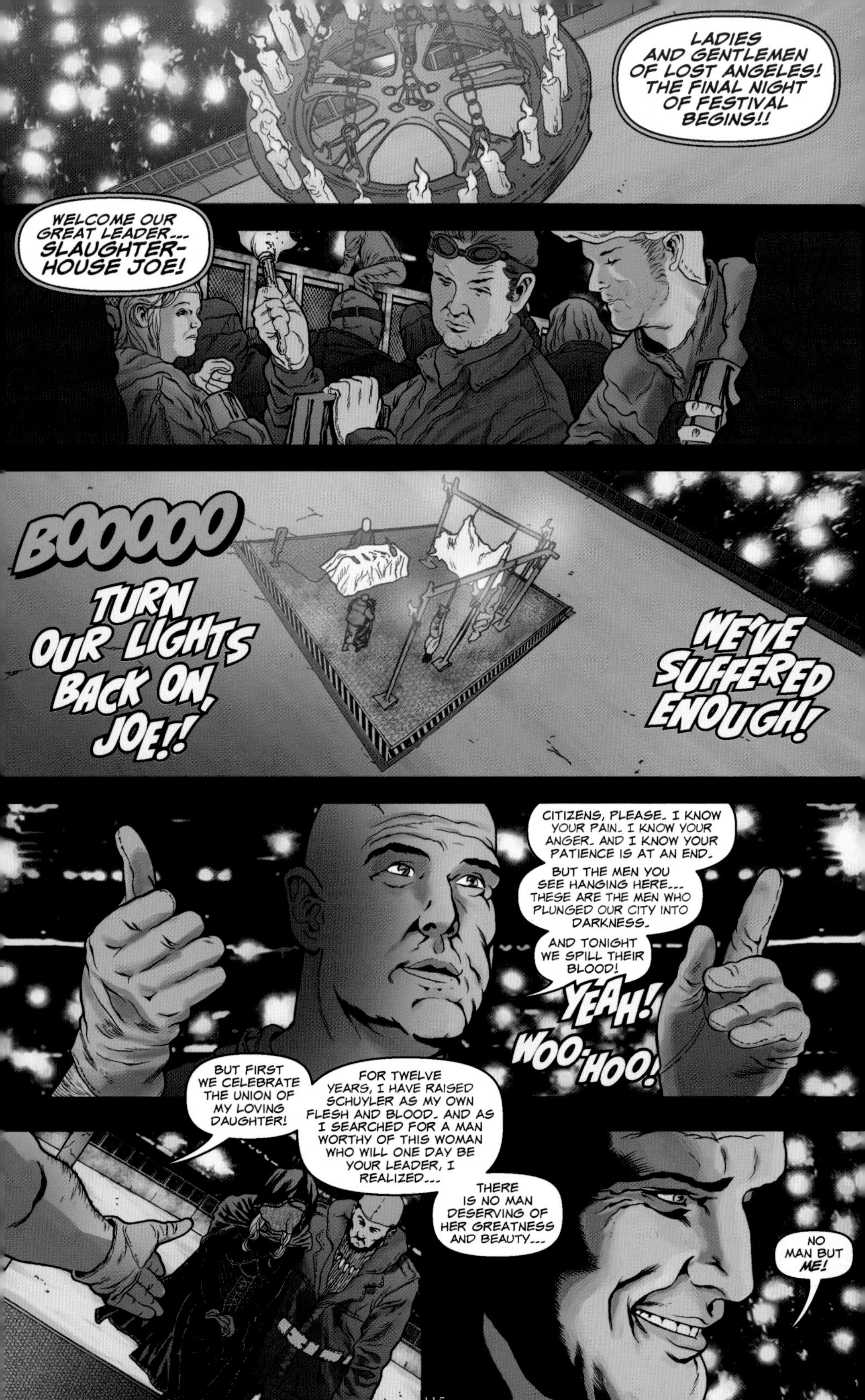
LADIES AND GENTLEMEN OF LOST ANGELES! THE FINAL NIGHT OF FESTIVAL BEGINS!!
WELCOME OUR GREAT LEADER... SLAUGHTER-HOUSE JOE!
BOOOOO
TURN OUR LIGHTS BACK ON, JOE!!
WE'VE SUFFERED ENOUGH!
CITIZENS, PLEASE. I KNOW YOUR PAIN. I KNOW YOUR ANGER. AND I KNOW YOUR PATIENCE IS AT AN END.
BUT THE MEN YOU SEE HANGING HERE... THESE ARE THE MEN WHO PLUNGED OUR CITY INTO DARKNESS.
AND TONIGHT WE SPILL THEIR BLOOD!
YEAH!
WOO-HOO!
BUT FIRST WE CELEBRATE THE UNION OF MY LOVING DAUGHTER!
FOR TWELVE YEARS, I HAVE RAISED SCHUYLER AS MY OWN FLESH AND BLOOD. AND AS I SEARCHED FOR A MAN WORTHY OF THIS WOMAN WHO WILL ONE DAY BE YOUR LEADER, I REALIZED...
THERE IS NO MAN DESERVING OF HER GREATNESS AND BEAUTY...
NO MAN BUT ME!

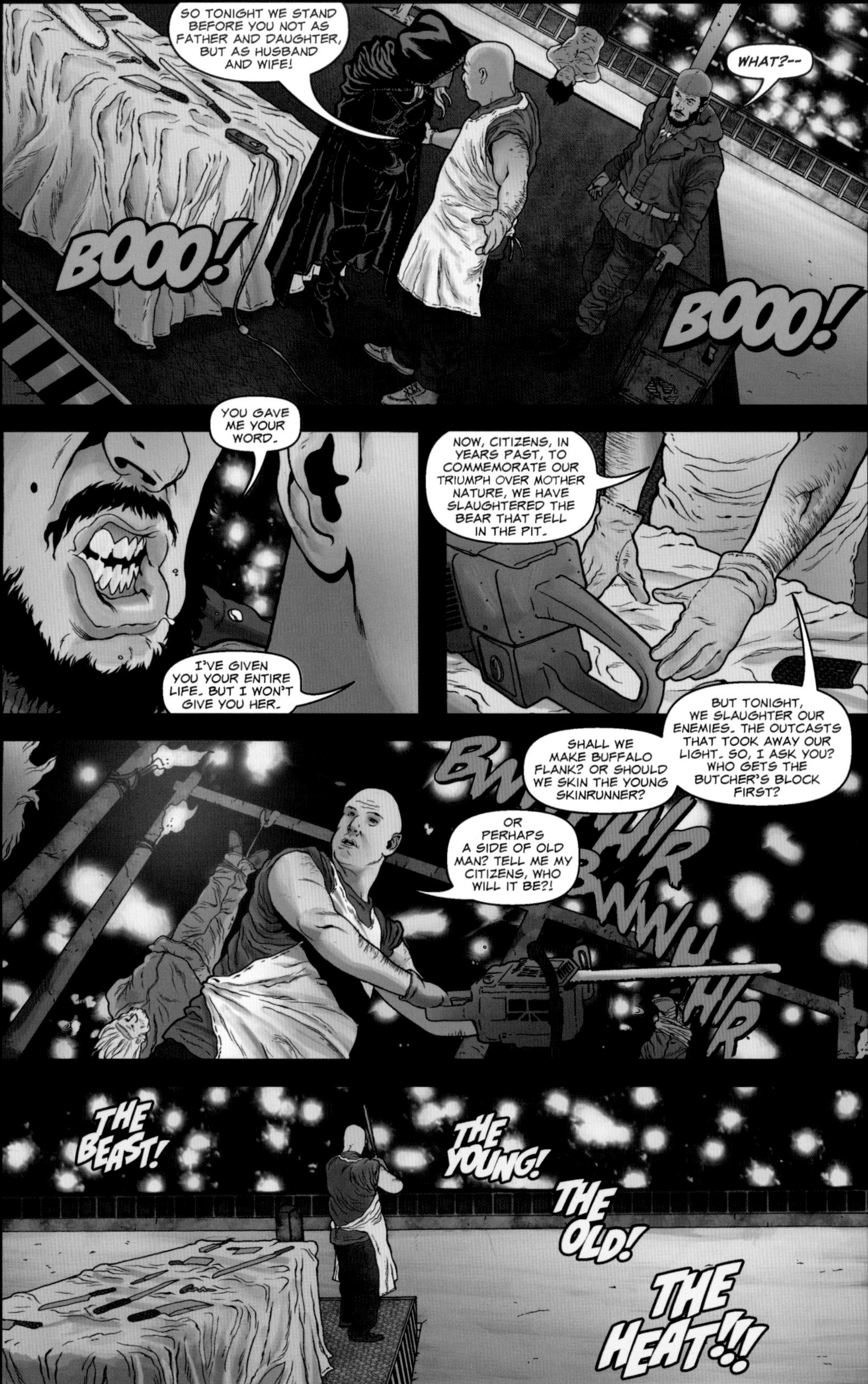
SO TONIGHT WE STAND BEFORE YOU NOT AS FATHER AND DAUGHTER, BUT AS HUSBAND AND WIFE!
WHAT?--
BOOO!
BOOO!
YOU GAVE ME YOUR WORD.
I'VE GIVEN YOU YOUR ENTIRE LIFE. BUT I WON'T GIVE YOU HER.
NOW, CITIZENS, IN YEARS PAST, TO COMMEMORATE OUR TRIUMPH OVER MOTHER NATURE, WE HAVE SLAUGHTERED THE BEAR THAT FELL IN THE PIT.
BUT TONIGHT, WE SLAUGHTER OUR ENEMIES. THE OUTCASTS THAT TOOK AWAY OUR LIGHT. SO, I ASK YOU? WHO GETS THE BUTCHER'S BLOCK FIRST?
SHALL WE MAKE BUFFALO FLANK? OR SHOULD WE SKIN THE YOUNG SKINRUNNER?
OR PERHAPS A SIDE OF OLD MAN? TELL ME MY CITIZENS, WHO WILL IT BE?!
THE BEAST!
THE YOUNG!
THE OLD!
THE HEAT!!!

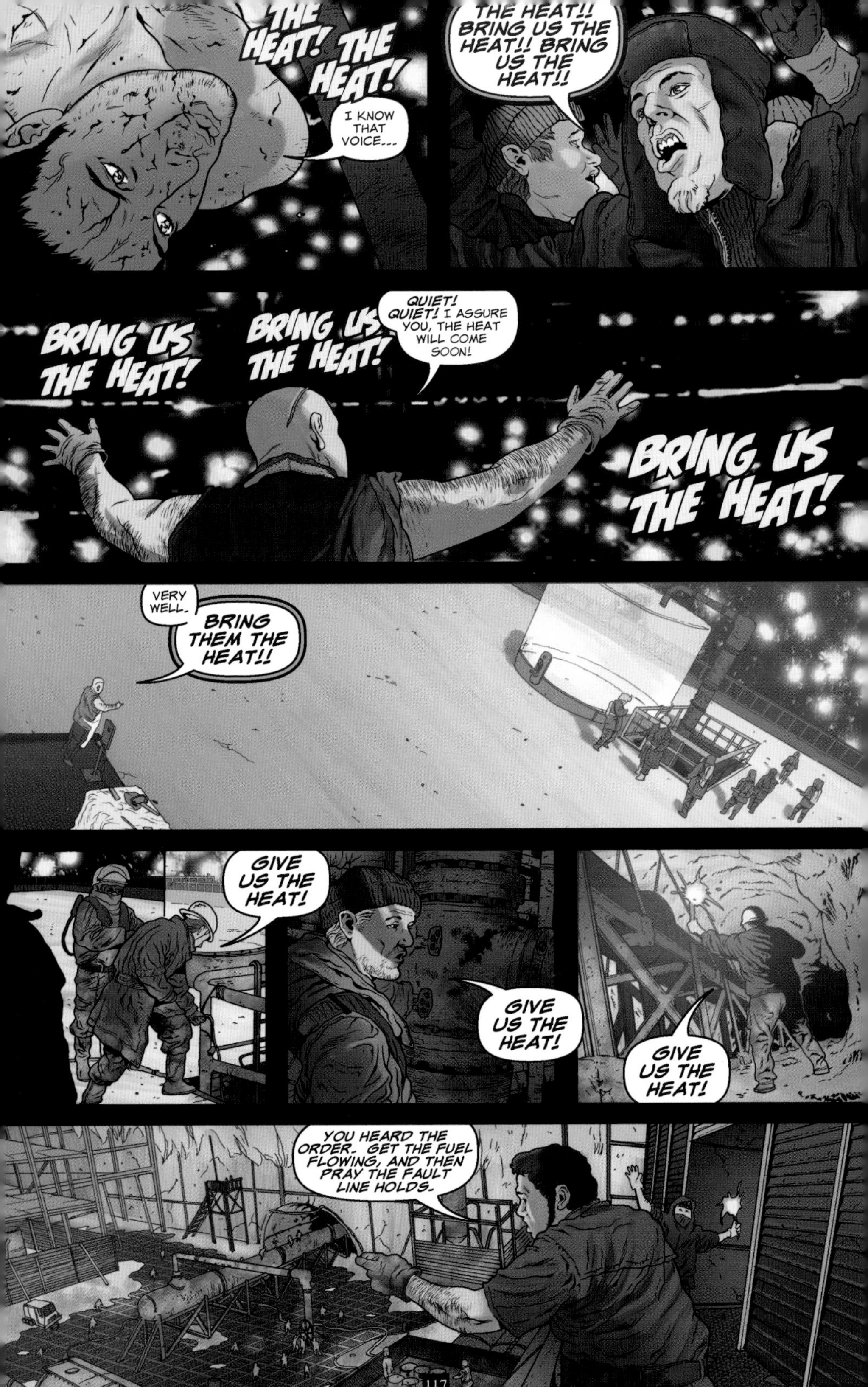
THE HEAT! THE HEAT!
I KNOW THAT VOICE...
THE HEAT!! BRING US THE HEAT!! BRING US THE HEAT!!
BRING US THE HEAT!
BRING US THE HEAT!
QUIET! QUIET! I ASSURE YOU, THE HEAT WILL COME SOON!
BRING US THE HEAT!
VERY WELL.
BRING THEM THE HEAT!!
GIVE US THE HEAT!
GIVE US THE HEAT!
GIVE US THE HEAT!
YOU HEARD THE ORDER. GET THE FUEL FLOWING, AND THEN PRAY THE FAULT LINE HOLDS.

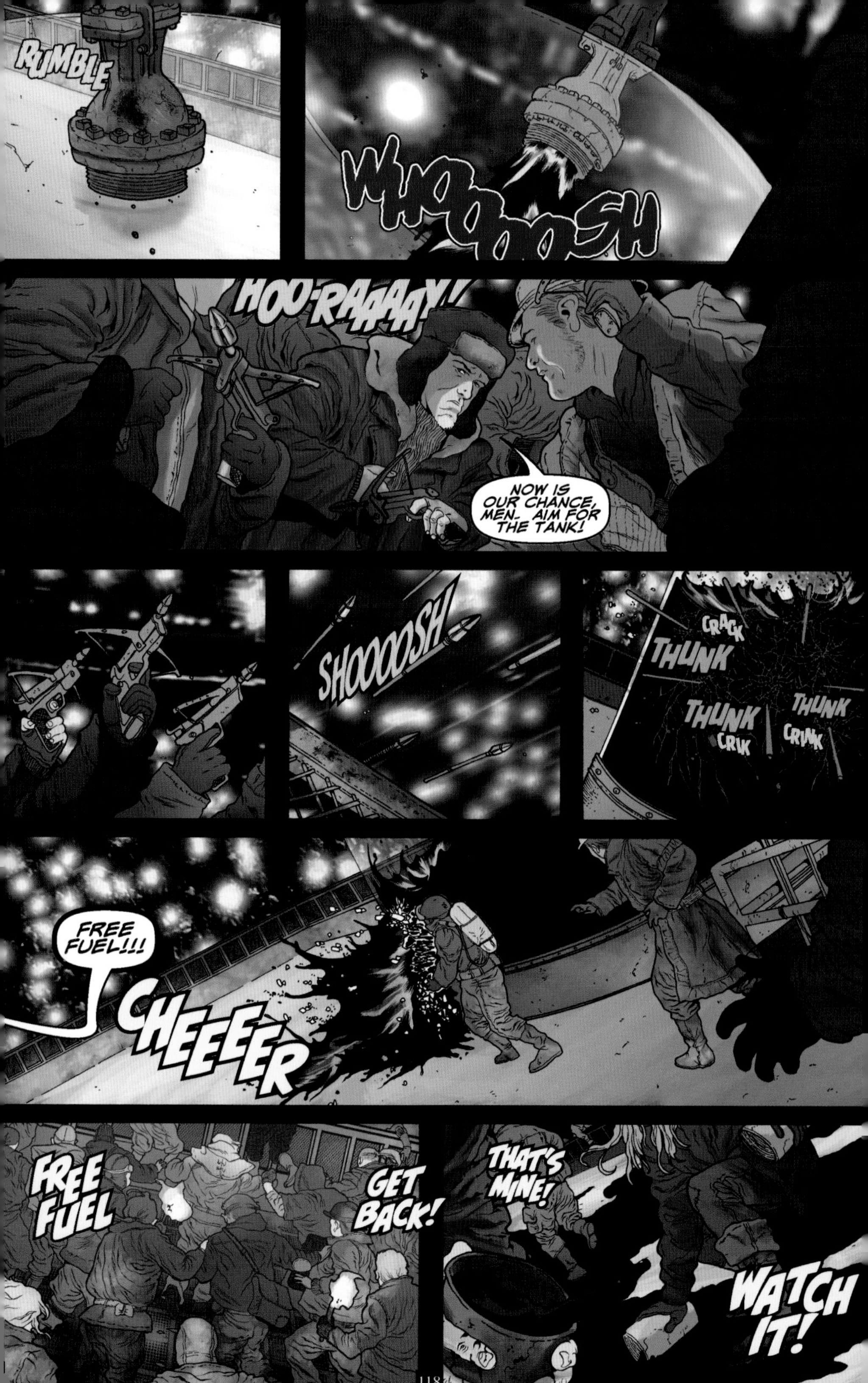
RUMBLE
WHOOOOOSH
HOO-RAAAAY!
NOW IS OUR CHANCE, MEN. AIM FOR THE TANK!
SHOOOOSH
CRACK
THUNK
THUNK
CRIK
THUNK
CRINK
FREE FUEL!!!
CHEEEER
FREE FUEL
GET BACK!
THAT'S MINE!
WATCH IT!

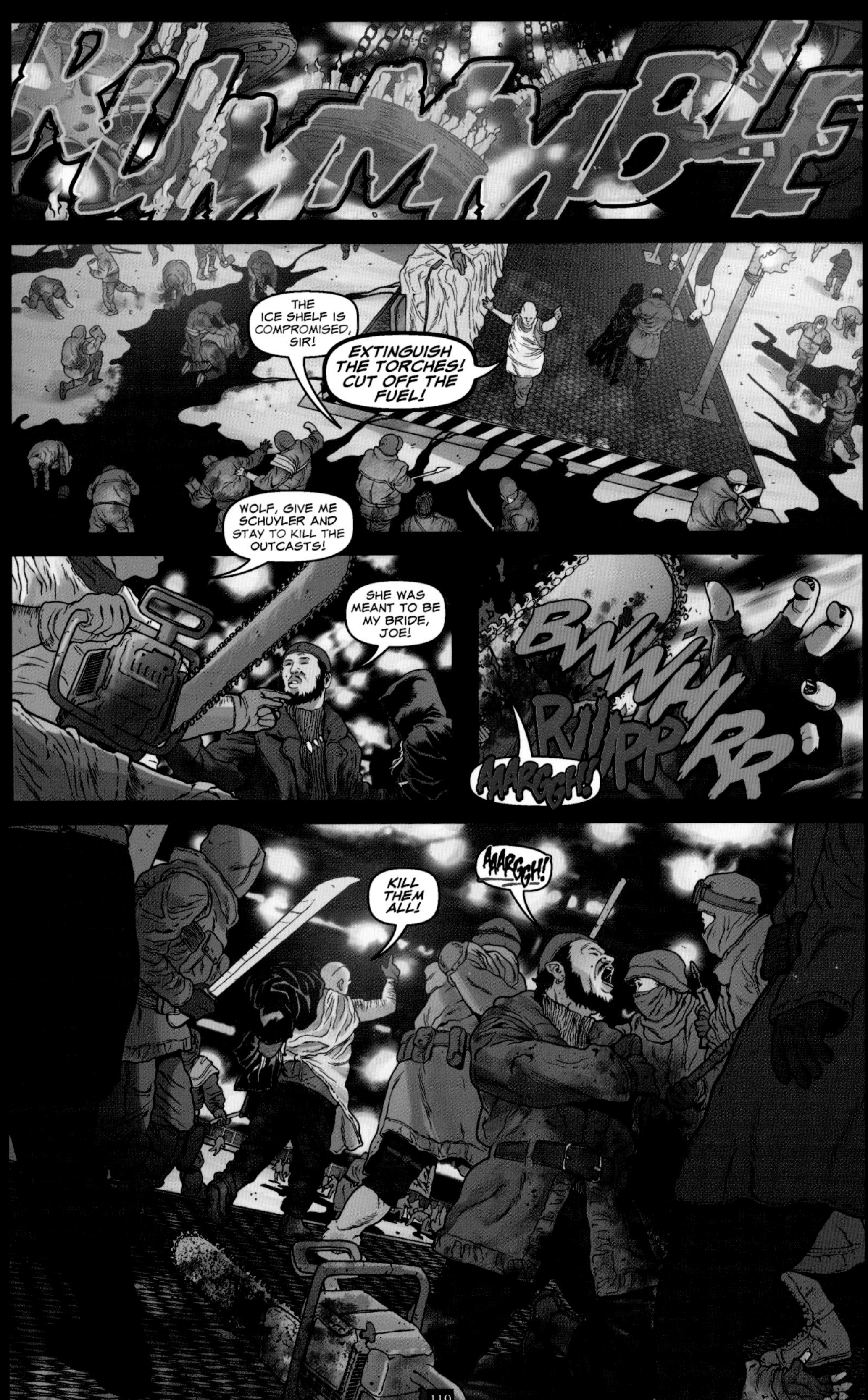
RUMMBLE
THE ICE SHELF IS COMPROMISED, SIR!
EXTINGUISH THE TORCHES! CUT OFF THE FUEL!
WOLF, GIVE ME SCHUYLER AND STAY TO KILL THE OUTCASTS!
SHE WAS MEANT TO BE MY BRIDE, JOE!
BWWH-RRIPPRRR
AAARGGH!
KILL THEM ALL!
AAARGGH!

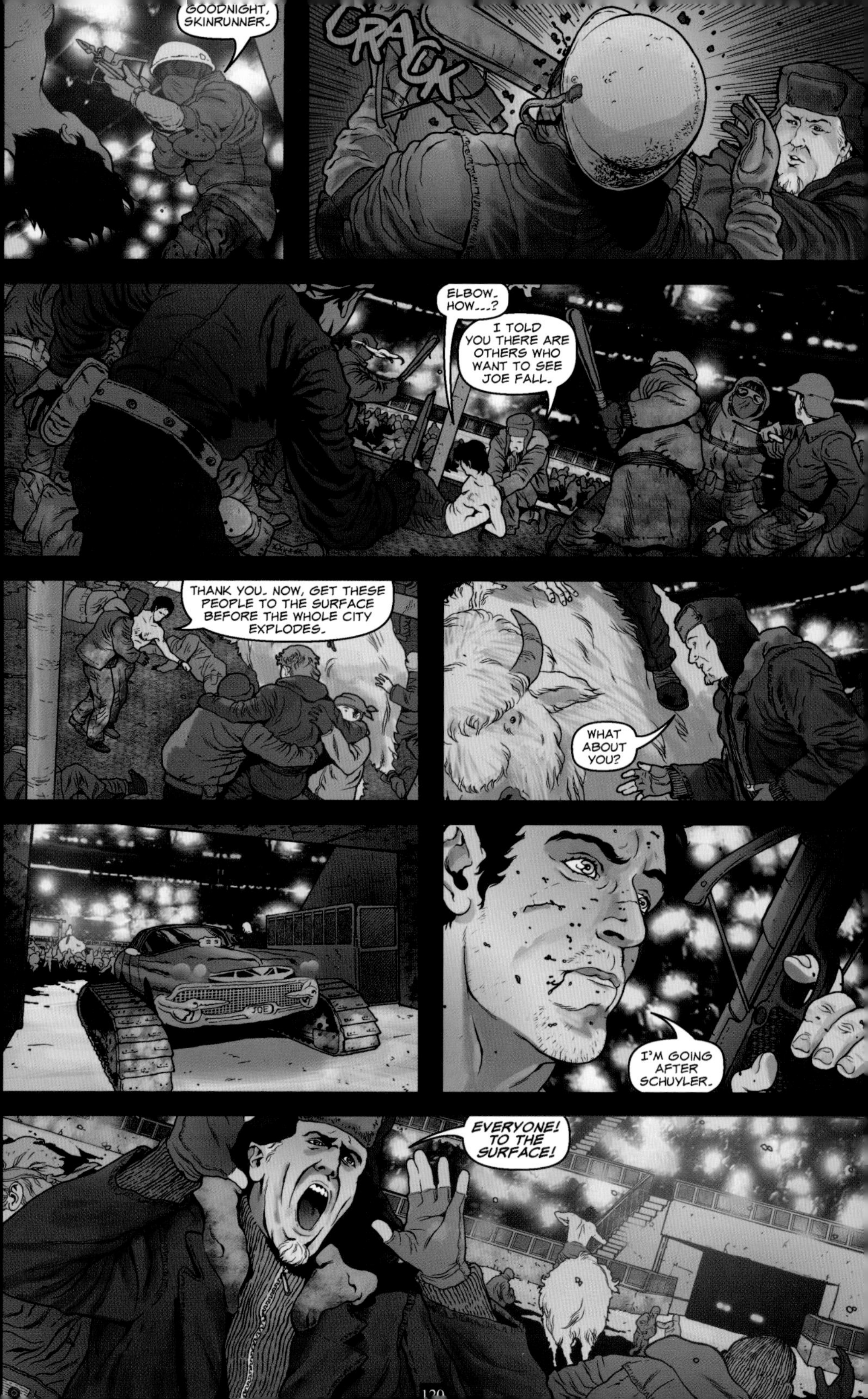

GOODNIGHT, SKINRUNNER.
CRACK
ELBOW. HOW...?
I TOLD YOU THERE ARE OTHERS WHO WANT TO SEE JOE FALL.
THANK YOU. NOW, GET THESE PEOPLE TO THE SURFACE BEFORE THE WHOLE CITY EXPLODES.
WHAT ABOUT YOU?
JOE
I'M GOING AFTER SCHUYLER.
EVERYONE! TO THE SURFACE!

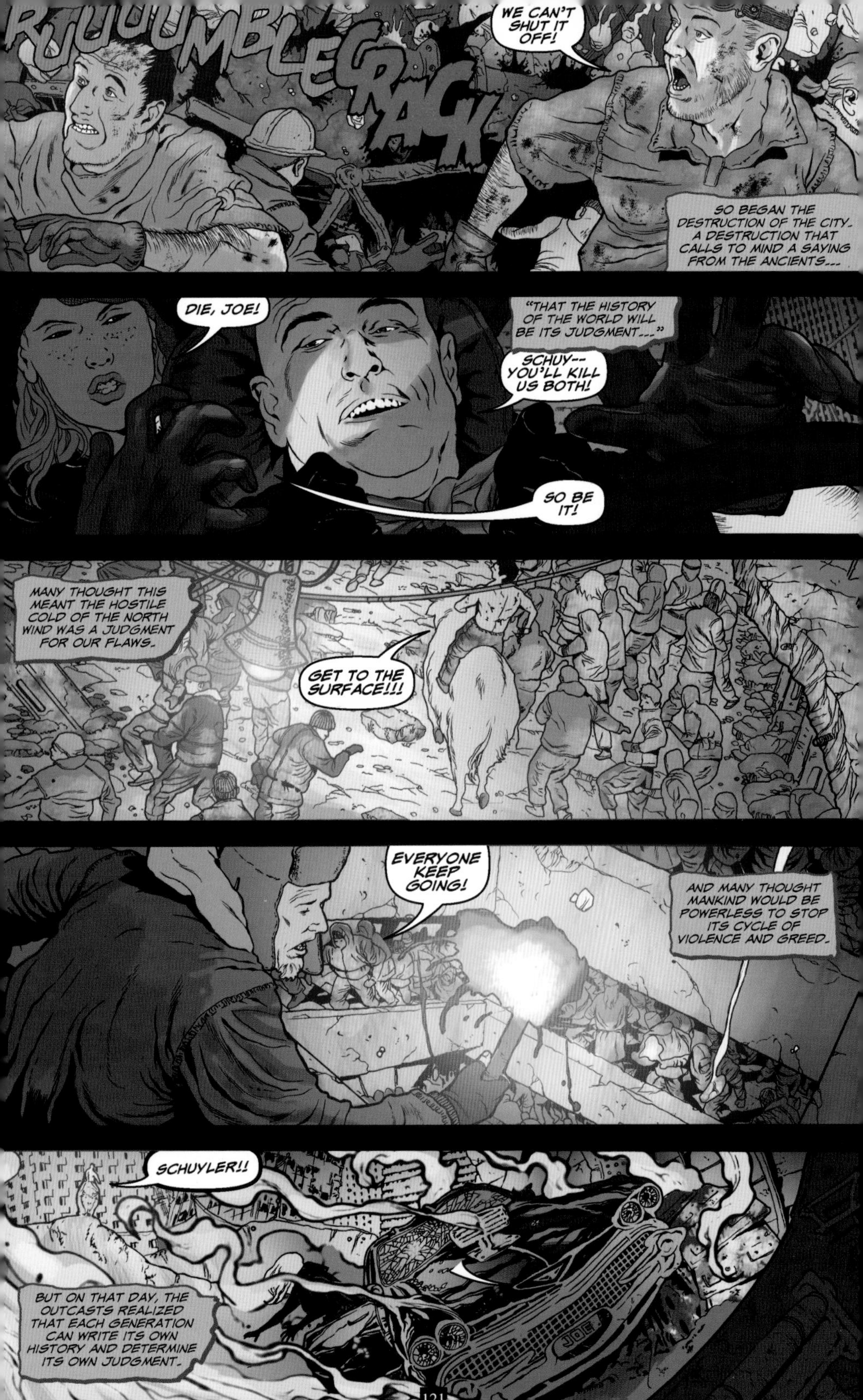
RUUUMBLE
WE CAN'T SHUT IT OFF!
CRACK
SO BEGAN THE DESTRUCTION OF THE CITY. A DESTRUCTION THAT CALLS TO MIND A SAYING FROM THE ANCIENTS...
"THAT THE HISTORY OF THE WORLD WILL BE ITS JUDGMENT..."
DIE, JOE!
SCHUY-- YOU'LL KILL US BOTH!
SO BE IT!
MANY THOUGHT THIS MEANT THE HOSTILE COLD OF THE NORTH WIND WAS A JUDGMENT FOR OUR FLAWS.
GET TO THE SURFACE!!!
AND MANY THOUGHT MANKIND WOULD BE POWERLESS TO STOP ITS CYCLE OF VIOLENCE AND GREED.
EVERYONE KEEP GOING!
SCHUYLER!!
BUT ON THAT DAY, THE OUTCASTS REALIZED THAT EACH GENERATION CAN WRITE ITS OWN HISTORY AND DETERMINE ITS OWN JUDGMENT.
JOE

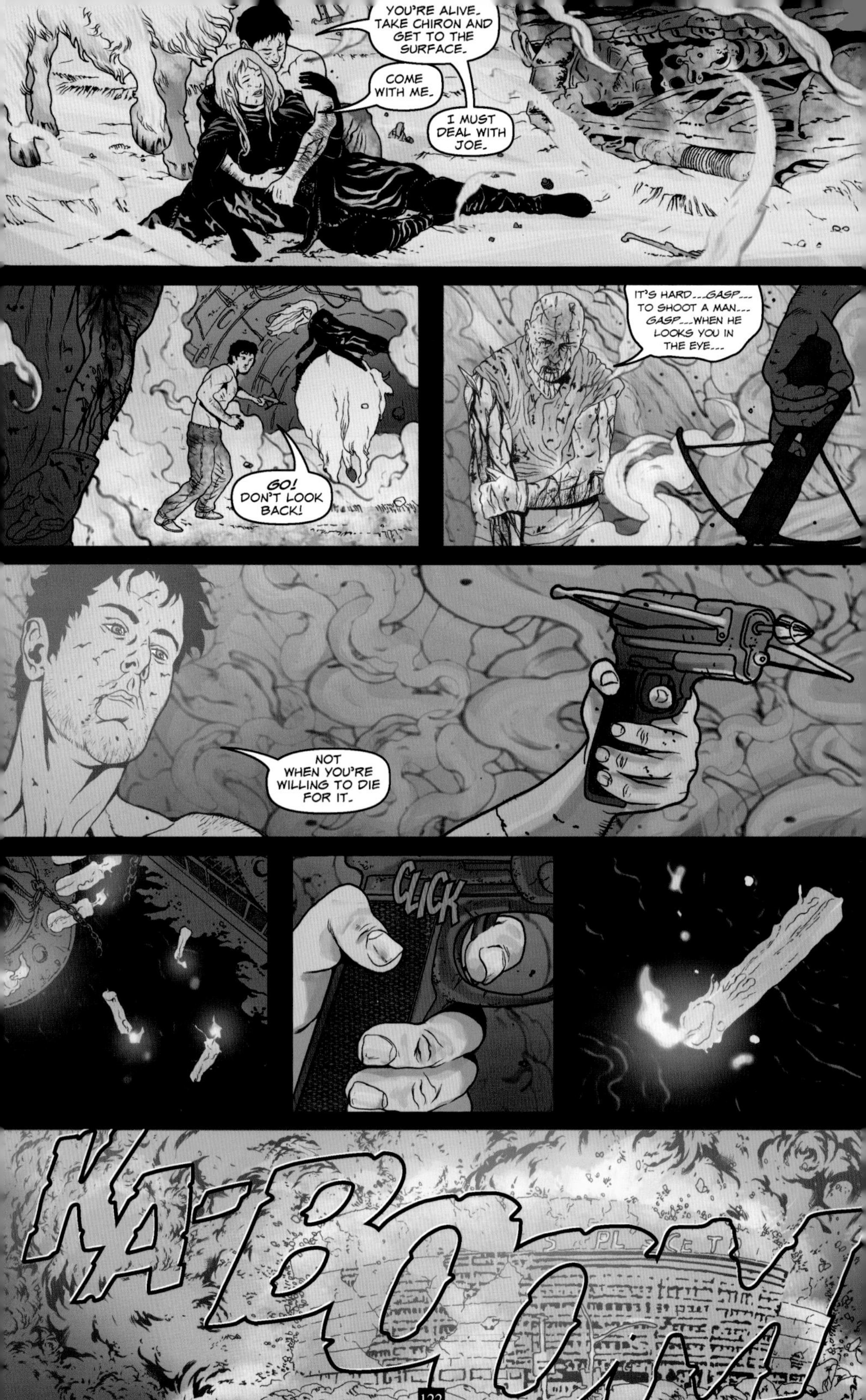
YOU'RE ALIVE. TAKE CHIRON AND GET TO THE SURFACE.
COME WITH ME.
I MUST DEAL WITH JOE.
GO! DON'T LOOK BACK!
IT'S HARD... GASP... TO SHOOT A MAN... GASP... WHEN HE LOOKS YOU IN THE EYE...
NOT WHEN YOU'RE WILLING TO DIE FOR IT.
CLICK
KA-BOOOM!

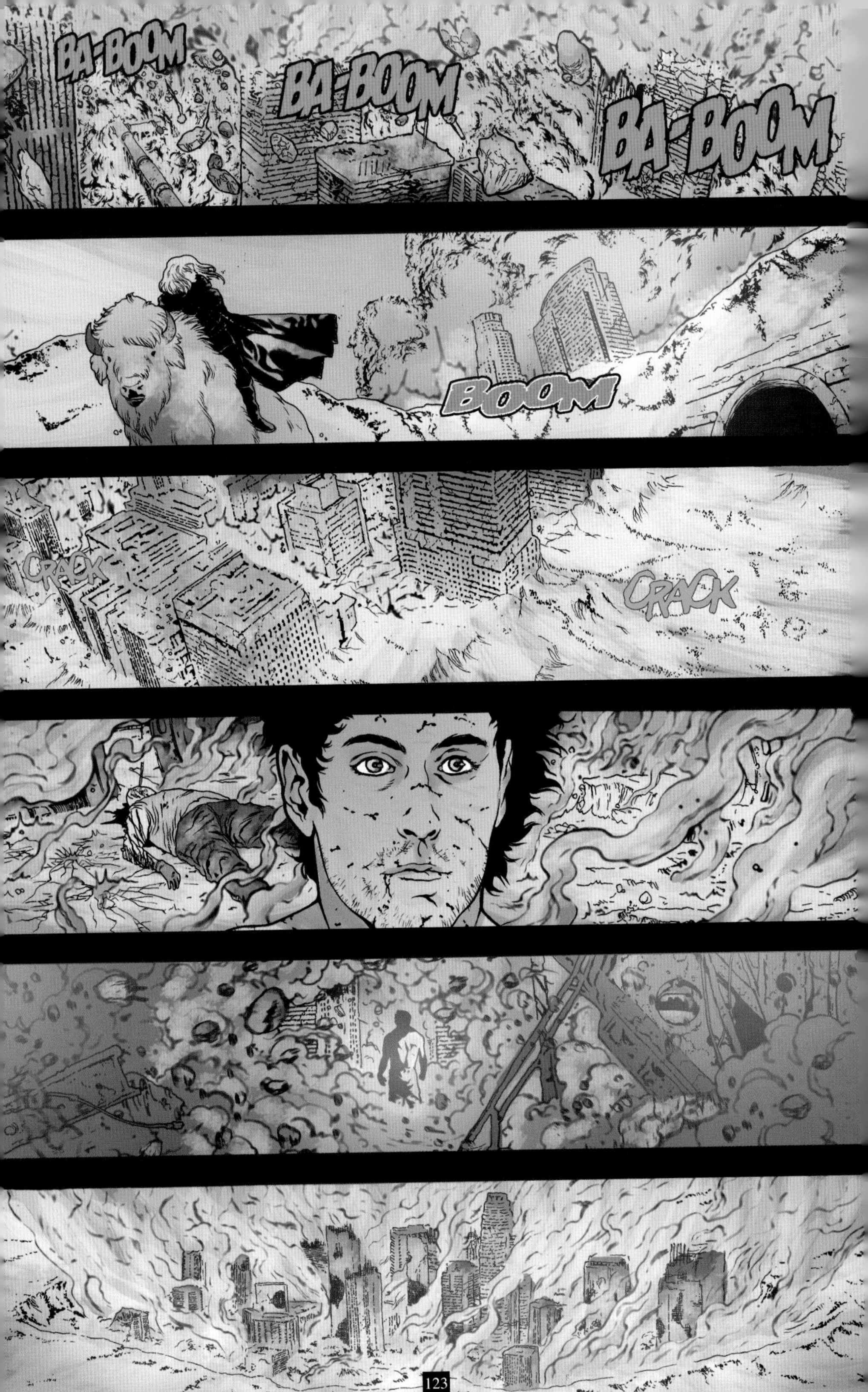
BA-BOOM
BA-BOOM
BA-BOOM
BOOM
CRACK
CRACK

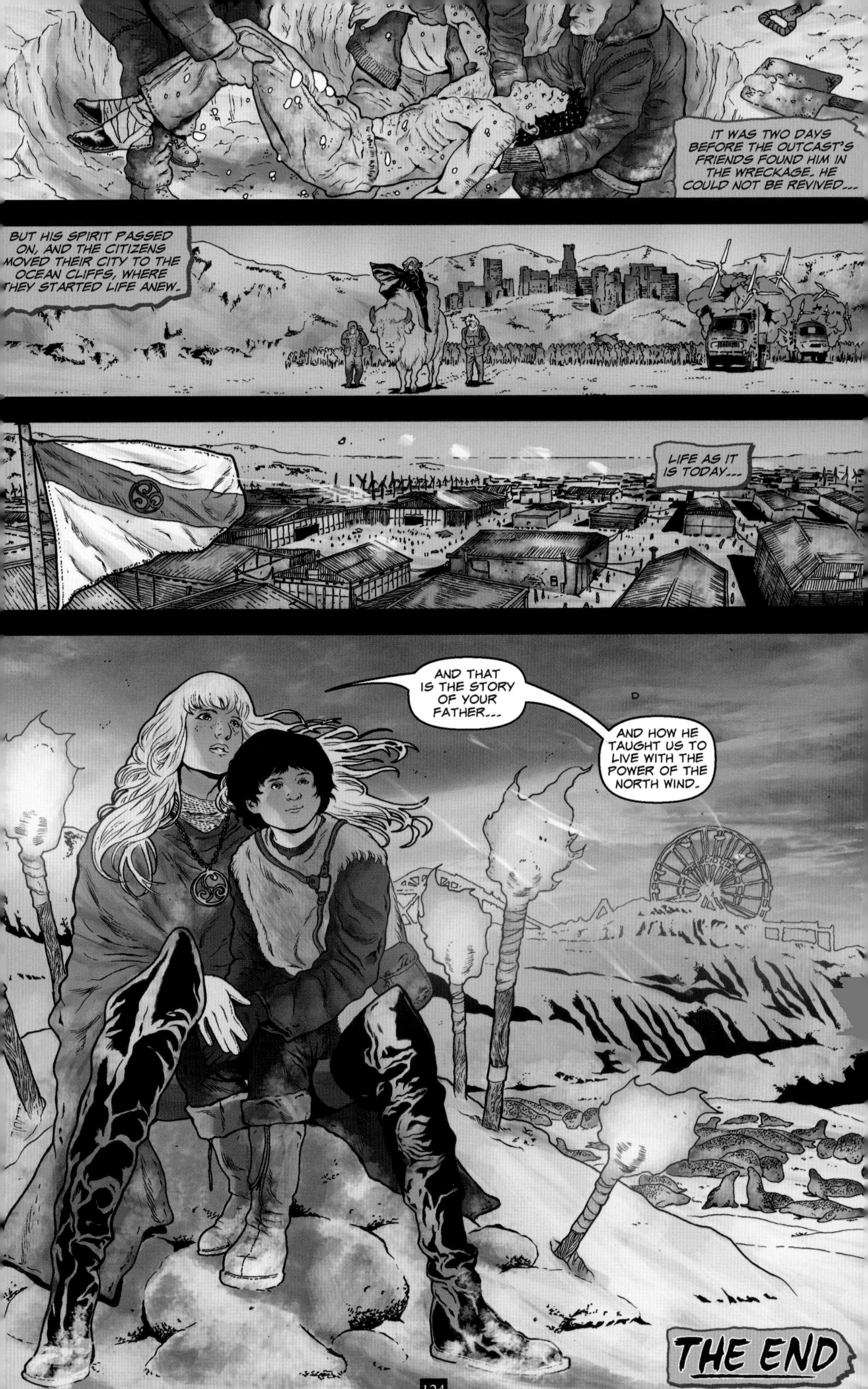
IT WAS TWO DAYS BEFORE THE OUTCAST'S FRIENDS FOUND HIM IN THE WRECKAGE. HE COULD NOT BE REVIVED...
BUT HIS SPIRIT PASSED ON, AND THE CITIZENS MOVED THEIR CITY TO THE OCEAN CLIFFS, WHERE THEY STARTED LIFE ANEW.
LIFE AS IT IS TODAY...
AND THAT IS THE STORY OF YOUR FATHER...
AND HOW HE TAUGHT US TO LIVE WITH THE POWER OF THE NORTH WIND.
THE END

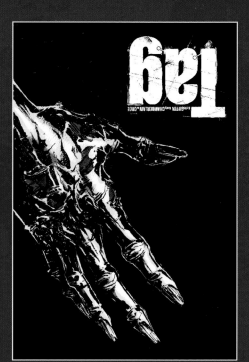

TAG
VOLUME I

written Keith Giffen
drawn by Kody Chamberlain
and Chee
$14.99, full color, 128 pages
ISBN13: 978-1-934506-03-5

An average Joe strolls down the street after a fight with his girlfriend when a random stranger TAGS him, handing off an ancient curse! He literally begins to die – and rot – seeing his body begin to decompose every day before his very eyes. Cursed, he must either surrender, or find the next victim to TAG... BONUS: Included in TPB form for the first time as an "extra" is Keith Giffen's "10" one-shot -- ten innocent people become unwilling contestants in a game of death. Given 10 bullets and a gun, it's kill or be killed as they're forced to hunt the other 10 contestants!

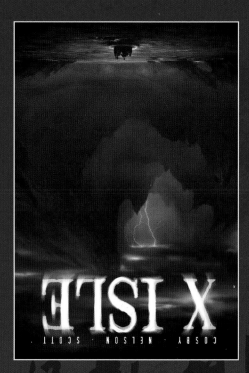

X ISLE

written by Andrew Cosby
and Michael Alan Nelson
drawn by Greg Scott
$14.99, full color, 128 pages
ISBN13: 978-1-934506-09-7

From EUREKA TV show creator Andrew Cosby and Michael Alan Nelson (Fall of Cthulhu, Second Wave) comes this tale of survival horror! A team of researchers drift on the ocean, lost, in their quest for an enigmatic island that's never been explored. Washing on its shores, they find a dense, terrifying jungle populated with animal and plant life that has evolved along a completely different path. What secret does this isle hold? Why are the life forms there so dangerous –and so alien? In the tradition of Alien and the recent horror-hit The Descent! Featuring art from Greg Scott (Gotham Central, Sword of Dracula).